Radical Theology

Radical Theology

An Essay on Faith and Theology in the Twenty-First Century

Ingolf U. Dalferth

Fortress Press
Minneapolis

RADICAL THEOLOGY

An Essay on Faith and Theology in the Twenty-First Century

Copyright © 2016 Fortress Press. All rights reserved. Except for brief quotations in critical articles or reviews, no part of this book may be reproduced in any manner without prior written permission from the publisher. Visit http://www.augsburgfortress.org/copyrights/ or write to Permissions, Augsburg Fortress, Box 1209, Minneapolis, MN 55440.

Cover image: Thinkstock © 2016: Abstract painted canvas

Cover design: Alisha Lofgren

Library of Congress Cataloging-in-Publication Data

Print ISBN: 978-1-4514-8881-4

eBook ISBN: 978-1-5064-1684-7

The paper used in this publication meets the minimum requirements of American National Standard for Information Sciences — Permanence of Paper for Printed Library Materials, ANSI Z329.48-1984.

Manufactured in the U.S.A.

This book was produced using Pressbooks.com, and PDF rendering was done by PrinceXML.

Contents

	Preface	vii
	Introduction	ix
1.	Hermeneutical Theology	1
2.	Trends within Twentieth-Century Hermeneutics	9
3.	Guiding Ideas of Understanding	39
4.	Theological Hermeneutics and Hermeneutical Theology	55
5.	The Hermeneutical Way of Thinking: Language as Word-Event	83
6.	Toward a Critique of Hermeneutical Theology	95
7.	On Hermeneutical Theology's Hermeneutical Approach	131
8.	Hermeneutical Theology as Radical Theology	147
9.	Radicalizing Modernity	161
10.	Phenomenology and Theology	177
11.	Resonance Analysis of Revelation	199

12. Radical Theology   213

   Bibliography   255

Preface

This book is a new version of my *Radikale Theologie* (Leipzig: EVA 2010). In the course of reworking a first translation by William D. Howden I made many changes and additions to the original text. I hope this has improved the intelligibility of the translation and clarified the issues discussed.

I am grateful to Deidre Green for her careful reading of the typescript, and to Marlene Block for her help with many problems, in particular with finding translations of the diverse literature I cite. The book would not have made it into print without their help. Whatever mistakes remain, I grudgingly acknowledge to be mine.

I thank Fortress Press for the willingness to publish the book. I hope the book will help to show the potential of hermeneutical theology for the elucidation of the Christian faith not only in the past, but also in the twenty-first century.

Ingolf U. Dalferth
Claremont, CA

Introduction

This book is a contribution to hermeneutical theology in the twenty-first century. It offers a critical analysis of this important movement within twentieth-century Protestant theology. The purpose of the analysis is not to assign this movement a place within the history of theology, thus consigning it to the past as theology moves on to face changing issues and new challenges. Rather, it is to make its concerns understandable and to point out their validity for the present. Hermeneutical theology in all of its versions has never attempted to adapt to the trends and fashionable topics of the time, but has rather taken up the task and assignment of Protestant theology with radical seriousness in the context of our present secular age. It is not directed toward the wishful thinking of more or less well-meaning contemporaries, whether those nostalgic for a bygone religious age or those critical of all religion. It seeks rather to develop itself from the roots of Christian theology in Christian faith. Its concerns were and are those of a radical theology. That is what this book is about.

Theology is intellectual work that involves hard thinking. However, one's thinking is not rendered radical simply by writing "RADICAL" in capital letters while leaving "thinking" in small letters. Nor do theologians become radical theologians by focusing all their energies on maximizing the *Logos* aspect of "theology" while minimizing the *Theos* aspect.[1] Such a strategy holds just as much promise as sawing off

---

1. The shift from the study of God (theology) to the study of religion (science of religion or religious studies) since the late eighteenth century has often been (mis)understood to mean that theology

the branch on which one sits. Nor are those theologians particularly radical who put all their efforts into demonstrating that it is not necessary, possible, useful, or appropriate to speak of God, but instead insist that human experiences, needs, problems, religious orientations, antireligious prejudices, or nonreligious ways of life must be placed at the center of theological thinking and church practice.[2] This alternative is a caricature. The two emphases are not mutually exclusive; instead, they require each other theologically.

The Reformation insight into the elementary and comprehensive correlation between the knowledge of God and the knowledge of human beings (*cognitio dei* and *cognitio hominis*) is not realized, however, simply by adorning our everyday experience and its scientific explanation with a cream topping of religion or some reference to transcendence. For Christian theology, the fact that religion and religions exist is not the greatest stroke of good fortune; this fact can serve to divert theology from its rightful task. So long as one understands "religion" as a special field of empirical research or as one segment of human life that is the subject matter of theology, one makes

---

has to be construed as anthropology (Feuerbach), as a systematic account of the history of religions (Troeltsch), as a version of the psychology of religiosity or religious emotions (Freud, Jung, William James, Otto, Erikson, Jaynes), as part of an evolutionary psychology of religion and religious convictions (Pascal Boyer, Barbara King), as a spiritual neuroscience (Persinger, Newberg, Geschwind), as a radical account of the decline, disappearance, or death of God in secular culture (Althizer, Hamilton), as a comparative account of what people believe in different cultures and traditions (theology of religions or comparative theology), and so on. Approaches of that kind, for all their differences, all agree that we cannot say anything meaningful about God but only about human belief in divinities, gods, or God or, more generally, about the empirical, experiential, and historical phenomena of religion, religions, and religiosity in human life and society. For methodological reasons, they hold, we can only study human activities but not divine activity. It is the accepted methodological axiom of the modern and postmodern mind alike that everything that can be studied, even God and trust in God, has to be studied *etsi deus non daretur* (as if there were no God). But this is self-defeating, as many have pointed out, and it misses the very point of religious convictions. Cf. Herbert McCabe, *God Matters* (London: Continuum, 1987); and McCabe, *God Still Matters* (London: Continuum, 2005).

2. English grammar creates well-known problems about the appropriate third-person reflexive pronoun for God. As the American poet Christian Wiman asks in *My Bright Abyss: Meditation of a Modern Believer* (New York: Farrar, Straus & Giroux, 2013), 2, what language is "accurate or helpful when thinking about how God manifests himself—or herself, or Godself, or whatever pronoun you want to use—in reality or in individual lives"? There is no general answer to this, and to use "Godself" just becomes too awkward in many contexts. Since Christians speak of God as Jesus did, and Jesus addressed God as father and not as mother, I shall use "he" and "himself" in this book wherever "God" or "Godself" sounds too clumsy. The reader ought not to conclude from this that I assume that God is male or that this gendered language is being used descriptively when applied to God.

the very possibility of theology dependent upon a debated reality, a reality that appears from a secular point of view to be shrinking and from a postsecular point of view to be gaining ground. Moreover, the field of religious studies has long established itself as the specialist for studying this empirical and historical realm of cultural phenomena, thus leaving theology, so understood, in an unfortunate battle for turf.

All this is unnecessary. Theology has no need to fight with religious studies about which can better, or more appropriately, or more rightfully deal with the religious phenomena of human life. Theology also gains no advantage by approaching the topic of religion with a sociological or anthropological fundamentalism that sees all people through the lens of religiosity (so that they are not really without religion, even though empirically they practice no religion) or that understands society to be fundamentally shaped by the function of religion (so that there can be areligious people, but no religion-free society). Theology has to do primarily with God, not with religion, with the one who alone rightfully deserves to be worshipped (a normative question), not with the empirical practices of worship and the gods people actually worship (factual questions). Theology's interest in religion(s) and religious practices is a mode of its interest in God, not an independent interest in its own right. It studies religion(s) because it seeks to learn something about God and, as theology, it does so for no other reason.

This is true of everything it studies, and it could study anything in this way. Without God, there would be nothing to study and nobody to study it. God is the one without whom nothing possible would be possible, and nothing actual would be actual. To be true to this is a formal requirement of any viable idea of God. To think God, therefore, is to think that without which one could not think—whether with respect to what one thinks (content) or how one thinks it (form) or how one thinks what one thinks (mode) or that one thinks (fact). To focus on God (or the question of God) is to focus on that without which one could not focus on God (or the question of God) or on anything else. This has to be taken in its most radical sense. There is nothing special about God, but everything is unique. "God makes no difference to anything," as Herbert McCabe held, "not because God is impotent, but because God is the reason why there is anything at all."[3] This is why theology does not assume any specialist knowledge about God from sources inaccessible to anyone else. What it thinks and says is public; it can be understood by anyone who cares, whether one agrees with it, dismisses it, or rejects it. But it does not think something that one could meaningfully affirm, ignore, or deny without affecting one's view about everything, including oneself. For theology, even to deny God presupposes the prior actuality of that which one denies. Therefore, theology cannot focus on God without understanding itself and everything else as being impossible without God. This is a unique claim made only about God, the prior actuality of everything possible and actual; or, rather, it is a claim made about the idea of God—that is to say, that which we think when we think God as the one without whom nothing possible would be possible, and nothing actual would be actual. But it does not assume God to be a self-evident reality that nobody could meaningfully deny. On the contrary, God is neither given in experience (God is not one god among others) nor accessible in thought (God is beyond everything that can be thought). God is not a token (this god) of a type (god), nor a particular (a Christian or a Jewish or a Muslim God) of something general (divinity), nor merely singular (one) but unique (the only one). This does not make God ineffable but rather inconceivable as God without God's self-disclosure. And it does not make theology impossible but allows it to see God present and at work everywhere, albeit in different ways. Just as the sciences explain everything *etsi deus non daretur* (as if there were no God), so theology discerns everything *etsi deus daretur* (as if there were God). On the one hand, therefore, theology has nothing more to do with religion, religions, or a particular religion than it has to do with other areas and aspects of human life that are explored in the humanities (culture) or the natural and social sciences (nature and society). On the other hand, the only way God can become its theme is because of God's self-

---

3. Herbert McCabe, *God Still Matters* (London: Continuum 2005), xiii.

disclosing relationship to human life and human life's relationship to God. God is not an entity among others in the world but that without which there would be no life and no world, and thus no way of dealing with God or religion or anything else.

It follows that theology, since it is directed toward God, must take *everything* into account, not just the limited field of religious phenomena within human life. In principle, then, the subject area for theological thinking extends far beyond religion and religions. The social sciences are no closer to the center of its concerns than the natural sciences or the life sciences. Theology focuses on God, not by making God a special topic among others but by perceiving everything, seeking to understand everything, exploring everything, and reasoning about everything in the light of God's effective presence. It is *theo*logy insofar as it concerns itself with bringing the *logos* of the phenomena of this world to expression as it is manifested or hidden in the light of God's presence.

Doing this makes theology *theology*. *How* it does this marks it as *radical* theology. Radical theology not only addresses everything in the light of the presence of God, but it does so within a certain horizon and from a very specific point of view, that of the radical reorientation from nonfaith or unfaith (unbelief) to faith (belief).[4] This transformation is not something that one can bring about on one's own; instead, it is a totally contingent experience that those affected, with good reason, do not attribute to themselves or to others, but to God alone. This by no means explains this contingency or theologically defuses it. In fact, it is just the opposite: through reference to God its inexplicable contingency is not only retained, but increased and deepened. Theology becomes radical by consistently and uncompromisingly reasoning on the basis of this event, whose contingency is not explained away but radically enhanced through reference to God. It explores an event horizon that through its very

---

4. I shall use the terms *non-faith*, *lack of faith*, and *unfaith* interchangeably as the opposite or negative complement of *faith*.

recourse to God makes room for absolute novelty and thus offers a new perspective on everything.

Radical theology aims neither to induce such a change of orientation from unbelief (lack of faith or nonfaith) to belief (faith) nor to deduce its possibility from given experiences or principles of reason. Both would be foolish expressions of a thorough confusion about what is and is not possible and useful for theological thinking. Rather, it sets out from this change of orientation and seeks from within it to shed light on the conditions of its possibility and to clarify the prerequisites and consequences of its reality. Without this change, there could be no radical theology. The given for radical theology, however, is not the mere empirical presence of certain life phenomena (conversion experiences), but rather the radical transformation of the framework of orientation through which all life phenomena are experienced and understood. This transformation is not confined to certain phenomena, but can appear anywhere and at any time, if it happens at all. Biographically, this change may occur as a sudden event or as an imperceptibly recurring process that others can hardly notice and that the persons themselves may recognize only in retrospect. It thus corresponds to the Christian paradigm for this change, the confession of faith in Jesus Christ, expressed in terms of the end of the old life and the beginning of a new life: the world came to an end and a new world began and hardly anyone noticed. If not for the church, no one would even remember. But the fact that the church exists is no merit of the church, and that it still exists after two thousand years is also nothing for the church to brag about.

This change is radical both in the biographical sense and the historical sense because it is a new beginning of life, not simply a change of life, a becoming new (an eschatological event), not simply a becoming different (a historical event). Of course, this transformation of orientation, in either life history or world history, can be described as an alteration or becoming different in such a way as to underscore the continuity of the life and of the history. Nonetheless, the essence of the experience is that the continuing sequence of "the old" is not extended, but a sequence that is entirely new begins. This is not merely a new series of the old things: both in life and in history, something radically new has come into being, not just another case of the old. Thus, neither life nor history can be described any longer as a simple unity; they must now be eschatologically differentiated (old and new). This does not mean, however, that the old is simply what came before while the new is what comes after. Instead, the distinction between the old and the new applies both to the life and history that came before and to the life and history that comes after: *everything* is seen in a new way in light of the eschatologically decisive point of view of the old and the new. This is what makes it a *radical* transformation of orientation.

This radical transformation of orientation, from nonfaith to faith, does not lead to a new life in a different world, but to a new worldview and view of life in which everything is seen anew, including the biographical or historical event that led to this new view. This change can be investigated by all the scholarly and scientific methods we normally use in studying the phenomena of human life, history, and culture. Nonetheless, if one does not recognize that this *becoming different* in faith is understood and lived out as a *becoming new* by those who define their new identity and life as believers by reference to it, then the crucial point will be missed entirely. One does not do it justice when this terminology is understood only as a hyperbolic way of expressing what "actually" is, in a scientifically strict sense, only a *becoming different*. After all, in life and in history there is no becoming new, only an ongoing becoming different. Once a life has begun, it can no longer become new; it can only become different so long as it exists and has not reached its end. If it is new, then it was previously not yet there (substantial becoming); if it was already there, then it can only become different, but not new anymore (accidental becoming). A life is new only at the beginning, and that lies always behind us. But each beginning is also a becoming different, if not for the new life itself, then for the context in which it appears. Thus, there are always two things one can say about the beginning of a new life: It is new because it now is, whereas before it was not; and it is a change in the world that now is different from what it was before. When new life makes its entrance, it enters into the context of a particular history. What is a becoming new for it is a becoming different for the context: it is not the new life that is changed, but the history that is changed. Every becoming new is thus a becoming different, but not every becoming different is also a becoming new. Nothing that is can become new, so wherever something new comes into being, the context in which it happens also becomes different. It is not the becoming new, but the becoming different, that is the dominant category. And since every change is an event that changes the state of the world, every becoming new from the perspective of a new life is a becoming different from the perspective of the world. The world permanently changes, but it only becomes different and never new.

Looking at the transformation from nonfaith to faith solely in terms of a life becoming different sets up the ordinary point of view as the measure of the theological point of view, and thus misses its point. Theology does not understand all becoming new, including the coming to faith, as "in the end" simply becoming different. It understands *this* becoming different *as a becoming new* of *this life*. This is true only because and insofar as the change from nonfaith to faith possesses a surplus in comparison with all other phenomena of life in the process of becoming different. Faith cannot be reduced to a set of empirically describable phenomena that initially are not there in someone's life and then are there (even though it certainly does not occur without such phenomena). Faith is not itself a phenomenon in life, an acceptance of what one has previously not thought true or what one has experienced as real (a cognitive and emotional becoming different that affects a person's will and attitudes), but a fundamentally new horizon within which all the phenomena of life are understood in a new way (a radical becoming new, and thus not to be traced back merely to a becoming different). Only within this horizon can one speak at all of a change from nonfaith to faith: neither faith nor lack of faith appears as an inventory of particular phenomena that can be specified by distinguishing them from other phenomena in life. Faith is much more a way of living and perceiving human life as a whole, a way that lives, understands and judges life in all of its dimensions and with all of its phenomena in relationship to God. Thus, in principle, faith brings more into view than human life within its own horizon can see and say about itself. Within the horizon of the phenomena of life, nonfaith or lack of faith does not become a topic of concern; it becomes so only in relation to faith. The phenomena of life neither define what faith is nor what nonfaith is; faith arises only in relationship to God, and so does nonfaith. Without recourse to God, then, there is no way of clarifying what is meant here by becoming new. If such recourse is denied, then the *becoming new* appears only as a *becoming different* and the theological point is lost.

Of course, this all depends upon what one means here by "God." Little would be gained if this God were only a theological construct and Christian interpretant—that is, an arbitrary point of view or way of thinking that could be dispensed with without losing anything essential with respect to the phenomena under consideration. To understand everything *coram deo* (before God) does not mean that one can do just as well without this *coram deo* reference, because everything can also be understood *coram mundo* (before the world) or *coram seipso* (before oneself): we still have the phenomena, but we do not determine their meaning by reference to God. Theologically, this is a fatal mistake—a mistake made by all those who think that believers and unbelievers share the same phenomena of life but differ only on their meaning. The difference is much more radical. Without such reference to God, one is not simply thinking differently about life and the world. Rather, one does not think theologically in the proper sense of the word at all because, strictly speaking, there is nothing to think about anymore nor anyone to think. Without reference to God, one does not simply lose a certain way of looking at things; the phenomena themselves disappear, and so does the subject to whom they appear. Believers and unbelievers do not share the same world of phenomena and differ only about the phenomena's relation to God. Rather, their difference goes all the way down to everything actual and possible.

They live in different worlds inasmuch as that believers hold that everything owes its existence to God whereas unbelievers ignore or deny this. For unbelievers there is a world but—perhaps, probably, very probably, or certainly—no God. For believers, there is no world without God and nobody to affirm or deny it. However, this cannot be read off or inferred from the phenomena but becomes clear only when one comes to see oneself and everything else as creation. Those who do, live in a creation that is distinct from but dependent on its Creator. Those who do not, live in a world whose fundamental character they miss, whether they speak of God or not. That they miss it neither is self-evident nor can be shown from the phenomena of life. It requires a total change of perspective on everything, including one's own point of view, to see the world and oneself as God's creation. Since nobody begins her life as a believer and nobody can achieve this change of perspective by herself, it is precisely the change from nonfaith to faith that discloses the character of the world as creation, and the character of God not only as Creator but also as revealer of Godself as Creator and the world as creation. Without the change from nonfaith to faith, nobody can see the world as creation, and this change cannot be brought about by anyone in the world, but is rightly attributed by believers only to the effective presence of Godself.

Radical theology thus understands reference to God neither as an arbitrary nor as a necessary horizon of interpreting the phenomena of life that it epistemologically and hermeneutically unfolds. Instead, it explores the reference to God as the horizon of the event of the transformation from non-faith to faith through God's effective presence. It is the horizon of an entirely contingent event that is not a creation of theology, but through which theology first becomes possible at all. To live and think *coram deo* (before God) does not mean to understand life in reference to God and to understand God within the horizon of life, but rather to understand God in reference to life and life within the horizon of the event in which God so manifests the divine presence in human life that it does not remain what it was but becomes what it is: the place within creation where the presence of the Creator is experienced by the creature.

The program of radical theology is to explore the meaning of the event in which human life becomes the place where God manifests divine presence. It does so not by grounding its thinking on anything it thinks, but by measuring its thinking by the event on which it is grounded. This makes its thinking radically experimental, at any time open to revision, should this be called for by the event that makes it think what it thinks. All theology can think only what is not self-contradictory but possible, and theology can think that only because its thinking is itself possible and not impossible. Radical theology is radical precisely by building on nothing but the actuality of this possibility. Without the silent power of the possible that it explores, radical theology would not exist. This power of the possible is given to it in the event that it contemplates and that makes its contemplation possible. Radical theology cannot contemplate this event without contemplating a prior actuality that precedes it and provokes it. And it cannot understand this event without understanding it in the way in which the event itself discloses its meaning (as a becoming new) against the misunderstandings (as a mere becoming different) by which it is covered up but in, with, and under which it is hidden and communicated. In order to discern and bring out the meaning of the event from among the manifold misunderstandings and failures to understand, radical theology must proceed with a critical hermeneutics that identifies misunderstandings as misunderstandings and understandings as understandings. That was the task that the hermeneutical theology of the twentieth century set for itself. I begin, therefore, with an analysis of twentieth-century hermeneutical theology.

1

Hermeneutical Theology

Everything has its time. Hermeneutical theology had its time—in the 1960s, 1970s, and 1980s. That is a significant duration. In contrast to some other theological movements, it did not simply remain an announcement and an agenda; it actually has a history that is worth remembering. But does it have a present that is worth mentioning? Or any future at all? Are there reasons to continue that which students of Rudolf Bultmann such as Ernst Fuchs, Gerhard Ebeling, and Eberhard Jüngel—and their own students—began two or three generations ago? And what would there be to continue, if one wanted to?

I am not suggesting that there is only one answer.[1] But to be able to answer at all, one must first take a look backward, for orientation, before looking ahead. What goes by the name of "hermeneutical

---

1. See U. H. J. Körtner, "Zur Einführung: Glauben und Verstehen. Perspektiven Hermeneutischer Theologie im Anschluß an Rudolf Bultmann," in *Glauben und Verstehen. Perspektiven hermeneutischer Theologie*, ed. U. H. J. Körtner (Neukirchen-Vluyn: Neukirchener Verlag, 2000), 1-18; H. Vetter, "Hermeneutische Phänomenologie und Dialektische Theologie. Heidegger und Bultmann," in Körtner, *Glauben und Verstehen*, 19-38; O. Bayer, "Hermeneutische Theologie," in Körtner, *Glauben und Verstehen*, 39-55; Körtner, *Theologie des Wortes Gottes. Positionen—Probleme—Perspektiven*(Göttingen: Vandenhoeck & Ruprecht, 2001); and Körtner, *Hermeneutische Theologie. Zugänge zur Interpretation des christlichen Glaubens und seiner Lebenspraxis* (Neukirchen-Vluyn: Neukirchener Verlag, 2008).

theology" within Protestant theology cannot easily be reduced to a single type or common denominator. Of course, there are similarities, but there are also significant differences.

In contrast to theological hermeneutics, which exists in many versions both inside and outside of Christianity,[2] hermeneutical theology is a movement within Protestant theology in the second half of the twentieth century that is tightly linked, theologically, with the development and deepening of Bultmann's theology along the lines of Reformation theology and, philosophically, with the history of philosophical hermeneutics in the twentieth century after Martin Heidegger.[3]

1. A Philosophical Perspective

These developments can be described under different aspects and from different standpoints; the same is true of that which was, is, or can be understood as hermeneutical theology. In his commendable book, Otto Pöggeler presents a philosophical narrative, rich in material and detail about the various threads of discussion, concerning what he, following Heidegger and Bultmann, calls "hermeneutical theology."[4] However, exactly what is to be understood by that term remains obscure, lost among the complexities of the extensive reminiscences from the history of theology and philosophy that Pöggeler shares. All the way through to the final chapter it remains unclear just what he understands "hermeneutical theology" to mean or how he wants it to be understood. True, he connects it to a number of theological and philosophical debates of the twentieth century and includes in his narrative not only different strands of twentieth-century Protestant theology but also recent publications of Pope Benedict XVI. However, within these complex discussions, "hermeneutical theology" is spoken

---

2. See, for example, J. Lauster, *Religion als Lebensdeutung. Theologische Hermeneutik heute* (Darmstadt: Wissenschaftliche Buchgesellschaft, 2005); and U. H. J. Körtner, *Einführung in die theologische Hermeneutik* (Darmstadt: Wissenschaftliche Buchgesellschaft, 2006).
3. In this book, "theology" is always understood as Christian theology. More specific definitions will be given as needed.
4. O. Pöggeler, *Philosophie und Hermeneutische Theologie. Heidegger, Bultmann und die Folgen* (Munich: W. Fink, 2009).

of in very different, sometimes contradictory, and often pejorative ways. Pöggeler fails to provide the clarity needed to guide us through this ambiguity.

Even his final chapter, presented as the systematic culmination of the work, remains vague on this point. To be sure, the publisher announces that at "the end of book stands the attempt to systematically define on the basis of philosophy what hermeneutical theology can be."[5] And Pöggeler himself announces that "it will be asked in systematic fashion how philosophy helps to bring a theology into play that claims for itself the adjective 'hermeneutical.'"[6] But this promise is never fulfilled. Pöggeler begins with Ebeling, who is said to have used "hermeneutical theology" to mean the fundamental theological "question about the ground of the necessity of theology at all."[7] Pöggeler criticizes Ebeling for answering that question in a way that was not only so Christian, but so narrowly Protestant, that it was not even able to value "the artworks of Christendom" or "Gregorian chant." Much less was it able—as had been the case since Heidegger—to value "the experience of nature and art," "Greek tragedy," "Zen Buddhism," or "Taoism."[8] And Pöggeler asks whether "today, when the continents have become closer, any talk of a 'hemeneutical' theology must not be developed from this world-wide conversation," and whether "what we call 'hermeneutical theology'" ought not be practiced "as a global hermeneutics" of a variety of religious and cultural traditions.[9] Hermeneutical theology, to put it succinctly, ought to be understood and practiced as the cultural hermeneutics of religions.[10]

However, Pöggeler correctly sees that the "focus upon 'theology'" can be "a problem."[11] "In a hermeneutical theology the very heart of the question must be whether the step to theology must be, or may

---

5. Ibid., back cover.
6. Ibid., 283.
7. Ibid., 295; See G. Ebeling, "Hermeneutische Theologie?," in *Wort und Glaube II* (Tübingen: Mohr Siebeck, 1969), 99–120.
8. Ibid., 296.
9. Ibid., 296–97.
10. Cf. I. U. Dalferth and Ph. Stoellger, eds., *Hermeneutik der Religion* (Tübingen: Mohr Siebeck, 2007).
11. Pöggeler, *Philosophie*, 297.

be, taken at all."[12] Would it not be better to restrict oneself to the hermeneutical and forgo the theological? Should one not concentrate on the understanding of religious, cultural, and anthropological phenomena and, as "a philosopher like Franz von Baader in opposition to Hegel and Schelling" rightly stressed, want "to see the effects of the religions not determined by metaphysical principles"?[13] Indeed, if theology is understood to be a metaphysical science of the principles of religion, one can only agree. But one can only understand theology in that way if one has not understood what hermeneutical theology of the Protestant sort is all about. Pöggeler's extensive survey actually misses the very point of the movement that he discusses in such detail. He fails to grasp it because he gets lost in the diversity of the historical material and in the vagueness of his view of hermeneutics, while simultaneously holding firmly to an understanding of theology that is not that of hermeneutical theology. In the end, therefore, for him there can only be an "interplay between philosophy and a hermeneutical theology" that remains "to be carried out again and again."[14]

The problem of this position lies neither in Pöggeler's understanding of philosophy nor in his completely legitimate request that the variety and diversity of cultures and religions be taken into account hermeneutically. Instead, the problem lies in his lack of a clear understanding of theology. Thus, he writes:

> Any effort may be counted as philosophy that takes up the questions humans ask while dismissing none of those questions. Such a philosophy always exists within a socio-historical context. It must offer instruction in the beliefs and practices which determine how people define themselves. This instruction can critically take into account the lived experience of people. If one is to speak of a hermeneutical theology, then it must be conceded that the theological approach itself is problematic. While individuals may distinguish themselves from one another by their religious decisions, they remain embedded in the comprehensive assumptions of their larger cultures. . . . As a result, philosophy has the obligation to engage with every fundamental approach in the dialogue and conflict of cultures, while allowing this dialogue and conflict to

---

12. Ibid.
13. Ibid., 26.
14. Ibid.

remain open, an openness that must be achieved again and again and often cannot be achieved without pain.[15]

As a specification of the task of a hermeneutically oriented philosophy, this statement is worthy of support, especially since not just the interpretative, but also the critical task of philosophy is emphasized. But while philosophy is concentrated on a problem-oriented instruction regarding the "beliefs and practices which determine how people define themselves," the task of hermeneutical theology is intended to be that it "critically take[s] into account" what is, in fact, experienced within the variety of cultures and religions. However, this critical account must by no means take on the problematic form of a theology that seeks to make normative statements and privileges one faith persuasion over another. Accordingly, hermeneutical theology is limited to remembering "that the theological approach itself is problematic." This self-critical function of seeing itself as a problem is all Pöggeler can get out of hermeneutical theology.

But that is too little. Hermeneutical theology is not simply that which should distinguish every critical theology. It does not exhaust itself in seeing itself as a problem. It has a positive task. But at this point, Pöggeler's account remains opaque.

2. Theological Perspectives

Pöggeler's book fails to address the challenges of clarifying how hermeneutical theology understands theology and of giving a theological account of hermeneutical theology. That challenge will be taken up in this study in light of German-speaking Protestant theology of the last century. Here, too, the task will not only be reconstruction but also criticism. But beyond this, I shall attempt to critically adopt the core insights of hermeneutical theology and to develop them in a constructive fashion. My aim is not only to report on the history of philosophy and theology in the twentieth century, but to make a theological contribution to the debate in the twenty-first century.

---

15. Ibid., 27.

A critical look to the past is a prerequisite for moving forward in a productive way. This look backward would, however, prove to be blind in crucial respects if it did not see that two clearly different tendencies can be distinguished within the theological tradition we are considering. They have two important features in common. Both follow the Reformation tradition of being oriented on the incarnate *verbum dei*,[16] because that is the only place at which (and from which) one not only can but *must* speak of God, if one wants to say anything at all.[17] And both place the basic relationship between *cognitio dei* and *cognitio hominis* at the center, although with characteristically different emphases. One of these tendencies is represented by Gerhard Ebeling, the other by Ernst Fuchs and Eberhard Jüngel.

The theological point of Ebeling's approach was to develop, with constant recourse to Martin Luther, Friedrich Daniel Ernst Schleiermacher, and Dietrich Bonhoeffer, those features in Bultmann's theology that are consistent with Reformation theology, and to integrate them into a Lutheran hermeneutics of the word of God based on the distinction between law and gospel. This was carried out within the framework of a *hermeneutics of reality* centered on the key concept

16. See Ebeling, "Hermeneutische Theologie?"; E. Fuchs, "Das Wort Gottes," in *Zum hermeneutischen Problem in der Theologie. Die existentiale Interpretation* (Tübingen: Mohr Siebeck, 1959), 323-33; Fuchs, "Das Sprachereignis in der Verkündigung Jesu, in der Theologie des Paulus und im Ostergeschehen," in *Zum hermeneutischen Problem*, 281-305; Fuchs, "Das Neue Testament und das hermeneutische Problem," in *Glaube und Erfahrung: Zum christologischen Problem im Neuen Testament* (Tübingen: Mohr Siebeck, 1965), 136-73, esp. 150-57; and Fuchs, "Neues Testament und Wort Gottes," *ThLZ* 97 (1972): 1-16. Fuchs's texts are scarcely accessible unless one reads the Swabian dialect. "One has the feeling that Fuchs would be saying something marvelously important if he were saying anything at all," as R. W. Jenson, *The Knowledge of Things Hoped For: The Sense of Theological Discourse* (New York: Oxford University Press, 1969), 196, aptly noted. Those who have difficulty with the reading of Fuchs's texts, and understand no Swabian, can rely on the works of E. Jüngel. There one can find, presented in accurate hermeneutical punctiliousness, all of the sentences between Fuchs's thoughts and insights that Fuchs himself left unwritten.

17. In the world of human experience, there is not a single point where you would have to speak of God or where there would not still be much important to say if one renounced speaking of God. But one cannot speak about the Word of God, or about God's self-revelation, without speaking of God. Whoever cannot or will not do so may without self-contraction completely renounce the use of the term "God," because everything that can be said with it can also be said without it. Conversely, Christian theology, which has to speak about the Word of God and divine self-revelation if it is to have anything to say at all, cannot *not* speak of God, but at the same time must here speak of God in a very particular way if it is really to speak of God. That is why, starting from here, theology has good reason to make God a topic of discussion throughout, even where there is no necessity to do so. In this formal sense, Christian theology is a theology of revelation, or it is superfluous, because its talk of God could be replaced by other interpretations of reality as it is experienced or might be experienced.

of the *word-event*, in which the *cognitio dei* is developed from the *cognitio hominis* as shaped by the dialectic of sin and faith.

The theological point of the approaches of Fuchs and especially Jüngel, however, was to develop, by means of a thorough exegesis of New Testament texts within the horizon of the reflections on language of the later Heidegger and the Trinitarian Word of God hermeneutic of Karl Barth, a revelation-oriented theological hermeneutics of the freely occurring and self-disclosing presence of God. Its central term was the *speech-event*, and it was elaborated as a *hermeneutics of possibility* in which everything, even the *cognitio hominis*, was developed from the *cognitio dei* disclosing itself as such.

These two currents of hermeneutical theology also differ in their philosophical emphasis. While Ebeling proposed a *relational ontology of reality*, developed in the footsteps of the subject-hermeneutics of modernity, Jüngel outlined a *dynamic ontology of possibility*, which opened the way to a postmodern hermeneutics of the event.

To explain what this means, let me briefly review in the next chapter some central lines of development within twentieth-century hermeneutics.

2
―――

Trends within Twentieth-Century Hermeneutics

In all of its versions, hermeneutics is the practice and theory of an art: the *art of a detour to understanding through interpretation* (hermeneutics as interpretative practice),[1] and the theory of this art, the *poetics of understanding through interpretation* (hermeneutics as theoretical reflection of interpretative practices).[2]

1. The Basic Hermeneutic Constellation: Self and Situation

We can understand, and sometimes we actually do. Yet we do not always understand, and we do not need to understand all the time in order to live our lives. Much of what we do in our shared worlds of meaning is governed by daily routines that we perform without understanding what they are and how they work and without feeling

---

1. As E. Fuchs, "Das Neue Testament und das hermeneutische Problem," in *Glaube und Erfahrung: Zum christologischen Problem im Neuen Testament* (Tübingen: Mohr Siebeck, 1965), 150, emphasizes, "At home, one does not speak in order to understand, but because one understands." When that no longer takes place, hermeneutical efforts become necessary.
2. This accounts for the somewhat ambiguous use of the term "hermeneutics" for both the practice of interpretation and the theory of that practice.

a need to understand them. Only when they break down, we begin to wonder. Then we need to understand what has happened, why things have changed, and how we could remedy the situation in order to proceed. The need to understand arises because things have gone wrong. Seeking to understand in such cases does not mean that we have understood before or that a previous understanding has broken down. It may merely indicate that we seek to understand in order to find a way out of a situation in which we cannot proceed. We seek a solution to a problem, but it need not be a problem of understanding, and understanding may not be the solution to the problem at stake but rather that without which we cannot arrive at a solution. However, we cannot try to understand without realizing that we can also misunderstand and fail to understand. Then our attempts to understand take the form of overcoming or avoiding possible or actual misunderstandings and failures to understand. These are indeed problems of understanding, but they are not the only problems that challenge us to understand. Thus, while it is not necessary for us to understand in order to be able to live our lives, we can only fail to understand because we are able to understand, and we need to understand when we are faced with problems of understanding or with problems that cannot be solved without understanding.

The need to understand arises in situations where people who can understand do not understand (any more). The basic hermeneutic constellation is thus the correlation of "selves" that can understand and of "situations" that can be understood against the backdrop of an actual lack or failure to understand them, or to understand them sufficiently. We live in a world that we can understand even if in fact we do not, and we can do so because the world is intelligible ("It is possible to understand the world") and because we can develop the capacity to understand it ("It is possible for us to understand the world"). This is not to say that the world is completely intelligible to us or that we can fully understand it. But without some intelligibility of the world we could not understand anything, and without some capacity to understand we would not understand anything. And just as the intelligibility of the world is not a consequence of our understanding but its presupposition, so our capacity to understand is not a consequence of our understanding but a prerequisite to it. We live in a meaningful world not of our making, and we can relate to it in meaningful ways because of our capacity to understand—a capacity that we share to differing degrees with other human beings who are also able to acquire to differing degrees the capacity to understand and live as selves who can understand in situations that can be understood.

Understanding is thus a fundamental means of carrying out our lives in relation to the situation in which we live—whether we mean by "situation" our natural *environment* (the natural world of events and entities surrounding us: *Umwelt*, or surrounding world), our *fellow human beings* (the social, historical, and cultural worlds in which we live: *Mitwelt*, social world; *Vorwelt*, primeval or past world; *Nachwelt*, afterworld or future world; *Kulturwelt*, cultural world), *ourselves* (our private and public worlds as subjects and the moral world of our life as persons among persons: *Subjektwelt*, subjective world; *Innenwelt*, inner world; *Außenwelt*, external world; *Selbstwelt*, world of the self), or the *presence of God* (the world of positive or negative relations to the one without whose presence there would be no persons and no natural, social, historical, cultural, subjective, or moral worlds: *Welt des Glaubens*, the world of faith, and *Welt des Unglaubens*, the world of nonfaith, *coram deo* [before God]).[3]

These various ways of construing the situation in which we live are not mutually exclusive but can coexist with one another and, indeed, require one another. What is more, they correlate with an equally sophisticated and complex account of us in our situations. For just as we can determine our situations in many differentiated ways, so

---

3. The different ways outlined of construing the situation in which we live cannot be understood as moving from the particular to the general or as being members of one and the same series of determinations. All sorts of naturalism that assume this are self-defeating. Rather, these ways of construing our situations differentiate the distinctive perspectives of *Umwelt*, *Mitwelt*, *Selbstwelt*, and *presence of God*, which cannot be reduced to one another and cannot be derived from each other. We cannot adequately understand our situations and ourselves from one point of view only, construed as comprehensive as it may be, but only from different perspectives and from different points of view. For we are not only complex beings (as seen from any of those perspectives), but highly precarious syntheses of radically different views.

too can we determine ourselves in our situations in a variety of ways: *as* entities in the *Umwelt* of others; *as* social, historical, and cultural beings in the *Mitwelt, Vorwelt, Nachwelt,* and *Kulturwelt* we share with others; *as* subjects or persons in our *Subjektwelt, Innenwelt, Außenwelt,* or *Selbstwelt*; and *as* believers or unbelievers in the world of faith or nonfaith. All these ways of seeing, construing, or understanding ourselves *as* something or someone are variations and concrete determinations of the fundamental correlation of self and situation. We always exist in a world, and we cannot exist otherwise: to be for us is to exist in a world (*Dasein*), and we cannot exist in a world without living in it in some way or other (*Sosein*). But in our world things can go wrong, expectations may fail, and routines break down. Therefore, we cannot live long in the world in which we exist without understanding the world and ourselves in specific ways, as we show in our everyday practices and dealings with the world, with others, and with ourselves. We always live in a world of meaning into which we are born and in which we can understand or fail to understand our natural environment, our fellow human beings, ourselves, and God *as* something or someone, and we cannot do otherwise.

2. Orienting Terms

As beings who exist and live in such a way, we refer to ourselves by using reflexive pronouns, to others by using personal pronouns, and to our world by speaking of our situations under some description that indicates how we access the world and are located in it: "I do it *myself*," "*He* has done it *to me*," "She lives *in her mother's house* at the bottom of *the next street to the right*." In each case we cannot use these locating terms without employing a whole scheme of orientation. We orient ourselves in the world by locating others and ourselves with the help of schemes of orientation that structure not the world but our relations to the world. Such schemes are established in communities by drawing relevant distinctions and by paying attention to important contrasts in common areas of life and practice. Thus, we orient ourselves in space in terms of spatial distinctions (left, right, behind, in front of, above, below); in time in terms of temporal distinctions (today, tomorrow, yesterday, past, present, future, earlier than, later than, simultaneous with); in social contexts in terms of family relationships (mother, father, sister, brother, uncle, aunt), professional functions (teacher, student, professor, administrator, fellow, provost), or personal pronouns (I, you, he, she, it, we, you, they); and in life in terms of distinctions such as good or evil, good or bad, pleasant or unpleasant, to be strived for or to be avoided, pain or pleasure, and so forth. The various sets of distinctions differ, but the important point for all of them is that we cannot use any distinction in order to locate others or ourselves in the respective scheme without using the whole set of distinctions.[4] Orientation is holistic, plural, and pragmatic; there is no orientation unless it is concretely enacted and performed, and we cannot do so or talk about it without employing shorthand formulas for us in our world ("self") and for the changing world in which we live and try to orient ourselves ("situation"). *Self* and *situation* are not descriptive terms that signify something that could be explored independently (*a self* or *a situation*) as David Hume was not the only one to discover. They are orienting terms that we use to structure the world in which we try to orient ourselves (situation) and that we employ to locate ourselves in the world structured in this way (self). Without actual human beings there are no selves, and since human beings live their lives in a permanently changing world, we cannot orient ourselves in our world without locating ourselves in changing situations.

The use of orienting terms has been the source of many misunderstandings and confusions in the history of philosophy and theology because of misconstruing the grammar of those terms according to the grammar of descriptive terms. However, it is not a mysterious self but *we human beings* who live in the world, and there is nothing special about the world that makes it our situation. The terms *self* and *situation* are not names for entities, phenomena, or structures

---

4. Cf. I. U. Dalferth, *Die Wirklichkeit des Möglichen. Hermeneutische Religionsphilosophie* (Tübingen: Mohr Siebeck, 2003), 463–66, 493–509.

alongside the human beings we are and the world in which we live. They are simplifying abbreviations to talk about our world and ourselves in certain respects, strategies for orienting ourselves in our world but not special features of the world.

Since human beings live their lives in changing situations, we cannot address concrete human existence as a self without locating it in a situation: a self is always a self-in-a-situation, and a situation is always a situation-of-a-self. Of course, these are—potentially oversimplifying—ways of talking about *la condition humaine* in the world. For just as *situation* is a term that refers to the complex and changing environments in which each of us lives, so the term *self* refers to those who live in such a way in those situations that they can develop an understanding of their situation and of themselves that guides their way of relating to their situations and to each other in their situations. We exist in situations, and we become human beings who can be addressed as selves by living in our situations in a certain way—a way characterized by human self-understanding, free self-determination, and moral self-orientation. Situations are always situations *of somebody*, they are *shared with others*, and we apply the term *self* to human beings who together with others live in shared situations that they experience and change by interacting with each other and their environment. We cannot do this without understanding ourselves, our situations, and those who share our situations in some way or other, for we determine ourselves as we understand ourselves, everybody else, and everything else in our situations. But different human beings understand differently, determine themselves differently, and orient themselves differently, and it is rarely possible to agree on only one acceptable way of doing this. Therefore, we cannot live as selves without participating in conflicts of understandings and self-understandings (What do we know? Who are we?), conflicts about determinations (How shall we live?), and conflicts about orientations (How ought we to exist?). And while there may be occasional solutions for some of these conflicts, there will never be an end to all.

However, the correlation of self and situation cannot be determined only in the variety of ways indicated; it can also be construed from the perspective of the situation (the world in which we live in certain ways) and from the perspective of the self (the human beings who live in their situations in certain ways). In the first case, situations are seen as impacting selves. This activity can be determined in different ways, depending on whether we construe the relation to our situation as a relation to our *Umwelt*, our *Mitwelt*, our *Selbstwelt*, or *God*. Accordingly, we understand ourselves to be affected differently in pain, suffering, receptivity, emotions, affects, feelings, perceptions, understanding, beliefs, or faith. All these are modes of passivity, and they show the differentiated ways in which we experience ourselves as part of the larger situation in which we live.

In the second case, selves are seen as impacting their situations. This shows not merely in the changes we cause and the alterations we effect in our situations, but also in how we interpret, determine, or describe the situation in which we live and act (as *Umwelt*, *Mitwelt*, *Selbstwelt*, or *God*) and our place and role in the situation thus understood (as organisms, human beings, selves, persons, believers, or unbelievers). These interpretations determine how we see and relate to our situation, to others, and to ourselves.

3. Self as Shorthand for a Specific Way of Living a Human Life

Selves are not mysterious entities that are hard to detect in the world. In English, the term *self* is neither a noun nor a verb nor a pronoun but an operator "that makes an ordinary pronoun into a reflexive one: 'her' into 'herself,' 'him' into 'himself' and 'it' into 'itself.' The reflexive pronoun is used when the object of an action or attitude is the same as the subject of that action or attitude."[5] In much the same sense the term *self* "is also used as a prefix for names of activities and attitude, identifying the special case where the object is the same as the agent: self-love, self-hatred, self-abuse, self-promotion, self-knowledge."[6] Thus, the grammatical operator *self* identifies a relation of sameness or

5. John Perry, The Self (1995) https://faculty.washington.edu/smcohen/453/PerrySelf.pdf.
6. Ibid.

a reflexive self-relation, but it does not name or refer to an entity or to a particular attitude or activity of an entity. It is neither a noun (that refers) nor a verb (that describes) but an operator (that qualifies)—that is, a linguistic device that allows or facilitates the expression of a pragmatic feature of a communicative situation (it was *me* and not somebody else who returned the book to the library) at the sematic level of what is communicated ("I returned the book myself").[7]

These grammatical observations should alert us when the term *self* is used as a noun that refers to a referent—to somebody, that is, a material body or (gendered) organism that represents the presence of something distinct from its materiality called "the self"—or when "the self" is used "for the set of attributes that a person attaches to himself or herself most firmly, the attributes that the person finds it difficult or impossible to imagine himself or herself without."[8] In all such cases, the *self* is contrasted to the *other*—whether in the sense of the body or the corporality or materiality of a human organism ("body"), or in the sense of other objects and organisms ("things"), or in the sense of other persons or selves ("the other")—and understood as the operator, "the agent, the knower and the ultimate locus of personal identity."[9]

This view raises a number of issues. First, there is the fallacy of mistaking grammar for description. The self, understood in this way, "is a mythical entity.... It is a philosophical muddle to allow the space which differentiates 'my self' from 'myself' to generate the illusion of a mysterious entity distinct from ... the human being."[10] Grammatical features do not depict reality but help to orient speakers in a communicative situation. We are human speakers who refer to

---

7. Grammatically, operators are defined as auxiliaries that facilitate, for example, the expression of a negation, interrogative, or emphasis (cf. http://heather-marie-kosur.suite101.com/verb-functions-in-predicate-verb-phrases-a136667). But operators are not restricted to this. Thus *negation* can be expressed by the operator *not* because in English a "clause is made negative by adding *not* or suffixed *n't* after its finite auxiliary verb" (http://www.phon.ucl.ac.uk/home/dick/aux.htm).
8. Perry, "Self."
9. Ibid. Cf. Galen Strawson, "The Self," *Consciousness Studies* 4 (1997): 405–28; and Strawson *Selves: An Essay in Revisionary Metaphysics* (Oxford: Oxford University Press, 2009).
10. Anthony Kenny, *The Self* (Marquette: Marquette University Press, 1988), 3–4.

ourselves by using the reflexive pronoun; but we do not refer to something distinct from us ("a self") when we do so.

Second, there is (what Whitehead called) the fallacy of misplaced concreteness: we notice that we are different from that which others, or we ourselves, perceive when we look at or interact with each other, and we turn this *marker of a difference*—which is at best a negative limit term ("self" = *not* a body)—into a description of something (object or substance) that is different from what we perceive by our senses.

Third, there is the question: what is meant by "personal identity" here? As Paul Ricoeur has pointed out, we must be careful not to confuse what he called our *ipse-identity* (what we take to be decisive for us from our own perspective) with our *idem-identity* (what is taken to be sufficient for identifying us over time from the perspective of others). The first is what we may express in an autobiographical account of our life, and this view has nothing to say about the beginning and end of our life. The second is what a biographer may present as the biography of our life, and this view has no access to how we experience our life. Things go badly wrong when we confuse these irreducibly different accounts and perspectives. The term *self* then becomes used interchangeably with *person*, and persons are understood as entities that possess certain characteristics, traits, or properties such as "agency," "self-awareness," "time-consciousness," "rights and duties," and the like by which they can be marked off from other entities that do not possess those properties.

This is a highly problematic view. As many have pointed out, selves are not physically or empirically detectable entities. This is not due to a failure of our empirical methods, which include scanning and brain imaging. *Idem*-characteristics of our personal identity can be directly observed; *ipse*-characteristics, on the other hand, can only be indirectly inferred from a person's articulation, manifestation, or communication of his or her self-understanding. In the latter sense, the term *self* does not name a natural entity, nor does it refer to a set of biological, psychological, or social facts that are descriptively accessible in a third-person perspective. The natural world does not include selves but only biological organisms of different complexity; some have brains, and those with the most complex brains we know we call "human beings."

But to restrict the use of the term *self* in the *idem*-sense of identity to human beings seems to be arbitrary, to say the least. If the self is defined by a set of (necessary and/or sufficient) properties, then every entity that shares these properties is a self; and if a human person, for whatever reasons, fails to possess these properties or fails to possess them to a sufficient degree, then he or she is not (or is no longer) a self and hence should not be called a person either. The danger of this view of the self is that it drives a wedge between the humanity and the selfhood of human beings so that there can be non-human beings that are selves and human beings who are not selves. Even if we want to defend something like this, we can no longer explain selfhood in terms of humanity or humanity in terms of selfhood. Instead, we are in danger of collapsing an *anthropological distinction with respect to human life*—a distinction that allows us to differentiate between human and inhuman ways of living a human life—into the *biological distinction between human and nonhuman life*, hence leading us to miss the point of the reflexive grammatical use of the term *self*.

Some have attempted to avoid this by construing the term *self* not as a noun but as a *verb*—as a sign not for an entity but for the *happening* of an event or the *performance* of an activity. As Antonio Damasio put it in *The Self Comes to Mind* (2010): "There is indeed a self, but it is a process, not a thing, and the process is present at all times when we are presumed to be conscious."[11] This process he construes from a neurobiological perspective as a "witness" to that which goes on in the mind that is produced by the brain: "The witness is the something extra that reveals the presence of implicit *brain* events we call mental."[12] Yet by identifying "that something extra" in the brain with what we "call self, or me, or I" in communicative contexts, he understands the self within the narrow confines of a neurobiological perspective that construes the self as a mental observer of mental

---

11. Antonio Damasio, *The Self Comes to Mind: Constructing the Conscious Mind* (New York: Random House, 2010), 8.
12. Ibid., 17.

events.[13] Moreover, by construing the difference between "observer" and "knower" perspectives on the self as "two stages of the evolutionary development of the self," he downplays the difference between being an observer and observing an observer and reduces his knower's insight into the process character of the self to an observer's account of the evolutionary process of the self.[14] Most importantly, however, Damasio still seeks to find in the brain "that something extra" that we "call self, or me, or I" in communicative contexts instead of looking at the ways in which we actually use the terms *self, me,* or *I* in concrete communications.[15]

If we do this and pay attention to grammar, then we can see that we use terms like *self* or *situation* not as names for entities but as simplifying abbreviations to talk about our human condition in this world in certain respects. In many cases, the term functions not so much as a noun that signifies an entity but as a way of referring to oneself (I, we) or to some other human being in a certain respect (he, she, them), or it functions as the abbreviation of a verb ("selfing," becoming a self) or as (part of) an adjective or adverb (selfish/selfishly, selfless/selflessly). Where it is used as a noun, the term *self* is a shorthand formula for human beings understood as centers of activity and passivity, as the originators of doings and the recipients of sufferings, as social and political subjects, moral agents, or religious persons. The term does not refer to a special substance or a thing (the self) distinct from the human being but to a particular way or mode in which human beings exist. Only we can be selves, as far as we know, and we become selves by living in a certain way. We do not have to do so in order to be human beings, and we do not cease to be human if we fail to do so. But we become selves where we begin to understand ourselves *as* human beings (self-understanding) and seek to determine our life accordingly (self-determination and self-orientation). That is to say, we refer to human beings as selves if they are able to understand themselves as human beings among human beings (self-understanding

13. Ibid., 17.
14. Ibid., 8.
15. Ibid., 17.

as a human being), if they seek to live their life in a self-determined way (self-determination as a moral agent), and if they are willing to orient their self-determining on the principle that a good human life aims at living in a selfless and not selfish way together with others (orientation toward selflessness as the mode of a truly human life). In all those respects we can manifest selfhood by degrees: our self-understanding can be more or less adequate or true; our self-determination can be more or less efficient and responsible; our self-orientation can be more or less appropriate and right. In short, to be rightly referred to as a self is not to exhibit a stable number of features but to participate in a human mode of living that admits of degrees—that is to say, that can be increased or decreased, intensified or mitigated in various respects. To be a self is to become a self and live more or less as a self. It is not to be a special kind of being but to live as a human being in a specific way—the way we call "self."

Without actual human beings, there cannot be selves. Humans exist in situations that they share with others, they experience and change their shared situations by interacting with each other and with their environments, and only in such situations they can learn to live as selves. Our situations impact us, and we impact them; they change us, and we change them. Through experiencing and communicating, acting and interacting we relate passively and actively to our situations as something different from us. We construe our situations and ourselves in terms of how they impact us and what we seek to impact by relating to what is different from us. We do so in different ways by understanding that to which we relate as our natural environment (nature), cultural context (culture), social context (society), historical situation (former, present, and future selves), or the Infinite Other (God), without whom there would be no self, no situation, and no way of relating to or distinguishing between self and situation. And we perform this constructive interpretative task, not exclusively but significantly, through two importantly different operations: the way of *perception* and the way of *understanding*.

4. Perceiving and Understanding

Both perceiving and understanding are understood here in the widest possible sense. They signify two modally distinct ways in which the correlation of our situation and ourselves presents itself to us from the side of the situation, and not primarily as construed from our side: we perceive what is actual, and we understand what is possible. And just as we do not make what we perceive in perceiving, so we do not produce what we understand in understanding. If we did, we would not perceive but imagine, and we would not understand but invent.

However, both perceiving and understanding have active and passive sides. They are attributed to selves not merely as passive recipients of what happens to them, but also as agents who actively shape what happens to them. We contribute to forming our perceptions and to how we perceive what we perceive, and we contribute to molding our understanding and to how we understand what we understand. The details may be difficult to sort out. But it is clear that it is not either an activity or a passivity but more or less of both, and we know how to make distinctions here. Just as there is a difference between *perception* and *observation* (*seeing* and *watching*, *hearing* and *listening*, *feeling* and *discerning*), so there is a difference between *understanding* and *interpretation*. When we observe, we turn perceiving into an activity, and when we interpret, we do the same with understanding. Whereas in observation and interpretation the center of activity is located in the self (though by no means exclusively), in perception and understanding the center of activity is located in the situation (though again not exclusively). In the latter case, the passive mode dominates the active mode. This is why we cannot help perceiving (or failing to do so) when there is something we can perceive—both in the sense of "There is something that can be perceived" (possibility) and "We are able to perceive it" (capability). And similarly we cannot help understanding (or failing to do so) when there is something we can understand—again, both in the sense of

21

possibility ("There is something that can be understood") and of capacity ("We are able to understand it").

Moreover, each of these two ways of relating to situations takes on different modes and comes in different degrees. There are different ways in which we perceive and understand phenomena pertaining to our environment (*Umwelt*), to others (*Mitwelt*), to ourselves (*Selbstwelt*), or to the presence of God (*world of faith and nonfaith*). And in each case, we can perceive more or less clearly and understand more or less adequately. In perceiving, we attain awareness of our situation and ourselves through the causal mechanisms of sensory information (environment), the signifying processes of communication and interaction (others), introspection and self-observation (ourselves as others), and negative, privative, or mystical experiences: we understand that God cannot be perceived or experienced (agnosticism), we experience only a lack (that there is no God) or a trace of God's absence (negative theology), or we experience the very absence of God as the presence of the unfathomable ground of all that is and can be present (mystical theology). In all these different ways, we relate to something actual in our situations—or something we take to be actual—that is independent of and precedes our perceiving and makes it the awareness of something happening to us rather than done by us.

This is different in understanding. In contrast to perception, we are concerned in understanding not with the actual but with the possible, or with the possibilities of the actual, not with that which is the case (being) but with that which can or ought to be the case (ought), not with the present as present but with the past and the future as absent and no more or not yet present. That is to say, understanding is not a means of accessing and unraveling reality but of detecting and unlocking possibility. It does not disclose that which is (being, actuality) and which in one way or another affects us in our natural, social, cultural, historical, subjective, personal, moral, or religious worlds (affectivity, receptivity, emotion, feeling, perception, belief), but instead opens up that which is not (negativity), that which is possible (possibility), that which ought to be or ought not to be (normativity), or that which was the case or will (perhaps) be the case (past and future possibility). We need all this, in one way or another, not merely in order to react to changing situations according to a pattern of innate affects or emotional responses that we all share to some degree (behavior), but in order to determine ourselves freely and responsibly as individuals and groups to lead a good and human way of life (freedom, activity, agency, humanity, morality). We perceive what *is* (contingent existence, actual being, changing situations) and understand that which for ourselves or for others is possible, meaningful, helpful, needed, a must or an ought. In short, whereas perception is governed by being and actuality and aims at knowledge, understanding is governed by meaning and possibility and aims at insight.

5. Meaning and Understanding

Meaning is what we understand when we understand something. Nothing has a meaning per se; rather, something has meaning only in relation to a possible or actual understanding. Of course, what can be understood is not only the actual but also the possible, the fictional, or the imaginary. But there is meaning only for those who can understand, and only those can do so who are not only possible but actual and, indeed, who cannot exist without understanding. Heidegger has called this *Dasein* (Being-there). Only for those who possess the structure of *Dasein* is there meaning. It is not being or existence per se that has meaning ("*p is meaningful*" or "If p exists, then p is meaningful"); rather, being and existence have meaning only within the horizon of *Dasein* ("*p is meaningful for* . . ." or "If p is meaningful, then there is someone for whom p is meaningful").

Although there is meaning only for *Dasein*, the meaning it understands is not of its own making. Only a world that is intelligible can be understood (ontological priority of the intelligibility of the world: there is *something that can be understood*); only for those who can understand is it intelligible (epistemological priority of the capacity to understand: something can be understood *by somebody*); it is intelligible for them precisely in that it can be understood as meaningful or meaningless (hermeneutical priority of meaning: something can be understood by somebody *as something*); and it is understood in the one way or the other by becoming disclosed as meaningful or meaningless in a sign-event that integrates the other three dimensions in a continuous process of signification that opens up the difference between signifier (signifying element of a sign), signified (object), and meaning (interpretant) in a way that constitutes the world as a shared world of meaning (semiotic priority of the sign-event: something *becomes* understood by somebody as something by disclosing itself as meaningful to somebody in the very act of being interpreted as meaningful by somebody).[16]

That is to say the following: Only for someone who can understand can something be *meaningful or meaningless,* but for those who can understand, *everything* can become meaningful or meaningless. Only in relation to a possible understanding can something be called meaningful or meaningless, but wherever there is a being who understands, there is nothing that cannot be placed within the scope of the orienting distinction of the sign-process between that which is *meaningful* and that which is *meaningless.* As understanding beings, we already live in a shared world of meaning, not in a neutral world of facts (or facts and values). Only because we live in a world of meaning is it possible that much within it can be meaningless for us. From the point of view of the natural sciences, there can be only events and facts, but no meaning. But scientific research is possible only in a world where that which exists is *in principle* meaningful and understandable for those who study it, because it exists within the horizon of a way of life in which everything that can be perceived can also be understood in one way or another.[17] Only those who understand can conduct

---

16. Cf. Ch. S. Peirce's definition of a sign: "I define a sign as anything which is so determined by something else, called its Object, and so determines an effect upon a person, which effect I call its interpretant, that the later is thereby mediately determined by the former." N. Houser and Chr. J. W. Kloesel, eds., *The Essential Peirce, Selected Philosophical Writings, Volume 2 (1893-1913)* (Bloomington: Indiana University Press, 1998), 478.
17. In fact, there is much that is and remains incomprehensible to us and has no meaning. But we can

scientific research, even when that which they study is not a phenomenon of meaning but a problem of being or a fact of existence. It is not *the world* that has meaning (that is, *that which* we perceive or can perceive), but rather the world has meaning *for us* (that is, for those who perceive it *in a certain way* in and through signs, whether in an everyday or in a scientific manner). Meaning is not an attribute of the world but rather of the relationship of understanding to the world mediated through signs.

Perceiving and understanding are two paradigmatic ways of our relating to the world or, rather, of the world relating to us. They give rise to different problems, which provide the occasion for epistemological and hermeneutical reflection. As our *perceiving* is guided by the key distinction between *existence* (being) and *nonexistence* (nonbeing) and oriented through the modality of *actuality* (we can only perceive what is actual; otherwise, we call it an illusion), so is our *understanding* guided by the key distinction between *meaning* and *existence* and oriented through the modality of *possibility* (we can only understand what is meaningful and, as such, possible). Perception locates us in a specific, concrete situation (we are where we perceive); understanding opens the horizon for us of how we can act within this situation (we are what we can be). Both belong together, and both can go wrong. Not everything that we think we perceive is actually the case—we can be mistaken. And not everything that we think we understand have we understood correctly—we can be deceived. We are mistaken if we take something for real that is unreal or if we take something for unreal that is real. And we deceive ourselves if we hold something to be meaningful for ourselves or for others that is not possible—that is to say, accessible as a possibility—for them or for us, just as we deceive ourselves when we consider something not to be meaningful which in fact is possible. We do not perceive everything that is, and we do not understand everything we perceive. Furthermore, we do not truly understand everything that we think we

characterize it as *incomprehensible* only against the background of that which we can understand; only by reference to that which is meaningful can it be understood as *meaningless*.

do, whereas everything we do understand might still be understood better than we or others understand it. Much remains incomprehensible for us, and it is not always clear if *we* simply have not understood something or if *it* truly cannot be understood.

Wherever understanding fails in this way, and not understanding or misunderstanding hinders human life, wherever direct ways of understanding are blocked or not to be found, hermeneutics seeks the ways and means to reach the goal indirectly and to make (better) understanding possible through a critical practice of interpretation and a methodologically reflected poetics of understanding.

6. Understanding as the Goal of Interpretation

In the different areas of life, this can be done in decidedly different ways, but it is always done by *interpretation*. Interpretation is the active performance of what happens in what is (to a large extent) a passive way in understanding. If understanding can be characterized as "A understands B with respect to C on the basis of D through E as F in context G," then interpretation can be characterized by the reverse order of understanding as "E interprets B for A with respect to C on the basis of D as F in context G." That is to say, interpretation is a sign-process in which someone (*interpreter*) interprets something or someone (*interpretandum*) as something (*interpretant*) through something (*interpretans*) for someone (*addressee of interpretation*) with respect to something (*point of interpretation*) on the basis of something (*basis of interpretation*) in a particular context and situation (*context of interpretation*). In each of those respects we can meaningfully ask questions about the processes of interpretation and understanding. And hermeneutics as a poetics of understanding seeks to give a systematic account of this complex practice in the different areas of our life.

Since different areas of our common life and culture pose different problems of understanding and interpretation, the type of hermeneutics practiced with respect to the specific problems of understanding in a given area will also be different, even though it will still be based on the fundamental relation of understanding to that which is possible in each case, as sketched above. The term *hermeneutics*, which is derived from the Greek word ἑρμηνεύω (explain, translate, or interpret), is often (but questionably) explained by reference to Hermes, the messenger of the gods in Greek mythology.[18] Hermes mediates between the gods, and between the gods and human beings. He is described as the inventor of language, a divine interpreter and exegete, a liar, the god of the thieves, and a trickster.[19] Since interpretation and understanding take place as sign-processes, they are intrinsically ambiguous and open to sense and nonsense, truth and falsity, understanding and misunderstanding, interpretation and misinterpretation. Thus, whatever the specific field, the task of hermeneutics is methodologically always about that which the word *hermeneutics* suggests: to make understandable, to explain, to exegete, to interpret, to translate or transfer a strange, obscure, or incomprehensible complex of meaning from another world of understanding into one's own. It is about the transformation of something dark or obscure into something light (or at least lighter) by means of interpretation, at the end of which something is understood or better understood that was either not understood or misunderstood previously—either because it was not understandable or because we could not understand it.

The questions hermeneutics attempts to answer, then, are always questions of understanding, even though such questions may differ greatly. Questions of understanding may be divided into at least the following different types (without making any claim that this list is exhaustive):

Concrete questions of understanding to eliminate a certain ambiguity or obscurity: What does *apokatastasis panton* or "Jesus is the Christ" mean? What does Leonardo da Vinci's *Mona Lisa* or Picasso's *Guernica* convey? What does this scarcely decipherable term paper seek to say?

---

18. The explanation is far from established. Cf. J. Grondin, *Einführung in die philosophische Hermeneutik* (Darmstadt: Wissenschaftliche Buchgesellschaft, 2001), 39.
19. Cf. D. Couzen-Hoy, *The Critical Circle: Literature, History and Philosophical Hermeneutics* (Berkeley: University of California Press, 1978).

Disciplinary questions of understanding concerning the appropriate methods for solving problems of understanding within a specific field: How should one proceed to properly understand Scripture, the Constitution, Bach's *Art of the Fugue*, the Mayan ruins on the Yucatán Peninsula, or the fresco cycle by Piero della Francesca in the Bacci Chapel of the Basilica of San Francesco in Arezzo?

Methodological questions of understanding for clarifying the processes, conditions, and limitations of understanding in general: What must one do in order to understand properly at all? How is one to understand a foreign culture? On what can or should one focus in order to understand one's own religion or another religion? Where, or at which points, do certain methods reach their limits?

Epistemological questions of understanding, which inquire about the methodology of an entire field of scholarship, such as the human sciences, cultural sciences, or life sciences: How are the artifacts of human cultural achievements to be understood as they are found in monuments, works, practices, writings, or discourses of the past or of the present? How is one to understand the achievements and the limitations of the procedures used by biology or neuroscience to investigate human life?

Philosophical questions of understanding, which seek to discover the meaning and limits of what it means to understand at all: What furthers understanding and what hinders it? What does it require? Where are its limits? Is it essential to human life, or is it simply a helpful orienting strategy that one can learn but which can (or even must be) dispensed with under certain circumstances?

Each of these types of questions leads, in different ways, to the problem commonly called "the hermeneutical circle." We must always take into account what is already understood in order to understand the meaning currently in question: we start from a given basis of understanding when we seek to understand, or to understand better, by interpreting what we do not, or do not yet sufficiently, understand. Nothing can be understood without a guiding *preunderstanding*, and nothing will be understood unless this preunderstanding is corrected, confirmed, or deepened in the act or process of understanding.

Accordingly, each of these questions brings with it a different understanding of hermeneutics. Two things are common to them all. First, each seeks to understand something (an *interpretandum*) through something (an *interpretans*) as something (an *interpretant*); in this respect, hermeneutics—the poetics of understanding through interpretation—is a subdiscipline of semiotics, the study of signs or processes of signification. Second, they all have a continual and problematic tendency to universalize, seeing everything as an *interpretandum* and each *interpretandum* itself as a condensed hermeneutical process of interpretation consisting of *interpretandum*, *interpretans*, and *interpretant*. Thus, not only is everything defined as a problem of understanding, but every problem of understanding is seen as the understanding of something already understood, thus presupposing a regression that continues ad infinitum.

However, that which is understandable is not only that which itself has the structures of understanding. Rather, *for us* there is nothing that we have not already understood in some way, so long as it plays a role in the context and practice of our lives. Understandability is not a property of things or situations, by which we could differentiate things or situations that are understandable from those that are not. Understandability is rather a character of the relationship of things and situations *to us* in specific life contexts, in which they have a particular meaning for us through our relationship with them. Nothing has meaning per se; rather, everything has meaning only *for us* (or *for someone*). That everything can be understood does not therefore mean that everything that exists is understandable; rather, only that can be understood for which there is someone *for whom* it is understandable. It is not "everything is understandable" that is true, but rather "everything is understandable (and only that) that is understandable *for someone*."

7. Types of Hermeneutics

The usage of the term *hermeneutics* frequently oscillates between designating what one does when one seeks to understand something or to make something understandable, and designating the theory of such a practice. While hermeneutics at first was the practice of concrete interpretation within everyday or scholarly processes of understanding, it became, during Hellenistic antiquity and especially during the course of modernity, the technique or method of (textual) interpretation, as in literary, theological, or legal hermeneutics. Since Schleiermacher, hermeneutics—the art of avoiding misunderstanding—has been seen as the theory and practice of the understanding of communicative expressions of life in general and those in language (discourse) and fixed in writing (texts) in particular. Since Dilthey, it has become the methodology of the nonexplanatory or interpretative human sciences as a whole, and since Heidegger and Gadamer—and in different ways with Ricoeur and Taylor—it has been construed as the philosophical theory of the basic human way of being in the world. We exist, in authentic and inauthentic ways, in the life worlds, histories, and cultures that make us (shape our identities) and at the same time are of our own making: they depend on our interpretative practices and institutions and in turn enable and inform the interpretative practices that shape our identities.

With the philosophical turn in hermeneutics, the task of a fundamental elucidation and explanation of the phenomenon of understanding as a whole, not just the analysis of the methods and procedures of understanding, becomes the focus. The latter has long been a central part of traditional hermeneutics, from the hermeneutics of myths in Greek and Hellenist antiquity to the pietistic hermeneutics of Holy Scripture in the seventeenth century. Preromantic pietistic hermeneutics, for example, described the steps of the process of understanding Scripture as *explication, understanding,* and *application,* and the required human capabilities for understanding as *subtilitas explicandi, intelligendi,* and *applicandi,* respectively. But questions about procedures for understanding lead only to methodical or methodological issues, and questions about human capacities only to psychological or neuroscientific answers. Philosophical problems arise first with the self-referential critical question of the understanding of understanding. On the one hand, this is marked by the step from reflection to self-reflection about understanding inasmuch as it self-referentially turns its attention to itself, thus requiring the transition from empirical or methodological considerations (hermeneutical poetics) to philosophical theories of understanding (philosophical hermeneutics). On the other hand, as Jürgen Habermas rightly stressed, precisely as such it implies the question of the "limits of hermeneutical understanding" and is therefore critically oriented through the key distinction between understanding and not-understanding (in its various concrete determinations).[20] Without asking about the limits of understanding, the phenomenon of understanding cannot be clarified philosophically.

In broad outline, the development of hermeneutics in the Western tradition comprises three distinct stages: the hermeneutical question moves from a focus on the problem of understanding *something* (classical hermeneutics), through a focus on the activity of *understanding* something (subjective hermeneutics of the modern period: nineteenth century), to the *understanding of understanding* (philosophical hermeneutics: twentieth century). This shift of focus does not mean that later problems and versions of hermeneutics supersede earlier ones. Rather, the field of hermeneutics becomes significantly enlarged over the centuries, each turn adding new problems and questions to hermeneutics and thereby opening up new avenues of research, debate, and insight. This is particularly true of the turn from methodological to philosophical problems in the twentieth century, which fundamentally changed the face and status of hermeneutics by turning understanding upon itself and inquiring into the understanding of understanding. This philosophical problem was

---

20. J. Habermas, "Der Universalitätsanspruch der Hermeneutik," in *Hermeneutik und Ideologiekritik* (Frankfurt: Suhrkamp, 1971), 120–59; here 133.

addressed in quite different ways during the twentieth century. Their general directions may be characterized through such key terms as *subject* (Lonergan), *language* (Wittgenstein), *existence* (Heidegger), *life-world* (Blumenberg), *effective history* (Gadamer), *objectivity* (Figal), and *mediation* (Ricoeur). In differing ways, they all raise questions about the universal and fundamental character of understanding, questions that led to the transformation of philosophical hermeneutics into hermeneutical philosophy. But they also provoke questions about the boundaries, the otherness, the mediality, and the dispensability or indispensability of understanding, questions that stand at the center of the critiques of hermeneutics in recent decades (postmodern antihermeneutics: twentieth and twenty-first centuries).

Thus, the basic problem of hermeneutics is, first of all and in a general sense, the understanding *of something*. When the question concentrates on the object or a particular range of objects to be understood (the *whom* or *what* of understanding), it leads, along with the processing of specific problems of understanding, to the development of specific material fields of hermeneutics, such as theological, legal, or literary hermeneutics, as well as to the differentiation of special kinds of hermeneutics according to the sign character of the phenomena studied and interpreted (hermeneutics of texts, of actions, of images, of architectural monuments, of works of art, and so forth).

On the other hand, if the question concentrates on *the understanding* of something—that is, on the subject (the *who* of understanding) or the procedures of understanding (the *how* of understanding)—it leads to the development of hermeneutical or interpretative methodologies as a particular means of the cognitive-epistemological or affective-emotional engagement with "the other" and "the self," with the natural, cultural, social, and personal dimensions of our *Umwelt*, *Mitwelt*, *Selbstwelt*, and *Glaubenswelt* and with our relations to them (cultural problems of meaning).

The basic problem of twentieth-century philosophical hermeneutics, however, is not the question of a methodology of understanding but of the *understanding of understanding*: what is understanding, what does it consist of, how does it take place, what does it provide, under what conditions is it possible, what are its limits, and what does it mean that something is understood or not understood and that we can understand or fail to do so (the *what*, *that*, *where*, and *how* of understanding)? A large number of philosophical approaches attempt to answer this question through quite different philosophical theories, namely those of Heidegger,[21] Hans-Georg Gadamer, Bernard Lonergan,[22] and Hans Blumenberg.

When the understanding of understanding is seen not only as one philosophical question among others but as the fundamental task of philosophical thinking, the undertaking is then transformed from a philosophical theory of understanding into a *hermeneutical philosophy*. Such a philosophy can (as with Günter Figal) develop the objectification-processes of understanding as the basic act of experiencing the objective at all.[23] Or it can (as with Ricoeur) concentrate on the phenomena of cultural mediation and limitation that characterize all concrete forms of individual and shared understanding and self-understanding. Or it can (as with Charles Taylor) focus on the human interpreters as self-interpreting animals in a shared cultural world of meaning that resists any attempt at naturalist reduction.[24]

If, however, as in the poststructuralist,[25] deconstructivist, and postmodern (anti)hermeneutics of recent decades (Derrida, Foucault), the accent falls not on the understanding of understanding but on the needlessness, the redundancy, or the impossibility of understanding, then the focus shifts to the rupture of styles and traditions, the

---

21. Within the framework of his hermeneutics of facticity, M. Heidegger, *Ontologie: Hermeneutik der Faktizität*, GA 63 (Frankfurt: Suhrkamp, 1995), 15, described understanding as "the wakefulness of Being for itself" that is shown in that it communicates and interprets itself, so that it is because of its (self-)interpretation that Being can make itself understandable.
22. B. Lonergan, *Insight: A Study of Human Understanding*, vol. 3 of *Collected Works*, ed. Frederick E. Crowe and Robert M. Doran (Toronto: University of Toronto Press, 1992), 22.
23. See the review by J. Zovko, *ThLZ* 135 (2010): 72–74.
24. Cf. Ch. Taylor, "Self-Interpreting Animals," in *Human Agency and Language: Philosophical Papers 1* (Cambridge: Cambridge University Press, 1985), 45–76.
25. See K.-M. Bogdal, "Problematisierungen der Hermeneutik im Zeichen des Poststrukturalismus," in *Grundzüge der Literaturwissenschaft*, ed. H. L. Arnold and H. Detering (Munich: dtv, 1996), 137–56.

deconstruction of all directness and immediacy, the circuitous structures of understanding, the role of cultural mediation, bodily practices, and social and physical embodiments of understanding, as well as to the manifold forms and kinds of "others": other selves or persons; other objects, things, or events; other social practices and cultural institutions; the natural world as the prehermeneutic or nonhermeneutic other of meaning and culture; and God—the Other of all others.[26]

8. Approaches to Philosophical Hermeneutics

Answers to the central questions of twentieth-century philosophical hermeneutics regarding the understanding of understanding, the limits of understanding, and the difference between understanding and not understanding were sought during the twentieth century in three exemplary ways.

First of all, there are the *subjectivity-based* or *subject-oriented approaches*, which follow in the wake of neo-Kantianism (Ernst Cassirer,[27] Nicolai Hartmann), the transcendental turn of neo-Thomism (Bernard Lonergan), or—in a very different form—the confluence of a Hegelian view of history, meaning, and culture with a phenomenological account of the postmodern expressive self striving for authenticity and a hermeneutical account of the interpretative practices in and through which we live our lives as human beings (Charles Taylor[28]). Especially those indebted to neo-Kantianism and neo-Thomism understand understanding as a web of fundamental cognitive and evaluative functions of the human subject that are linked

---

26. G. W. Bertram, *Hermeneutik und Dekonstruktion: Konturen einer Auseinandersetzung in der Gegenwartsphilosophie* (Munich: Fink, 2002); and E. Angehrn, *Interpretation und Dekonstruktion. Untersuchungen zur Hermeneutik* (Wielerswist: Königshausen & Neumann, 2003).
27. E. Cassirer was of course not a hermeneutical philosopher but his *Philosophy of Symbolic Forms* (1923–1929) defends and develops the claim that humans are "symbolic animals." Cf. Cassirer, *An Essay on Man* (New Haven: Yale University Press, 1944). Whereas animals relate to their environment in direct sensory perception and behavior governed by instinct, humans create a universe of symbolic meaning through language, myth, religion, art, and science.
28. Ch. Taylor, *Hegel and Modern Society* (Cambridge: Cambridge University Press, 1979); Taylor, *Sources of the Self: The Making of Modern Identity* (Cambridge, MA: Harvard University Press, 1989); and Taylor, *A Secular Age* (Cambridge, MA: Harvard University Press, 2007).

to a pattern of a priori and universally valid, self-referential, interwoven, and unchangeable operations of the human mind in its construing engagement with the world and itself. Accordingly, the limits of understanding arise out of the conditions that establish the possibility and the validity of these cognitive and evaluative functions. As Bernhard Lonergan paradigmatically put it: "Thoroughly understand what it is to understand, and not only will you understand the broad lines of all there is to be understood but also you will possess a fixed base, an invariant pattern, opening upon all further developments of understanding."[29]

The *approach of linguistic phenomenology* replaces the focus on the subject with a focus on the language community. It criticizes the conception of the subject as an individual center of operations for not adequately recognizing the intersubjective makeup of human life and the specific historical forces that shape each individual. Thus, questions about the specific patterns of understanding of a linguistic community take the place of questions regarding any a priori and universally valid pattern of understanding. The later Wittgenstein, for example, understands understanding as a linguistically and socially mediated interpretive relationship to reality, in which we see, construe, interpret, and experience something as something. Such understanding always takes place in and through language (in the widest sense); since there is no purely private language, understanding always occurs in and through intersubjective communicative practices. One learns a language from others and, since one learns to understand along with the language, one inherits from others the competence to understand and to make something understandable. All individual processes of seeing, construing, interpreting, translating, explaining, and so forth take place within the framework of a linguistically mediated social form of life. In this, understanding also has its limits

---

29. Lonergan, *Insight*, 22. Cf. a number of articles by Fr. G. Lawrence in *Divyadaan: Journal of Philosophy and Education* 19, nos. 1–2 (2008): "Martin Heidegger and the Hermeneutic Revolution" (7–30), "Hans-Georg Gadamer and the Hermeneutic Revolution" (31–54), "The Hermeneutic Revolution and Bernard Lonergan: Gadamer and Lonergan on Augustine's Verbum Cordis—the Heart of Postmodern Hermeneutics" (55–86), and "The Unknown 20th-Century Hermeneutic Revolution: Jerusalem and Athens in Lonergan's Integral Hermeneutics" (87–118).

insofar as it ultimately leads to immediacies, which one cannot "say" but only "show"—that is to say, which one can, at most, name or point to or gesture at within such an approach, but which one cannot penetrate. One can only make manifest such immediacies, allowing them to show themselves through the act of naming them. Methodologically guided understanding therefore means showing how something is understood, showing which rules govern this understanding and where its limits are found: it means to describe the language game or form of life and to reconstruct the grammar in which the understanding in question takes place and is expressed.

The *approach* of *existential phenomenology*, finally, understands understanding as the fundamental ontological mode of human existence in this world. It precedes all specific actions of the human subject and all ontic formations of human linguistic communities by making them possible and ontologically grounding them in the first place. This approach was represented in the twentieth century by Heidegger, Gadamer, and Figal in three different versions:

Heidegger's existential-ontological "hermeneutics of facticity" or, as he calls it in *Being and Time*, the "analytic of *Dasein*," recognizes a primordial connection between understanding and self-understanding that precedes all splitting of subject and object.[30] Understanding, in which *Dasein* "has always" understood itself in its being-in-the-world, is not an epistemic relationship of a subject to certain objects of cognition, but rather is the mode of *Dasein*'s being-in-the-world. *Dasein* is marked off from other things that are (entities) because it is the place where being (*Sein*) fulfills itself as existence—that is, as the relationship of the understanding of a concretely present life to its contingent being in the world and to its specific possibilities for living that are given there within the horizon of time. This understanding mode of *Dasein* as such is the ontological condition of the possibility of every concrete act of understanding. Whatever "is encountered in the world is always already in a relevance which is disclosed in the understanding of the

---

30. See the reconstruction of these efforts by P. Stagi, *Der faktische Gott* (Würzburg: Königshausen & Neumann, 2007), and my review thereof in *ThLZ* 134 (2009): 737–39.

world, a relevance which is made explicit by interpretation."[31] This embeddedness in a meaningful world manifests itself in the conduct of life in the movements of the preunderstanding that precedes and continuously determines each act of understanding. A methodologically aware understanding must take account of these presuppositions. It must critically monitor its expectations about that which it is seeking to understand, and it must guard the thematic focus of its interpretation against the arbitrariness of sudden ideas or of unnoticed narrow-mindedness through the methodological unfolding of our *"fore-having"* (*Vorhabe*), *"foresight"* (*Vorsicht*), and *"fore-conception"* (*Vorgriff*) in the case of the interpretation in question, that is to say, of "what we 'have' in advance," "what we see in advance," and "what we grasp in advance" of any particular understanding.[32]

Gadamer's focus on effective history in his hermeneutics of conversation develops the primal relationship of understanding and self-understanding more precisely by means of an analysis of the context of transmission in which each one who understands as such already stands. Understanding is "never a subjective relation to a given 'object' but to the history of its effect; in other words, understanding belongs to the being of that which is understood."[33] We are always engaged in a conversation in which that which is to be understood takes part as it has already been understood. A methodologically guided understanding must elaborate the structure of this dialogue, its character as mediated through time and history, and its inherent dialectic of question and answer. One must always be aware that the understanding of self and the world passed on to us consists not only of questions and answers that develop between those who are speaking,

---

31. M. Heidegger, *Sein und Zeit* (Tübingen; Max Niemeyer, 1967), 150; Heidegger, *Being and Time: A Translation of* Sein und Zeit, trans. J. Stambaugh (New York: State University of New York Press, 1996), 140. J. Macquarrie's translation is better: "When something within-the-world is encountered as such, the thing in question already has an involvement which is disclosed in our understanding of the world, and this involvement is one which gets laid out by the interpretation." Heidegger, *Being and Time*, trans. J. Macquarrie and E. Robinson (London: SCM, 1962), 190–91.
32. See M. Heidegger, *Sein und Zeit*, 150–52; *Being and Time*, 140–41.
33. H. G. Gadamer, "Vorwort zur 2. Auflage [von Wahrheit und Methode]," *Gesammelte Werke 2, Hermeneutik II* (Tübingen: Mohr Siebeck, 1986), 437–48, here 441; Gadamer, *Truth and Method*, 2nd rev. ed., trans. rev. by J. Weinsheimer and D. G. Marshall (London: Sheed and Ward, 1989), xxviii.

but in significant ways also from the things spoken about whose history of effect is the context in which we find ourselves always already placed in our conversation.

Figal's hermeneutical philosophy of objectivity took up this point from Gadamer's hermeneutics and developed it into a fundamental discipline of philosophy. The subject matter of all understanding (*what we seek to understand*) is an "object," and an object, according to Figal, is "no random thing but rather something insofar as it is opposite us. An object (*Gegenstand*) is something in opposition (im *Gegen-Stand*)."[34] Everything so objectively encountered is an "objectivity of the world," which opens up the possibility of understanding.[35] This understanding-provoking objectivity of objects is to be preserved as the objects are interpreted and explained, and is not to be replaced by the formation of theories, as the de-objectifying processes of modern science have often been accused of doing. Hermeneutics becomes the fundamental philosophical discipline insofar as it seeks to "rescue" the phenomena of the objective "other" from the de-objectifying tendencies of modern theorizing. "That we are drawn to things and are at the same time impacted by them, that we are surrounded by things yet are different from them, is a key to understanding what 'life' means in reference to us and for us."[36]

---

34. G. Figal, *Gegenständlichkeit. Das Hermeneutische und die Philosophie* (Tübingen: Mohr Siebeck, 2007), 126.
35. Ibid., 135.
36. Ibid., 361.

3

Guiding Ideas of Understanding

Understanding can occur only within a specific context, under particular conditions, and with some guiding assumptions. A central task of critical hermeneutics is to consider these factors and address their impact. The (mostly unthematized) contextual conditions of the attempt to understand show up in many places: in the standpoint of the interpreter, in the process of interpretation, in that which is assumed to be already understood, and also, most decisively, in how the *interpretandum* is defined. How one defines what one is trying to understand determines which questions of understanding arise and are investigated. The guiding preunderstanding, which is manifest in how the object to be understood is defined, I call the *guiding idea of understanding*.

1. Psychological and Grammatical Interpretation

Obviously, such guiding principles vary widely. Schleiermacher defined the task of understanding as the reproduction of the original mental production of a meaning communicated in discourse, based upon the congeniality of minds.

> 5. As every discourse has a dual relationship, to the totality of language and to the whole thought of its originator, then all understanding also consists of the two moments, of understanding the discourse as derived from language, and as a fact in the thinker.
>
> 1. Every discourse presupposes a given language. One can admittedly also invert this, not only for the absolutely first discourse, but also for the whole of the discourse, because language comes into being through discourse; but communication necessarily presupposes the shared nature of the language, thus also a certain acquaintance with the language. If something comes between the immediate discourse and communication, so that the art of discourse begins, then this rests in part on the worry that something might be unfamiliar to the listener in our use of language.
>
> 2. Every discourse depends upon previous thinking. One can also invert this, but in relation to communication it remains true, because the art of understanding only begins with advanced thought.
>
> 3. According to this every person is on the one hand a location in which a given language forms itself in an individual manner, on the other their discourse can only be understood via the totality of the language. But then the person is also a spirit which continually develops, and their discourse is only one act of this spirit in connection with the other acts. . . .
>
> 6. Understanding is only a being-in-one-another of these two moments (of the grammatical and psychological).[1]

Accordingly, all understanding is to be viewed as an unending process that moves along two axes: the placement of the *interpretandum* within the context of the works and life of the author (psychological interpretation) and its placement within the overall linguistic context of the treatment of the topic that is being discussed (grammatical interpretation). In the first case, one understands a text as the *work of an author* (work-understanding), in the second as *a text among texts* of a certain type (text-understanding).[2] Understanding is to be found only within the *"being-in-one-another of these two moments,"* the grammatical

---

1. F. D. E. Schleiermacher, *Hermeneutik*, ed. H. Kimmerle (Heidelberg: Carl Winter, 1959), 80–81. The English translation is Friedrich Schleiermacher, *Hermeneutics and Criticism and Other Writings*, trans. and ed. A. Bowie (Cambridge: Cambridge University Press, 1998), 8–9. I have improved the translation where necessary.
2. This text-understanding is the ground for further diversity in understanding: one can relate texts to one another in a variety of different ways, whether by form (language, structure, genre, and the like) or content (topic or theme).

and the psychological.[3] *"Both are completely equal, and it would be wrong to call grammatical interpretation the lower and psychological interpretation the higher."*[4] Accordingly, for the "successful practice" of the art, the interpreter needs both "a talent for language" and a "talent for knowledge of individual."[5] Both are required at all times, for the two perspectives of interpretation cannot be separated, but can only be given differing weight relative to one another according to the insight of the interpreter in each case. "Psychological is the higher when one regards language only as the means whereby the individual communicates his thoughts; grammatical interpretation is in this case just the removal of passing difficulties."[6] On the other hand, the "grammatical interpretation is the higher when one looks at ... the individual person only as the location of language and his discourse only as that in which language reveals itself. Then the psychological is completely subordinated, like the existence of the individual person.... From this duality complete equality follows as a matter of course."[7] However, this equality is far from obvious. For Schleiermacher, the notion that both efforts toward understanding would in the end lead to the same understanding remained more an expectation unaccounted for than a demonstrated fact. Although he is aware that the interpreter is involved in two infinite processes, he assumes that in the end there must be one and only one complete understanding of an *interpretandum*, whether it is a written text or a spoken discourse. Diversity of understanding is always a sign that we are at best on the way but have not arrived at the end yet. This keeps the movement of interpretations open. But the complete equality of grammatical and psychological interpretation in one and the same complete understanding is at best a heuristic principle and not a realistic goal to strive for.

Without intending to do so, this distinction between psychological

---

3. Schleiermacher, *Hermeneutik*, 81 (*Hermeneutics and Criticism*, 10).
4. Ibid., 10.
5. Ibid., 11.
6. Ibid., 10.
7. Ibid.

and grammatical interpretation prefigured two of the major directions in which philosophical hermeneutics in the twentieth century would move. If one follows the focus of hermeneutical efforts as it shifts from linguistic and nonlinguistic *works* (texts), to the *subjects* who produce them or make use of them (authors and recipients), and then to the *event-context* of life, without which there would be nothing to understand nor anyone who could understand (the process of life in which producing and understanding texts is embedded), then three characteristic guiding ideas of twentieth-century hermeneutics may be distinguished—namely, *Work*, *Subject*, and *Event*. These have also shaped the formation of hermeneutics within theology, as is evidenced by the approaches of classical *hermeneutics of works*, modern *hermeneutics of the subject*, and transmodern *hermeneutics of event*.

2. Hermeneutics of Works (the Understanding of *Something*)

A hermeneutics of works understands the *interpretandum* as the product of a producer, using the actor-act model as paradigm. Actions, texts, letters, poems, pictures, musical scores, buildings, cities, and cultural phenomena in general are *produced by someone* from whom they are distinct. They are realities in their own right and with their own meaning even though they exist only because they are *made by someone*. It is therefore always possible, and sensible, to ask about the intention of the producer in order to understand the product. This intention determines or codetermines the existence, the character, the mode, the meaning, and the significance of the product (that is, that it is, what it is, how it is, what it means, and what it signifies), and guides the way it is to be rightly understood in the light of its original context of production.

From this perspective, distinctions such as those between texts, writings, pictures, or monuments are secondary. While they are indeed works of different character, styles, media, and function, so long as they are considered the works of an author, one can, in principle, seek to understand them guided by the same interpretive questions. What did Dante intend in writing the *Divina Comedia*? What was

Michelangelo's intention in painting *The Last Judgment* in the Sistine Chapel? What intention(s) governed Palladio's design of the Palazzo Chiericati in Vicenza? Even a systematic distinction between the author's intention (*intentio auctoris*), the work's intention (*intentio operis*), and the recipient's intention (*intentio lectoris*) does not fundamentally depart from the works-hermeneutical approach, since it is made in light of a work whose existence (that it is) and character (what it is) are essentially determined by the producer.[8]

Theologically, this is the dominant model in classical exegesis and biblical studies, both in the traditional form, in which God was considered the author of both books (*liber scripturae* and *liber mundi* or *naturae*), and in the modern form of historical-critical exegesis, in which biblical texts are understood as the writings of specific authors or redactors in specific times and under specific historical circumstances. But it also is a fundamental characteristic of all theological approaches that are guided by the distinction between producer and product, especially those that emphasize the distinction between Creator and creature, distinguishing between the divine author of Scripture and the human authors of the texts. Since for God, and God alone, there are no changing circumstances, God is continuously active as divine author, and the divine authorship of God's creative activity is always present to creatures under their changing circumstances. Understanding God's intentions from the book of nature is thus possible at all times in the same way if this book is read properly by paying attention to its divine author and to the language of mathematics and the laws of nature in which it is written. Understanding God's intentions from the book of Scripture, on the other hand, requires readers not only to understand the historical languages of the texts of the Old and New Testaments but also to differentiate between the diverse intentions of their human authors and the divine intention of the Spirit who is believed to have governed the mind of the human authors then and there and the understanding

---

8. On the issue of *intentio lectoris*, cf. U. Eco, *Lector in fabula* (Munich: dtv, 1998); Eco, *The Role of the Reader: Explorations in the Semiotics of Texts* (Bloomington: Indiana University Press, 1979); and Eco, *The Limits of Interpretation* (Bloomington: Indiana University Press, 1990).

of the recipients of those texts here and now. This is traditionally the task of a *hermeneutica sacra* of the book of Scripture, whether in the sense of interpreting the texts in the fourfold mode of patristic exegesis (*sensus historicus* or *literalis*, *sensus allegoricus*, *sensus tropologicus* or *moralis*, *sensus anagogicus*) or in the theological sense of the Protestant emphasis on Scripture as the word of God in terms of law and gospel.[9] Scripture has to be read with respect to the divine intentions that govern this unique collection of human writings used by the church as the source and norm of its creed. If it is merely read as a collection of texts by ancient writers, as it came to be studied in post-Enlightenment exegesis, then it is read as a monument of human culture and history but not as canonical scripture. It may tell us something about the intentions of their ancient authors but not disclose anything about those of a divine author. At best, we can find (some of) their ancient authors to believe that they are inspired or prophetic instruments of divine intentions. But this is a questionable belief and not a validated fact on which to build a defensible interpretation of those texts. From a hermeneutical point of view, to look for divine intentions in these writings is misleading and of no help in understanding them.[10]

---

9. In the fourth century, John Cassian summed up the interpretative tradition of patristic exegesis in his *Collationes patrum in scetica eremo* (*The Conferences of John Cassian*, part II, conference 14, chap. VIII: "Of spiritual knowledge") by distinguishing not only between the literal and spiritual senses of the biblical texts, but by subdividing the spiritual sense into the tropological (moral), allegorical, and anagogical (future-oriented) senses. This fourfold sense of Scripture was handed down through the centuries by a Latin rhyme: "Littera gesta docet / qui credas allegoria / moralis quid agas / quo tendas anagogia." Or, in a free English translation: "The *letter* shows us what God and our fathers did; the *allegory* shows us where our faith is hid; the *moral* meaning gives us rules of daily life; the *anagogy* shows us where we end our strife." In modernity, the literal sense became increasingly problematic. Whereas Thomas (and Luther) emphasized that the "sensus litteralis est, quem autor intendit" (the literal sense is the one which the author intended) (*S.Th.* I, q.1 a.10), later interpreters identified it with the historical sense of the words in the original situation in which they were written. This created special problems with respect to the interpretation of biblical texts. For Thomas, it was clear that the "auctor ... sacrae Scripturae Deus est" (the author of the holy Scriptures is God) (*S.Th.* I, q.1 a.10) so that the literal sense of Scripture was precisely the theological sense of what God intended to communicate through Scripture. Later interpreters distinguished more sharply between the *sensus litteralis* of the individual human authors of the biblical writings (the historical sense) and the *sensus litteralis* of God, the author of Scripture (the theological or divine sense). They then had to relate the human literal sense of the biblical writings to the divine literal sense of Scripture as a whole, and they tried to do so by showing how the unique divine or soteriological sense of Scripture was communicated through the historical sense of the plural canonical books of Scripture.
10. This is why one must distinguish as clearly as possible between different key notions of biblical

Whether one follows the classical view of God as author of the book of Scripture or the modern view of the Bible as a canonical collection of ancient writings spanning the time of more than a thousand years, for a hermeneutical theology so oriented the central category is the *meaning* that is found in a particular signifier (medium) because the meaning has *been given* to it or *will be given* to it—by the author or the recipient or both. All meaning owes its existence to a gift of meaning and thus to a giver of meaning; nothing has meaning to which no meaning has been, or will be, given.

3. Hermeneutics of the Subject (the Understanding of *Self-Understanding*)

A hermeneutics of the subject understands the *interpretandum* as the self-understanding displayed within every understanding. In order to understand something, the self-understanding that resonates within the understanding of something must also be understood. In fact, this self-understanding is truly that which is to be understood, as the analysis of prejudices and the hermeneutics of preconceptions demonstrate. This is true not only for the self-understanding of the author of a work (*sensus auctoris*), but also for that of its recipient (*sensus lectoris*). The understanding of self, and its mostly indirect forms of expression, thus moves to the center of hermeneutical interest, bringing along the task of understanding an author or recipient, if possible, better than they understood themselves.

---

hermeneutics and the different questions they pose: the literary notion of the *Bible* (a book that can be bought, read, ignored, or burned); the liturgical and theological notion of *Scripture* (the—different—canonical collections of texts used as sacred texts in Judaism and Christianity); the theological notions of *Old and New Testaments* (the terms do not signify special collections of texts but a theological way of understanding certain groups of texts to manifest the will of God for God's people—for Israel or for all humankind); the theological and dogmatic notion of the *word of God* (addressed to specific persons in their specific situations); and the dogmatic notions of *law and gospel* (the theological shorthand for how to read the canonical texts with an eye to the will of God expressed there for the contemporary reader). Just as *law and gospel* are theological determinations of the *word of God*, so the *Old and New Testaments* are liturgical determinations of *Scripture*. But neither *Scripture* nor the *word of God* can be identified with the *Bible* (they cannot be printed, for example, or burned, or torn asunder). This is why Christianity is not the religion of a book but the (re)orientation of human life by the word of God, and the word of God is understood properly only if one knows how to distinguish between law and gospel with respect to the ways in which the word of God is communicated.

The twentieth-century philosophical hermeneutics of Martin Heidegger, Hans-Georg Gadamer, and Hans Blumenberg have so been read and understood by many: as versions of a subject-hermeneutics that—whether by analysis of being, effective history, or phenomenology of variation—has to do with the self-understanding of people in the world, in the world of culture, or in history.

Theologically, this model is dominant where, following Schleiermacher, the *understanding* of something is conceived of as understanding within the context of an author's life-history (anthropological version of self-understanding), or where, as in cosmo-theological approaches from Hegel through Schelling up to Pannenberg, it is proposed as a process of the self-becoming, self-realization, or self-understanding of God (cosmo-theological version of God's self-understanding), or where, as in revelational-theological approaches, revelation is interpreted as God's self-revelation of the truth of divine eternal life under the conditions of history (revelation-theological version of God's self-understanding).

The central category of a hermeneutical theology so oriented is the word-act, in which and through which a faith-subject is constituted and made capable of distinguishing between sin and grace, lies and veracity, untruth and truth. *Meaning* is then defined more precisely through the distinction between truth and falsehood, while *true meaning* is understood as the result of truth-making. This *truth-making*, however, is not conceived of semantically in terms of correspondence (*adaequatio intellectus ad rem*) as the confirmation of a more-or-less-likely possibility through the contingent fact of its reality (truth-maker), but rather it is conceived of existentially in terms of the creative process by which the giver of meaning (the human person) is defined in light of the distinction between truth and lies as he or she truly is *coram deo*. A meaning is true when it owes its existence to a trustworthy and truthful giver of meaning, and whether this is the case or not is determined by his or her relationship to God (or, more precisely, by a person's relationship to God's relation to this person).

Considered grammatically then, the ideas of *God, human,* and *devil* symbolize the three constellations that are fundamentally possible: only truth and no lies (God), both truth and lies (human), no truth and only lies (devil). God always speaks truly, the devil constantly lies, and with humans you do not know where you stand. When it comes to God, understanding coincides with the recognition of truth: whoever understands God knows the truth. When it comes to the devil, understanding is to understand that there is nothing true to understand: whoever understands the devil knows that he lies. When it comes to humans, every act of understanding comes with the question of how to distinguish between truth and falsehood, truth and lies, true and untrue. This is the permanent hermeneutical predicament of the human subject: the fundamental problem of understanding is not understanding God or the devil but understanding ourselves. Whereas post-Cartesian epistemology has assumed that we can be certain with respect to ourselves and never be certain with respect to God, the situation is just the other way round from the point of view of a hermeneutics of the subject: we can be absolutely certain with respect to God (and the devil), and never know for sure with respect to ourselves. The real riddle of human life is not God but the human person. We do not know who we are, but we can know who and how God is.

4. Hermeneutics of Event (the Understanding of *Understanding*)

A hermeneutics of event draws on the second of the two main strands of Schleiermacher's hermeneutics: the understanding of something as a particular web of meaning within the context of the entire history of the texts in which a theme has been addressed in writing. However, recognizing Heidegger's distinction between the *sense of containment* (Gehaltssinn), the *sense of relation* (Bezugssinn), and the *sense of enactment* (Vollzugssinn) within the total intentional act of the *sense of temporalization* (Zeitigungssinn),[11] they take the central point and object

---

11. M. Heidegger, *Phänomenologie des religiösen Lebens*, GA 60 (Frankfurt: Vittorio Klostermann, 1995), 248, analyzes the triple-sensed intentionality of content (or containment), relation, and enactment (or actualization) in his "Introduction to the Phenomenology of Religion" (WS 1920–1921) by distinguishing between the sense of containment, or *Gehaltssinn* (containing sense:

of understanding to be not the resulting text but rather the concrete act of entextualizing an experience. The focus is not on the resulting construct of meaning but on the dynamics of constructing meaning, and indeed not primarily on the active aspects of those dynamics but on the passive-pathic aspects.[12]

This appears most clearly in the text-hermeneutical variants of event-hermeneutics, which understand texts as multilayered constructs of meaning that present a temporal (and thus continuously changing) process of connecting, condensing, and interweaving possibilities of meaning into a specific and determinate texture of meaning. It is not the author, but the text, that stands in the foreground, and indeed in such a way that neither the producer (*sensus auctoris*) nor the product (*sensus operis*) is the hermeneutical *interpretandum*, but rather the meaning-event of the production of the text. However, this is not understood *as someone producing*, and the resulting text thus is also not seen as the work of an author. On the contrary. It is not that someone makes or made it that is of interest, but rather the creative process of meaning that takes place—that is, the concrete weaving of units of meaning into a text and the manifold connections to other signs, texts, images, monuments, or other units of meaning that are thereby made use of but also made newly possible.

Every text comes out of a history of meaning and is at the same time the possible beginning of a new history. In every text, strands of earlier

---

the "what" of the experience); the sense of relation, or *Bezugssinn* (relational sense: the "how" of the experience); and the sense of actualization, or *Vollzugssinn* (enactment sense: the "how of the how" of the experience). The sense of temporalization (*Zeitigungssinn*) comprises all three elements in a unity and thereby shows the sense of enactment to be, as M. Jung, *Das Denken des Seins und der Glaube an Gott. Zum Verhältnis von Philosophie und Theologie bei Martin Heidegger* (Würzburg: Königshausen & Neumann, 1990), 46, puts it, "the way in which the relational sense (the relation in the intentional act) itself becomes enacted."

12. In an intentional differentiation from Dilthey's hermeneutics of experience and, in fact, from Husserl's phenomenology of experience (cf. the category of the "intentional experience" in Husserl's *Logische Untersuchungen* [Tübingen: Max Niemeyer, 1986], II.1.343ff.), Franz Rosenzweig, as early as 1918 and 1919, had placed the term *event* at the center of his work *Der Stern der Erlösung*, and indeed in the significant intensifying form of "occurred event" (*ereignetes Ereignis*), which emphasizes the passive-pathic character of the event. Rosenzweig, *Der Stern der Erlösung*, GS2 (Frankfurt: Suhrkamp, 1993), 178. On this point, see B. Casper, "Transzendentale Phänomenalität und ereignetes Ereignis. Der Sprung in ein hermeneutisches Denken im Leben und Werk Franz Rosenzweigs," in *Vom Rätsel des Begriffs. FS F.W. von Herrmann*, ed. P.-L. Coriando (Berlin: Duncker & Humblot, 1999), 359; and Caspar, "Die Gründung einer philosophischen Theologie im Ereignis," *Dialegesthai: Rivista telematica di filosofia* 5 (2003), http://mondodomani.org/dialegesthai.

concretions of meaning coalesce and new relationships of meaning are opened. Both must be taken into account if one wants to understand a text-event. Only because such relationships exist can one understand a text at all: if everything were new, it would remain fully inaccessible. However, since the references backward and forward are potentially inexhaustible, a text outside a concrete situation or in changing situations can never be conclusively understood. The conditions that make it possible to understand a text prove also to be the conditions that make it impossible to understand it conclusively or in only one way."[13]

Currently, the best example of such event-hermeneutics is presented by the sign-events within the global web of the Internet, which constitutes a repertoire and resource for unlimited webs and relationships of meaning. Texts appear on the screen as momentary webs of meaning whose strands may be traced in all directions across other texts into unfathomable realms of possibility. That they have authors or particular occasions, how many authors contributed to a text, or how a text may already have been understood and by whom—all of that has little relevance for how they are understood hermeneutically. Every text, in fact, has other texts behind it, stands in the context of other texts, and makes new texts possible. The variety of meaningful connections to other products of meaning is potentially infinite; accordingly, a text's plasticity of meaning can hardly be limited. It is not the text's framework of meaning that determines what is understood, but rather the understanding-event and thus the concrete act of understanding here and now, even though one knows that it can also be understood differently by another or at another time: the meaning of a text does not determines the understanding;

---

13. This is the point of Derrida's antihermeneutically intended contrast of word versus writing, which attempts to understand meaning not as an event of the present but only as a clue from the past. This approach is also followed by the dominant strategies of understanding of so-called postmodernity, which shift meaning away from texts and trace the opposing processes of meaning construction and deconstruction without which no specific meaning of a text exists. No meaning of a text is stable, but each meaning of a text is a snapshot made by a recipient at a particular time of one of the text's possible meanings; within the context of the possibilities offered by the given structure of a text, meaning can become fluid again at any time, and by bringing in new references, a different recipient may come to a different meaning.

rather, the concrete act of understanding here and now that decides the meaning of a text is.

If all understanding is in this sense bound to the concrete act of understanding and if understanding lives on the understandable possibilities of meaning that are put into its court, then there are paradoxical consequences. One can only understand here and now, but that which one understands or thinks one understands cannot be understood here and now. If the totality of the references of meaning make a text what it is, then not only can no text be understood exhaustively but each concrete act of understanding appears to be little other than an arbitrary act: even though here and now one cannot understand otherwise than how one does understand, one understands only because, in light of the possibilities of meaning offered, one could understand differently. However, if one can *always* understand something differently, then one has never understood it. The conditions of the possibility of understanding are also the conditions of its impossibility.

It is possible, in extreme cases, that this can lead to the irresponsible handling of texts: "I take (as author) whatever is offered to me" and "I understand (as reader) as I wish."[14] But it does not have to be so. It can also be just the opposite: a process in which, in a given situation, a meaning present through a symbolic medium may so impress an interpreter that instead of the interpreter interpreting the text, the text interprets the interpreter, perhaps even constitutes such as person for the first time as a specific subject of understanding: "I understand in this way because I cannot do otherwise." Instead of the interpreter explaining the text, the text explains the interpreter—and that, too, must be understood.

This hermeneutical orientation on the concrete-contingent event of understanding implies a fundamentally different approach to handling texts, for recipients as well as for producers. It effectively decouples authorship and property,[15] authorship becomes "one choice from a

---

14. Under the aspect of authorship and intellectual property, the problem sketched here has by now become a topic of public discussion. See the debate about H. Hegemann, *Axolotl Roadkill* (Berlin: Ullstein, 2010), and D. Shields, *Reality Hunger: A Manifesto* (New York: Vintage, 2010).

menu,"[16] and forms of collective authorship replace "the romantic model of the individual author working alone," which, after all, held "only a very small place in the history of human culture."[17] Consequently, quotations are no longer marked as quotations because the production model of works-hermeneutics, with its unambiguous distinctions between author and recipient, original text and copy, possessor and possession, owner and owned, has disappeared.[18] Everything depends on the meaning-event in the present that nonetheless may be retrospectively analyzed as a multifaceted doubling and connecting of other lines of meaning within the differentiated realm of possibility of the meaning of the signs. The hermeneutically decisive question is not from whom a construct of meaning stems or what it "really" says, but rather where and how and by whom and on what grounds it is understood, which new possibilities of meaning it opens up, and which old possibilities thus are taken up and developed or excluded as dead ends. The event counts, along with the future that it opens up and what becomes of the past because of it. Understanding becomes dynamic, and this dynamic is to be understood hermeneutically.

This hermeneutical conception has parallels in the approaches of Ernst Fuchs and Eberhard Jüngel, although with an additional theological point. They, too, pay attention not to the producer but to the product (the text); they, too, understand this text not as a work but as the manifestation of an event. However, they understand this event not only as an occasion for understanding but also as the concrete

---

15. I. Schneider, "Konzepte von Autorschaft im Übergang von der 'Gutenberg-' zur 'Turing'-Galaxis," in: *Zeitenblicke* 5, no. 3 (2006), http://www.zeitenblicke.de/2006/3/Schneider/index_html.
16. L. Manovich, *Black Box—White Cube* (Berlin: Merve Verlag, 2005), 10. Cf. Manovich, *The Language of New Media* (Cambridge, MA: MIT Press, 2001), 116ff.
17. Manovich, *Black Box*, 7.
18. From this perspective, the usage of Old Testament citations in New Testament contexts should be considered in a new way. Decisive for their understanding is not, as traditionally, the original context, which in the citation is re-presented and thus actualized, but rather the new construction of meaning through its usage in a fresh expression, which in this usage first receives this meaning, a meaning that is not transported with it from other contexts. The christological usage of Old Testament prophecies is thus not, from the outset, an abject abuse of the earlier texts, but rather a new meaning-event, a new concentration of meaning in a new context that creates and suggests new relationships of meaning that were not to be found earlier, thus opening up new and unpredictable possibilities for understanding.

expression of a speech-event that reveals its meaning to others so that they can understand it and thereby also come to understand themselves in a new way. The elusive moment of the event, of the free occurrence, of self-giving and of self-revelation dominates, and that means, on the part of human beings, being encountered by an experience that passively makes one anew so that one sees and understands one's self, one's world, God, and everything else in a radically different way than one has done or could do thus far.

What occurs there and how that is to be understood—what one in this way experiences as an interruption of one's own life—can be misunderstood, not understood, or falsely understood in every conceivable way. Every impulse toward a hermeneutics of suspicion, every suggestion of hermeneutical criticism and self-criticism, is fully justified here. However, suspicion and criticism lose their point and their criteria if they do not aim at disclosing that which is experienced as an event and the process thus set in motion of revisioning, of understanding otherwise, and of interpreting anew everything that has already been understood and understandable. The decisive question in dealing with texts is thus neither the question about the guiding intention of the author, nor the effort to determine the original setting of the text in history, nor the quest for a dogmatic meaning fixed in the text. Much more decisive is paying attention to the event to which the text owes its existence and to which it bears witness through its reality as a text, as well as paying attention to the possibilities of understanding, self-understanding, and life that are set free and put into play by this event, possibilities that can never be discovered except by extracting them, through correction and criticism, from the misunderstandings, false understandings, and not-understandings. Theologically, the meaning of a text is not to be sought in the presumed intent of the author or in the facts of its composition, but rather in what is revealed through it to the one understanding it as the truth of his or her life. Through my understanding and engagement with the text, my previously operative views of self, world, and God are critiqued and corrected. Thus, the "real" meaning of a text is that which reveals who I really (tha is, *coram deo*) am.

Trinitarian theology is also understood and conceived not as a hermeneutics of the self-understanding of a super-subject, but as the event-ontology of the self-revelation of God. God is not to be sought either behind or in front of the revelatory event; God *is* the event of the divine self being revealed insofar as it repeats for human beings what God is in and of Godself: God reveals Godself as the one who reveals Godself. This revelatory event does not occur in such a way that one can speak of it in the past tense; it is present wherever God becomes understandable as God for people through their engagement with the *verbum externum* of the gospel (text-understanding) through the speech-event of being exegeted by the gospel (word-of-God-understanding). The theological *interpretandum*, accordingly, is neither behind nor in front of the text, as though the text stood only as a sign for it, but the text itself, the text as the event in which it becomes what it is for someone by opening the eyes of a person to that which they had not seen and understood, or had not seen or understood in that way, about their situation before God. It is not that an author explains herself in a text (expressive meaning); it is much more that the one addressed is so changed by the text-event that he can no longer understand himself and his world as he had before (transformative meaning). He or she is compelled to make critical distinctions between those understandings that are right and those that are false, those that are adequate and those that fail, those that lead astray and those that lead further.

The central category of a hermeneutical theology so oriented is the speech-event or truth-event. In this event that becomes present which makes understanding in its full scope as self-understanding, world-understanding, and God-understanding possible but at the same time unavoidable: where the truth occurs, one cannot avoid relating to it, and one cannot relate to it without understanding. Truth is that which makes one true, that changes what one is into what one becomes through this encounter with truth. Whoever has been affected by the truth finds himself or herself changed, with a new perspective that requires responding in an understanding way: In light of this truth-event, everything that was, is, and will become is understood in a concrete way by differentiating between that which furthers the true and contributes toward the new that has occurred and that which obfuscates or hinders the true and is discarded as old in the light of what has occurred. Only those who begin to thus understand themselves anew understand themselves at all. Therefore, understanding this transformative event is what theological event-hermeneutics is all about.

4

Theological Hermeneutics and Hermeneutical Theology

Theological hermeneutics is not the hermeneutics of a particular field (religion) or set of sacred texts (the Bible) such as biblical hermeneutics (*hermeneutica sacra*) or the hermeneutics of religion(s)[1] but of everything that we can (or cannot) understand in a theological perspective—the perspective of the creative presence of God.[2] If the fundamental problem of philosophical hermeneutics is the understanding of understanding, then the fundamental issue of modern theological hermeneutics is the *understanding of the understanding of God.*

1. Understanding the Understanding of God

This is an ambiguous formulation in need of clarification. For what

---

1. Cf. I. U. Dalferth and Ph. Stoellger, eds., *Hermeneutik der Religion* (Tübingen: Mohr Siebeck, 2007).
2. Regarding the hermeneutics of religion, cf. I. U. Dalferth and P. Stoellger, eds., *Hermeneutik der Religion* (Tübingen: Mohr Siebeck, 2007). To say "everything that we can (or cannot) understand" is not to say that theological hermeneutics helps to understand what cannot be understood but that it helps to understand why we fail to understand what we cannot understand.

is the meaning of the term *God* here, and how are we to understand the genitive in the phrase "understanding of God"? Various readings suggest themselves:

Does the phrase signify an understanding *of the way in which God understands Godself* (gen. subjectivus) or *of the way humans understand God* (gen. objectivus)? Two sets of distinctions are combined in this contrast: the distinction between *God and us*, and the distinction between *understanding and self-understanding*. In the first case, the issue at stake is divine self-understanding and God is understood to be something like a mind characterized by moral predicates of personhood such as understanding, reason, will, or desire (the moral idea of God as a person); in the second, this is not necessarily so. People understand God, or what they take to be God and take God to be, in many different ways. Moreover, whereas different people can understand something that is intelligible in the same way even though they do so from their different points of view, they can understand the self-understanding of somebody else only if and as it is communicated to them. However, it is one thing to understand oneself (first-order self-understanding from a first-person perspective) and quite another to understand the self-understanding of somebody else on the basis of his or her communication and testimony (second-order self-understanding from a third-person perspective). This is also true in the case of God. We cannot speak of God's self-understanding without raising the problems of how it is communicated to us (the problem of revelation) and how we can make sure that what we understand on the basis of what is communicated to us is not a human construction but indeed God's self-understanding as God (the problem of the *testimonium internum spiritus sancti* [the inner testimony of the holy spirit]). Thus, while the notion of divine self-understanding appears to be clear, it is meaningful only within a web of other theological ideas.

Or does it signify an understanding *of the understanding that God gives* (gen. auctoris) or *of the fact that it is God who makes it possible for us to understand at all?* In the first case, it refers to an understanding we have whose source and author we believe to be God, whether the understanding at stake is a particular understanding of something specific (God is the author of *this* insight) or of everything we can and do understand (God is the author of all our insights). In the second case, it means an understanding of God (*gen. objectivus*) as the creator of all intelligibility (everything that is intelligible), of all we actually understand, or of the possibility and capacity to understand at all (*gen. auctoris*).

Or is it about an understanding *that it is God who makes it possible for us to understand God* and thus an understanding *in which humans so understand God as God gives them to understand*? In this case, it signifies an understanding of God (*gen. objectivus*) as the comprehension and appropriation of God's self-understanding (*gen. subjectivus*) on the basis of God's giving of Godself to be understood (*gen. auctoris*).

Each of these readings implies a different understanding of God (God as the divine subject of understanding, as the ground of human understanding, as the fountainhead of the event of intelligible creation that makes understanding possible, as the original event of self-understanding, as a self-understanding conveying itself), and each plays a role in theological hermeneutics. In regard to the *understanding of the understanding of God*, and thus in regard to that which distinguishes theological hermeneutics from philosophical hermeneutics, the issue is a *human understanding* of the understanding of God—however that may be understood. Such human understanding can be conceived either as the understanding of God by those who put their faith and trust in God (first-order understanding of faith from a first-person perspective) or as the understanding of their understanding of God (second-order understanding of the understanding of faith from a third-person perspective). Furthermore, this second-order understanding can be pursued either within the context and horizon of the understanding of faith (as theological understanding) or from another point of view (as, for example, a historical, empirical, religious studies, psychological, or sociological understanding). Insofar as the second-order understanding is not only *about* the understanding of God in faith but takes place *from within the* horizon of this first-order understanding, it is a mode of the theological self-reflection of faith that attends to itself in thinking about itself in order to understand itself, its object, its basis, and its practice.

Such theological efforts toward understanding the understanding of faith are also critically interested in the scope and limits of this understanding and thus are oriented by the key distinction between the understanding of God in faith and the misunderstanding or failure to understand God in unfaith or nonfaith. Faith is the mode of human life that results from becoming aware of God's presence through God's self-communicating and self-disclosing presence in God's word; unfaith is the mode of human life that is not informed by the mode of faith.[3] Faith and unfaith are not independent modes of life, and they do not originate at the same time. Rather, one cannot identify a life of unfaith without recourse to faith, nor identify a life of faith without distinguishing it from unfaith. Faith exists only as a radical change from unfaith to faith, a change that shifts everything into a new light. This change can occur as a disruptive interruption of a life (dislocation) or as a scarcely noticeable development in it (reorientation). In either case, it takes place during a life. No one is born a person of faith; rather,

---

3. If living a human life means there exists somebody who lives her life in a particular way, then modes of life can be differentiated into *modes of existing* (modes of *being somebody*) and *modes of living* (modes of *living as somebody*). Modes of living are the set of ways in which humans can live their lives: interested, bored, full of humor, sad, happy, angry, satisfied, friendly, miserable, and so forth. Modes of existence, on the other hand, are not a subset of our modes of living but modes of being that function as operators of our lives lived in particular ways. They are qualifiers of the whole series of ways in which we can live our lives. Kant's distinction between real predicates and positing predicates may be of help here. Just as existence is not a defining or determining predicate of somebody (a real predicate in Kant's sense), so modes of existence are not modes that define or determine how we live our lives. Rather, just as existence is a locating or positing predicate that tells us *that* somebody exists but not *what* he or she is, so modes of existence are modes of being posited (that is, modes of contingent being) that determine the fact *that* somebody exists but not the way in which he or she is *what* she or he is. Both *faith* and *nonfaith* (or *unfaith*) are *modes of human existence* that determine how a human life in all its possible modes is in fact lived with respect to the presence of God without which it would not and could not be. Faith is a *mode of existence*; boredom or gratitude or resentment are *modes of life*. Modes of existence are defined in terms of a person's way of relating to his or her place *coram deo* as expressed in his or her actual way of living. Modes of life, on the other hand, are defined in terms of the multitude of ways in which persons can live together with other persons in the world. In the first case, the focus is on a person's relation to God, in the second, on persons' relations to the world. However, whereas there are many modes of life, there are only two modes of existence (faith and unfaith) because with respect to God persons can exist only by ignoring or not ignoring God's presence, even though they may live their lives of ignorance or awareness of God in many different ways and in many different degrees of certainty, conviction, doubt, or skepticism.

whoever becomes a person of faith becomes so during the course of his or her life. However, this change is not simply one further event in the sequence of life's events (even though it can always be described in such a way), nor it is the beginning of a new sequence of events within this life (even though such is always the case). Instead, it is a radical transformation of position, horizon, and orientation so that everything past, present, and future is seen in a new light: the light of the salvific presence of God's creative and transforming love. This makes it necessary to distinguish with respect to the past, present, and future of a human life between what is appropriate to such presence (faith) and what is not (unfaith). This is possible only in an autobiographical perspective from within that life (participant) and not in a biographical perspective from without (observer). Not from the biographical beginning, nor from any neutral perspective, but only by looking back from this change within a life does it become possible—indeed, necessary—to distinguish between faith and unfaith, between the life of a sinner (unfaith) and the life of a justified sinner (faith). For—to summarize the most fundamental aspects of the "grammar of faith" focused on this distinction—all people live either in faith or in unfaith; no one lives in faith who did not come out of unfaith; no one can change from unfaith to faith on his or her own account or by his or her own power; and no one who lives does so neutrally, that is, neither in unfaith nor in faith.

This has two important consequences. First, every understanding of God in faith is a critical correction and transformation of the misunderstanding and lack of understanding of God in unfaith. The understanding of God in faith can thus never be defined in and of itself, but only in critical contrast to the misunderstanding or failure to understand God in unfaith: faith is not merely a contrast term to unfaith but a success term of overcoming unfaith through the help of God.[4] Second, the understanding of God in faith cannot be separated

---

4. Even though it has been attempted repeatedly to argue from a set of phenomena to that which they are said to presuppose or imply as their contraries or contradictories, no negative phenomenology of faith may be derived from the phenomena of unfaith, which are assumed to contain within them, or to presuppose, the alternative of faith. This could only be done, if at

from the change from unfaith to faith, a change that does not come from oneself but instead befalls one, and thus is determined hermeneutically in a significant way by this radical change. A life of unfaith has, as such, no idea of such a change, it sees and provides no occasion for it, nor even a possibility of changing itself to faith. It does not know itself as unfaith, it cannot even be named so independently of faith, and faith is only an actuality if the change from unfaith to faith has taken place.

For this change to be meaningful and possible, the referent *God* must be understood not as we ourselves think or imagine God. Rather, God must be so known and accessible as God knows Godself and makes Godself accessible in occasioning the change from unfaith to faith in a human life: as God in whom one can put one's faith of one's own free will because God makes Godself manifest as a good God who concerns Godself with the concerns of those who ignore God. Thus, persons who live in faith perceive and know the change from unfaith to faith not as their own accomplishment, but only as an undeserved and unexpected gift from God. Accordingly, "God" is understood as the one who leads people from unfaith to faith, from a life ignorant of or estranged from God into nearness to God, from death into life. The understanding of God in faith, as distinct from not understanding God in unfaith, knows God as the object of faith only because it knows God as the ground of this faith—that is to say, as the originator of the change from unfaith

---

all, if phenomena of unfaith could be identified independently of faith. But that is impossible. Faith and unfaith are not descriptive terms but orienting terms; they do not name distinct sets of phenomena but signify the way in which human persons to whom phenomena are given relate to the presence of God's love and, in its light, to themselves and to their fellow creatures. Only faith knows about the contrast to unfaith and can thus distinguish between phenomena of faith and unfaith. Without faith there are neither any phenomena of faith nor any phenomena of unfaith but only phenomena of life. In order to define the phenomena of life as phenomena of unfaith, reference must be made to faith. And in order to describe the phenomena of life as phenomena of faith, there must not only be differentiation from unfaith but also explicit reference to God, to whom the change from unfaith to faith is owed, thus making possible the distinction between faith and unfaith. Without recourse to God, this distinction cannot be clarified nor used in any theologically meaningful way: It is not a descriptive differentiation within the classification of life phenomena that can be cashed out in terms of particular sets of phenomena. It is rather an orienting distinction of the life of faith, which understands itself and everything else in the light of, and within the horizon of, the change from unfaith to faith that it owes to God. *Unfaith* is the term used by believers for the past from which they find themselves saved by the love of God, *faith* the term they use for the gift received from God to be able to distinguish between faith and unfaith in their relationship to the presence of God's love.

to faith in a human life. To have faith in God is to have faith in the originator and initiator of that faith, and to understand God in faith is to understand God to be the one who is to be thanked for bringing about the change from unfaith to faith.

2. Approaches to Theological Hermeneutics

This is not always seen with sufficient clarity. The truth of the understanding of God is not insensitive to the mode in which God is understood as God (faith) or is not so understood (unfaith). For the analysis of the understanding of God in faith as distinct from not understanding God in unfaith, all of the philosophical approaches named are not only important philosophically but must also be employed theologically.

From the *subjectivity-theoretical approach*, God is understood as the ultimate ground of the reality and possibility not only of the human subject and its cognitive operations that constitute our understanding (self) but also of everything that is and can be understood with and through these operations (world). The understanding of God is thus developed either within the scope of a cosmological scheme of explanation (God is the one who explains the intelligibility of the world) or within the scope of a transcendental (that is, subjectivity- and reflection-based) scheme of justification (God is the one who grounds human self-understanding). In the first case, the understanding of God is construed according to the grammar of *understanding something*; in the second case, according to the grammar of *self-understanding*. Bernard Lonergan's philosophical theology is an example of the former, while the latter is represented in different ways by Karl Rahner's transcendental-hermeneutical theology of God's self-revelation mediated through intersubjective communication and by Eilert Herms's transcendental-semiotic theology of experience with its focus on the absolute transcendental dependence of the semiotic self.[5] The fundamental problem of these attempts is not merely that

---

5. B. Lonergan, *Insight: A Study of Human Understanding*, vol. 3 of *Collected Works*, ed. Frederick E. Crowe and Robert M. Doran (Toronto: University of Toronto, 1992). K. Rahner, *Grundkurs des Glaubens*.

they construe the understanding of God in terms of the epistemological contrast between subject (self) and object (world) based on the subject-predicate grammar of European languages. Even more so, they shift the key distinction of theological hermeneutics away from *understanding God* versus *not understanding God* to *understanding God* versus *understanding not-God* (that is to say, understanding something different from God). Accordingly, their efforts at understanding are no longer oriented toward the problem of distinguishing between true and false understandings of God, as Gerhard Ebeling and Michael Trowitzsch do in terms of sin and grace in the wake of Luther, Calvin, and Schleiermacher.[6] Rather, drawing on creation theology, their efforts are oriented toward the cosmological or anthropological difference between God and the world or God and the self. Formally, this may amount to little more than a differing determination of the range of the operator of negation used in the key distinction of theological hermeneutics (understanding / not understanding God versus understanding God / understanding not-God). But the material theological consequences are significant.

From the *phenomenology of language approach*, the understanding of God is explicated as understanding the manner in which people actually speak of God. Which understanding of "God" governs their religious use of language in speaking to and about God? Following Wittgenstein, a number of people, including Peter Winch, Rush Rhees, and D. Z. Phillips, have argued that this can only be answered concretely through a descriptive analysis of actual religious discourse, life, and speech behavior.[7] However, if this is to yield anything more

---

Einführung in den Begriff des Christentums (Freiburg: Herder, 1977), 122ff. E. Herms, *Theologie—eine Erfahrungswissenschaft* (Munich: Kaiser, 1978); Herms, "Die Einführung des allgemeinen Zeichenbegriffs. Theologische Aspekte der Begründung einer reinen Semiotik durch Ch. W. Morris," in *Theorie für die Praxis. Beiträge zur Theologie* (Munich: Kaiser, 1982), 164–88.

6. G. Ebeling, "Wort Gottes und Hermeneutik," in *Wort und Glaube* (Tübingen: Mohr Siebeck, 1967), 319–48, here 334, 341; Ebeling, "Theologie zwischen reformatorischem Sündenverständnis und heutiger Einstellung zum Bösen," in *Wort und Glaube III*, 173–204; Ebeling, "Das Problem des Bösen als Prüfstein der Anthropologie," in *Wort und Glaube III*, 205–24; Ebeling, *Dogmatik des christlichen Glaubens I* (Tübingen: Mohr Siebeck, 1987), 156–57. M. Trowitzsch, *Verstehen und Freiheit. Umrisse einer theologischen Kritik der hermeneutischen Urteilskraft* (Zürich: TVZ, 1981).

7. D. Z. Phillips, *The Concept of Prayer* (London: Routledge & K. Paul 1965); Phillips, *Faith and Philosophical Enquiry* (London: Routledge & K. Paul 1970); Phillips, *Religion without Explanation* (Oxford: Blackwell, 1976); Phillips, *Faith after Foundationalism* (London: Routledge, 1988).

than the bare normativity of the factual, the factual understandings of God in a religious practice must be critically assessed in terms of how God must be understood if it is truly God who is to be understood. This requires a normative grammar of the proper usage of the term *God* in a given religious tradition. Not everything believers think or say about God is adequate or to be taken seriously and at face value. Thus, a critical reconstruction of the grammar of a religious or (in the case of Christian faith) a Christian way of life can be attained only when the linguistic phenomenological analysis of actual religious discourse is judged against the backdrop of theological norms derived from the self-elucidation of the self-understanding of faith. In short, a theological analysis of religious discourse that aims at being normative rather than merely descriptive must have a dogmatic foundation (in the good sense of the word).[8]

Finally, *the phenomenology of existence approach* seeks to explicate the understanding of God in light of the fundamental connection between understanding and self-understanding by means of existential-ontological, effective history, or hermeneutics-of-objectivity analyses. Thus, Bultmann, assimilating the intellectual heritage of the Reformation, not only stresses the indissoluble link between the knowledge of God and the knowledge of self but also emphasizes this in such a way that the analysis of human self-understanding is presented as the key to understanding God.[9] The implications of this are twofold. On the one hand, Bultmann takes the preunderstanding existing within our particular self-understanding, or our prior life relationship to that which stands in question, to be the condition of the possibility of all understanding. Understanding something, according to Bultmann, fundamentally means "to understand it in its relationship to the one who understands, to understand oneself with or in it."[10] He seeks to develop this critically by drawing on Heidegger's analysis of being and

---

8. Cf. I. U. Dalferth, *Religiöse Rede von Gott* (Munich: Kaiser, 1981), 269–494.
9. R. Bultmann, "Welchen Sinn hat es, von Gott zu reden?" in *Glauben und Verstehen I* (Tübingen: Mohr Siebeck, 1980), 26–37; Bultmann, "Das Problem der Hermeneutik," in *Glauben und Verstehen II* (Tübingen: Mohr Siebeck, 1952), 211–35.
10. R. Bultmann, "Das Problem der 'natürlichen Theologie,'" in *Glauben und Verstehen I*, 294–312, here 295–96.

preunderstanding in *Sein und Zeit*. On the other hand, he describes the special nature of Christian faith and its understanding of God as the enabling and opening of a new, faithful self-understanding through which the person attains authenticity; this topic, formulated in terms of sin and faith, is also developed by Bultmann, using the formal conditions of existence from *Sein und Zeit*.

This orientation toward an existential-ontological understanding of *Dasein* and its theological interpretation in terms of sin and faith within the horizon of a critical analysis of self-understanding soon became questioned. The effective-history approach developed by Gadamer crticized it as a misunderstanding of Heidegger as a philosopher of subjectivity in disguise. The human self is not the reference point and fulcrum of all understanding but is itself constituted through a chain of occurrences: the occurrence of conversation or of tradition. As this takes place primarily in and through language, the analysis of understanding and self-understanding should also focus on language understood in terms of the later Heidegger's "history of (forgetting of) being." Thus, language, rather than existence, or the self, becomes the primary focus and frame of reference for the analysis of understanding.

This is also true of the hermeneutics of objectivity approach, which stresses that conversation has its point in being *about* something, and that clarifying this reference is the hermeneutical uncovering of the basic conditions under which something within this range of reference is spoken of, thought of, and known. The questions posed by the hermeneutics of objectivity approach definitely lead theological hermeneutics away from concentrating on the subject or self to a focus on the sign-medium of language and, furthermore, to a focus on that toward which the hermeneutical efforts of the first-order understanding of faith are directed in response. That which is to be understood is precisely that which gives the impulse to understand, in that it first provokes the question of understanding at all: in order to understand the understanding of God in faith, one has to understand that to which faith responds in speaking of God in prayer (speaking to God), in confession (speaking of God to others), and in reflection (speaking about God). This hermeneutical insight informs, within theology, both the phenomenological dogmatics of Karl Barth, which pretends to be antihermeneutical, and the hermeneutical theology of revelation of Eberhard Jüngel; within philosophy, it informs the responsive phenomenology of perception of Bernhard Waldenfels and the fundamental hermeneutics of objectivity of Günter Figal—regardless of the far-reaching differences between these approaches.[11]

3. The Understanding of Faith and Theological Understanding

If *theological hermeneutics* seeks to *understand the understanding of God*, it is *the human* understanding of God that it seeks to understand. Contrary to what some have thought, this does not mean that it must then be either about *the impossibility of understanding God* (because the infinite God cannot possibly be an object of finite human understanding) or about *the understanding of human constructions of God* (because we can only understand what we ourselves symbolically construct). It is not necessarily the case that humans either cannot understand God at all or can understand only their own constructs of God. Our understanding is always mediated by signs, but we do not therefore understand only signs; rather, through signs, we understand what is actual or possible or necessary. If there is human understanding of God, then it is mediated by signs. But that does not mean that it can only be an understanding of human signs for God. It would be equally erroneous to presume from the outset that human understanding of God necessarily fails because God is *semper maior* and there is always more that we do not understand. It is hardly true that the most that one can hope to understand with respect to God is that God cannot be

---

[11]. E. Jüngel, *Gottes Sein ist im Werden. Verantwortliche Rede vom Sein Gottes bei Karl Barth. Eine Paraphrase*, 4th ed. (Tübingen: Mohr Siebeck, 1998); Jüngel, *Gott als Geheimnis der Welt. Zur Begründung der Theologie des Gekreuzigten im Streit zwischen Theismus und Atheismus* (Tübingen: Mohr Siebeck, 72001). *Gottes Sein* is translated into English by John Webster as *God's Being is in Becoming: The Trinitarian Being of God in the Theology of Karl Barth* (Edinburgh: Bloomsbury T&T Clark, 2004). *Gott als Geheimnis* is translated into English by Darell L. Guder as *God as the Mystery of the World: On the Foundation of the Theology of the Crucified One in the Dispute Between Theism and Atheism* (Eugene, OR: Wipf & Stock, 2009).

understood. If speaking of God is to have any relevance for life at all, it is the exact opposite. Only because God can be understood can we know that there is always more than we in fact understand, and God can be understood precisely because God makes Godself understandable as God.

Here is the parting of the ways between the classical tradition of theological hermeneutics, which sets out from the nonunderstanding of God (hermeneutics of negativity), and hermeneutical theology, which starts its thinking with the understanding of God (hermeneutics of divine self-revelation). This difference is manifested also in the ambiguity of the phrase "understanding of God," which can be understood in two ways—as the understanding of *something as God* or as the understanding of *God as something*.

In the first case, human understanding is directed toward *something* that it understands *as God*. This approach can take the form of the interpretive understanding *of something* (the conceptual objectification of something as God) as it did in early modern theistic metaphysics. Or it can follow the idealist path of a self-elucidating unfolding of *self-understanding* (the understanding *of oneself*) that seeks to understand God not (as an object) in the mode of understanding nor (as a subject) in the mode of self-understanding but instead as the dynamic idea of the absolute that integrates object- and subject-based understandings of God into a transcendental account of God as the beginning and end of all understanding and self-understanding. In either case, a coherent conception of God—as a concept of understanding (*Verstand*) or an idea of reason (*Vernunft*)—is required in order to be able to understand something as God.

Alternatively, human understanding directs itself toward *God*, whom it understands *as something*. Then no preliminary conception of God is required, but—since God is not presented as simply one thing to be understood among others—it can only truly be God who is understood and not just a historical understanding of God or a term for God, if God *makes Godself understandable (intelligible) and understood as God*. That this is indeed what occurs is the strict meaning of revelation as *self-*

revelation: God makes Godself *understandable as God in Christ, and understood as God in Christ through the Spirit*. All religions that claim to speak *to God and of God* and not just about something as God refer in a similar sense to a revelation of God that they assert as that to which they respond.

The difference between the two understandings of the phrase "understanding of God" has nothing to do with the difference between an indirect and mediated or a direct and unmediated understanding.[12] All understanding is mediated by signs, and nothing is understood *as something* that is not understood *through something* as something: "to understand something as something" always means "to understand something through something as something." That applies to the phrase "to understand something as God" just as it does for the phrase "to understand God as something." In either case, God is understood mediated through sign, word, writing, or image, never directly in an unmediated way.

4. Negative and Radical Theology

For thinkers in the tradition of *negative theology*, this implies that we are always dealing with *signs* for God, not with the God to whom they refer.[13] If God, however, is always beyond the signs through which we seek to understand God, then God is, in the end, not understandable. Signs are finite, but God is infinite. Negative theology is, accordingly, the basic form of all theology.

In contrast, *radical theology* emphasizes not some sign-free immediacy in the understanding of God, but instead a use of signs in which the signs do not disguise God but rather make God present. In the event of God becoming understandable as God—that is, in the event of God's self-revelation—the distinction between sign and God

---

12. Cf. V. Hoffmann, *Vermittelte Offenbarung. Ricoeurs Philosophie als Herausforderung der Theologie* (Mainz: Matthias-Grünewald-Verlag, 2007), ch. 1.
13. Classical theology was well aware that there was more to it than this, as seen in the Augustinian tradition in which those signs wherein the signified and signifier were to be systematically distinguished were set apart from *sacramental signs* in which the signified (God) was present in the concrete signifiers (bread and wine).

is not withdrawn, but rather intensified to the point that the signs in question are fundamentally *overdetermined*: God does not disappear behind the signs, but *becomes so present with them* that through these signs, for the one understanding, God becomes understandable as God.[14] Signs mediate God not because they cease to refer to God and thus to be distinct from God, but rather because, in using these signs, something occurs that the ones affected retrospectively bring to expression in the confession that God has made Godself understandable to them.

In this respect, *revelation* is a theological category for analyzing the responsive confessional structure of faith ("not I, but God," "not through my own intelligence and power, but rather the Holy Spirit through the gospel"), not a descriptive category for a historical, empirical, or—in the widest sense—phenomenal event of the world of experience.

Revelation is repeatedly described as such a disclosure-event or an experience of opening in the tradition of Ian Ramsey's "Christian empiricism" or by followers of Schleiermacher.[15] They thereby highlight an occurrence that is not some experience or insight that the

---

14. This has sometimes been overgeneralized and turned into the highly problematic view of the "sacramental shape" of creation as such and the sacramentality of all things. Cf. Denys Turner, *Faith, Reason, and the Existence of God*, 2004. But this shifts the emphasis away from God and God's self-revealing activity to the materiality and character of creation and the diagnostic capacities of human reason. It is not a big deal to infer the creator from creation; indeed, that is an analytic move that explains nothing but unfolds the creation view from which one starts. The real challenge is to see the world *as creation*, and to give reasons for doing so. The world does not manifest its createdness; to see it as creation is impossible without *understanding oneself* as God's creature, and to understand oneself in this way is impossible without God opening one's eyes and mind to it. Of course, Denys Turner knows that one has to start not from creation but from the creator and hence from the person who sees and experiences the world as creation because she sees herself as God's creature through the grace of God. Without God illumining the human mind, humans cannot see themselves and their world as God sees them: as God's creation. Cf. Turner's later books: *Julian of Norwich, Theologian* (New Haven: Yale University Press, 2011), and *Thomas Aquinas: A Portrait* (New Haven: Yale University Press 2013).
15. On disclosure-events, cf. I. Ramsey, *Miracles: An Essay in Logical Map Work* (Oxford: Clarendon, 1952); Ramsey, *Religious Language: An Empirical Placing of Theological Phrases* (London: Macmillan, 1957); Ramsey, *Christian Discourse: Some Logical Explorations* (London: Oxford University Press, 1965); Ramsey, *Models and Mystery* (London: Oxford University Press, 1964); Ramsey, *Models for Divine Activity* (London: SCM, 1973); J. H. Gill, *Ian Ramsey: To Speak Responsibly of God* (London: Allen and Unwin, 1976); and Dalferth, *Religiöse Rede*, 19. On Christian empiricism, cf. I. Ramsey, *Christian Empiricism*, ed. J. H. Gill (London: James Clarke, 1974). On the followers of Schleiermacher, see E. Herms, "Offenbarung" (1985), in *Offenbarung und Glaube. Zur Bildung des christlichen Lebens* (Tübingen: Mohr Siebeck, 1992), 168–220, here 176ff.

subject has won, built up, or developed over the continuity of his or her life, but rather an occurrence that so interrupts everything one has experienced that it enters into awareness as something unexpected and surprising. The penny drops, and everything looks different. But that is too nonspecific to be theologically convincing. As right as it is to stress that the event that produces such an experience is beyond grasp, it remains too vague, in everyday language, and theologically unclear for it simply to be designated "revelation" as such. The character of a disclosure-event in this sense can be found not only in religious experiences but also in aesthetic experiences, even, most broadly, in every act of experiencing, so that "revelation" and "experience" threaten to become coextensive. It is precisely this breadth and continuity that is understood as the strength of this understanding of revelation, and the theological task is seen only as the effort to distinguish special religious experiences from other types of experience. However, no phenomenology of religious experiences can hide the fact that it does not describe a separate class of phenomena (religious phenomena) but rather deals with experiences that owe their interpretation to a contingent cultural and religious context (religious interpretations of phenomena). In other words, it is not the experience per se that is religious, but what is experienced is interpreted in religious ways. A religious experience is not an experience of something that is religious but a religious interpretation of something that is experienced.

All recourse to general or to special "experiences of revelation" thus loses its point. Whether the experience originates "directly from above," "vertically," or "horizontally" is secondary to the fact that it always occurs mediated by particular media and becomes a "religious revelation" only in connection with culturally contingent processes of interpretation. "Revelation" is thus determined not by *what* is experienced, but by *how* something is experienced. Accordingly, the theologically decisive question is not how "religious disclosure-experiences" are to be described so as to be distinct from other, similar experiences, but rather how that which is experienced is understood or must be understood so that it can rightly be called "revelation." This question cannot be answered without recourse to a contingent tradition of religious interpretation. Therefore, in decisive ways, the term *revelation* must be seen as an interpretation (to experience *something as revelation*), not as the designation of that which is to be interpreted (to experience *revelation as something*). It is an interpretation that makes clear that *more* is seen in particular phenomena than what they show in and of themselves: they are seen as signs of the hidden presence of God.[16]

In a theological sense, *revelation* designates no particular phenomenon, no special experience nor special type of experience, but instead a new point of view on everything—namely, the point of view of the one to whom faith anaphorically owes its existence, and the one whom, in response, it articulates as its ground, its object, and its content. In this overall context of the theological self-interpretation of faith, theology unfolds the category of revelation, first of all, as being about that to which faith owes its existence (its ground) and that toward which faith is directed (its object): God. And it understands God in the way in which God, through the Holy Spirit, makes Godself accessible in Jesus Christ and believable to human beings: as merciful love that overcomes evil by good, creates justice out of injustice, and makes wrong things right. However, it cannot understand God in this way without also understanding human beings in a new way: as God's creatures who pay no attention to their Creator. Human beings are sinners who ignore God and do not want to believe in God. They do so only when God makes them change from unfaith to faith. This is why they cannot understand God without understanding God to be the one to whom they owe their existence and their faith. Second, theology, within the horizon of this category, unfolds the self-interpretation of faith with respect to how humans are therefore seen (namely as sinners and faithful), how the God in whom they have faith is therefore understood (as creative fatherly love directed toward them), and how

---

16. Cf. I. U. Dalferth, "Understanding Revelation," in *Revelation*, ed. I. U. Dalferth and M. C. Rodgers (Tübingen: Mohr Siebeck, 2014), 1–25.

the world in which they live thus comes to be seen (as God's creation). As the first brings the ground and object of faith into view, so the second brings the content of faith to speech and develops it in theologically differentiated ways.

5. Understanding within the Horizon of Revelation

Because they so understand themselves, people of faith see *everything* differently. They do not distinguish in a theologically relevant sense with respect to their experiences in nature and history between the holy and the profane, the religious and the political, the sacred and the secular but instead see and relate to everything as God's creation. All those distinctions mark differences within creation. They cannot replace or compete with the fundamental difference between Creator and creation that revelation, understood as divine self-revelation, elucidates. It is this self-revelation to which believers respond in confessing faith and trust in God, and they fall into idolatry if they mistake any of the differences within creation for the creature-Creator difference elucidated by revelation, acknowledged by faith, and explicated by theology. Only in the overall context of this theological self-interpretation of faith does it make sense to speak of revelation. The theological category of revelation marks the point of reference of the horizon within which everything is understood in a new and different way, a point of reference that is unavailable and inaccessible to us because it marks the fundamental self-disclosing and self-communicating activity of love that faith calls "God." In Christian thought, wherever the term *revelation* is used theologically, there is accordingly a process of explication opened up that addresses God, faith, Jesus Christ, the Spirit, creation, the sinner, the kingdom of God, the church, death, and eternal life. *Everything* must be said anew because that to whom faith understands itself as a response effected the change from unfaith to faith, from death to life, from the old to the new.

Recourse to the mere formal structure of a disclosure situation of the type "A discloses in situation B the content C for the receiver D with result E" contributes nothing toward clarifying the understanding of revelation in a theological sense because these structural features sketch the pattern of a communication situation but not the hermeneutical structure of *the self-interpretation of Christian faith*, which seeks by means of this category to understand the passivity that constitutes it.[17] There are all sorts of disclosures. Revelation in the Christian sense, however, is only that to which faith understands itself to be a response when persons come to acknowledge God to be their loving Creator in whom they trust, since it is thus that the change from unfaith to faith has come about: a process of signification becomes the self-revelation of God's love when the signified one (God) becomes present as creative love, in, with, and under the signs. It is in the concrete usage of these signs that God becomes understandable as God to a person, so that she understands herself and her world in reference to God in a new and different way.

There is no set of rules or conventions that can make signs function in this way. Revelation can only occur *extra ordinem*.[18] But when it occurs and when signs function in this way, transforming the self-understanding and world-understanding of a person, then they do not conceal God but rather make God present by disclosing God's presence as the presence of creative and transforming love. Signs then are not a hindrance to understanding God as God; instead, they are precisely what make it possible. They make it possible, however, in such a way that God—or Transcendence, Truth, the Source of Life, the Absolute, or whichever expression one chooses to speak of the one who has thus disclosed Godself as understandable—is not understandable as ontological object, as an abstract other, or as something epistemologically inaccessible, but rather as the reverse and the background of the understandable. More precisely: the event of self-interpretation makes it is possible to speak religiously of and to God,

---

17. C. Schwöbel, "Offenbarung und Erfahrung—Glaube und Lebenserfahrung. Systematisch-theologische Überlegungen zu ihrer Verhältnisbestimmung," in *Marburger Jahrbuch Theologie III: Lebenserfahrung* (Marburg: N. G. Elwert, 1990), 68–122, here 72.
18. "Who can explain it, who can tell you why? Fools give you reasons, wise men never try." These lyrics are from "Some Enchanted Evening," a showtune in the Rodgers and Hammerstein musical *South Pacific*.

or theologically of the God who reveals Godself, or philosophically of a self-disclosing transcendence, or in terms of philosophy of religion of the inaccessible making itself present in the accessible. For this event is experienced as an interruption of experience as a whole such that it opens up a new way of viewing all that has been or can be experienced. That without which there could be no usage of signs discloses itself not beyond the signs, but rather within and through their usage. The distinction between sign and signified is thereby not dissolved, but rather specified in that the contingent *that* of this distinction, which exists only because that has taken place which was not inevitable, is disclosed as understandable and thus meaningful.

The difference between negative theology and radical theology in understanding the expression "understanding of God" thus does not consist in the antithesis of an understanding that is mediated by signs and one that is not. The difference is to be sought elsewhere, and has parallels to how we understand people: to understand a person does not mean to understand something (a material body) *as* a person but to understand a person in the way persons can be understood within the context of our interactions with people. In both cases, the understanding is mediated by signs, but the human brain is hardwired, with good reason, for distinguishing those signs through which people express themselves and give themselves to be understood from other signs. We are "self-interpreting animals" (Charles Taylor) precisely because we know how to make this distinction—in respect to others and in respect to ourselves. Long before we have a concept of person, we can understand people and thus learn how other understandings differ from this understanding.

Similarly, to say that God is intelligible does not mean that we can infer who and what God is from something that is not God. Just as we do not infer the presence of persons from the empirical data given to our senses, so we do not infer the presence of God from the material world we experience. Rather, to call God intelligible means that God makes Godself understandable as God to humans through concrete sign-events that are understood to disclose God's self-understanding as God in relationship to others—an understanding that normally does not leap to the eye in the actual experience of such events but becomes clear only in retrospect. Just as we cannot understand persons as persons without also understanding ourselves in this way, we cannot understand God as God without also understanding our world and ourselves in relation to God. To interact with persons is to be a person, and to understand God is to be a creature who knows herself or himself to be a creature. In this sense, one cannot understand God without understanding oneself differently, and to understand God on the basis of God's self-communication in and through particular sign-events is to understand oneself as the addressee of this self-communication (God's creature) and one's world as the place where this self-communication takes place (God's creation). Humans who understand themselves as the addressees of God's self-communication understand their world as that through which God addresses them and God as the one who addresses them. In the light of their altered understanding of themselves and their world, God is understood as the one who reveals Godself in relationship to others as "*God for* . . ." This concretizes who and what God is in such a way that it can be symbolized with the help of time-bound media and, in this form, communicated to others and passed on by tradition. In this sense, Judaism, with reference to the revelation of Moses, understands itself responsively as the *people of God*; Christianity, with reference to the revelation of Jesus Christ, understands itself as *the body of Christ*; and Islam, with reference to the revelation of Mohammed, understands itself as *the faithful who subject themselves to God with fullest devotion* (that is to say, as Muslims). Accordingly, in Judaism God is confessed as *the Lord and deliverer of Israel*, in Christianity as *creative and redeeming love*, and in Islam as the *merciful and compassionate ruler of the world*. And just as *faith* is the mode of human existence in which persons live their lives by understanding and trusting God as the self-communicating love that God reveals to humankind in Jesus Christ and through the Spirit as his divine self-understanding, so *unfaith* is the lack of this God-trusting mode of existence.

In all its proper versions, faith is normatively *faith in God*. This is also true in the Christian context, where this faith is expressed as *faith in Jesus Christ* because God is known as the love of the divine Father disclosed in Jesus Christ through the Spirit. Trinitarian theology puts it in a nutshell: there is no way of trusting God (Father) without trusting the one who reveals God to be eternal love (Son) and the one who makes humans trust in God's love (as revealed in Jesus Christ) and in Jesus Christ as the revealer of this love (Spirit). When Christians speak of God, they refer to the one who is disclosed in Jesus' message as loving Father, in Jesus' life and death as obedient Son, and in faith in Jesus as Christ as the Spirit who makes people trust in God's love by making them trust in Jesus as Christ, that is, as the revealer of God's heart toward the creatures who ignore and despise God. Thus, the name "Jesus" stands for the concrete, historical events that people, who then became Christian, experienced as disclosing God's self-understanding as creative and redeeming love to them in such a supreme, comprehensive, and definitive way that they gave Jesus the title of Christ. In and through the life and death of Jesus they came to understand God's presence as the presence of creative and redeeming love. One cannot accept this as true according to one's own lights or in one's own right, but rather only by undergoing a fundamental alteration of one's own self-understanding and mode of existence from a God-ignoring to a God-adoring life. If one understands oneself as someone who receives God's creative and redeeming love for no apparent reason, then one is no longer who one was (a person who ignores God) but instead is one who has become aware of God's presence in his or her own life, thus learning to observe and understand that life in the light of the distinction between sin (a God-ignoring way of life) and grace (a God-given life of responsive love of God and God's neighbors).

Both the understanding of God in faith and the misunderstanding or failure to understand God in unfaith are to be distinguished from the *theological understanding* of this understanding or failure to understand God. Theological understanding is not as such a faithful understanding of God. It is rather a critical and reflective understanding of this understanding of God in faith that also involves an effort to understand the nonunderstanding of God in unfaith. One cannot intellectually understand faith without also considering the opposite of faith. Therefore, efforts at theological understanding are always critically interested in the limits of the understanding of faith, and focus therefore on the key distinction between the understanding of God in faith and the failure to do so in unfaith.

6. The Hermeneutical Heritage of Bultmann and Barth in Hermeneutical Theology

The analysis of understanding God and not understanding God within twentieth-century theological hermeneutics was closely related to the profound alterations taking place within philosophical hermeneutics. This is true of all phases and forms of theological hermeneutics in its efforts to understand the understanding of God. The turn to language, to "subject matter," "cause," and "concern," and (later) to a responsive hermeneutics of objectivity was shared by theology, but most explicitly by *hermeneutical theology*. Bultmann, according to the critique of Ernst Fuchs, had not sufficiently appreciated "the linguistic nature of human existence."[19] And Ebeling thought that Bultmann had not gone far enough in his Reformation focus and had not truly grasped the word-event character of God's Word and the linguistic nature of human existence.[20] In regard to the "subject matter" of faith, he had not given enough emphasis to the basis of the christological kerygma in the event of the Word of God coming to speech in Jesus,[21] nor had he

---

19. E. Fuchs, "Das hermeneutische Problem," in *Zeit und Geschichte: Danksgabe an Rudolf Bultmann zum 80. Geburtstag*, ed. E. Dingler (Tübingen: Mohr Siebeck, 1967), 357–66, here 364; Fuchs, "Was ist existentiale Interpretation?," in *Zum hermeneutischen Problem in der Theologie. Die existentiale Interpretation, Gesammelte Aufsätze I* (Tübingen: Mohr Siebeck, 1959), 107–15, here 113–15; Fuchs, "Was ist ein Sprachereignis? Ein Brief," in *Zur Frage nach dem historischen Jesus, Gesammelte Aufsätze II* (Tübingen: Mohr Siebeck, 1960), 424–30, here 427ff; Fuchs, *Jesus. Wort und Tat* (Tübingen: Mohr Siebeck, 1971), 141: "The difference between Bultmann and me is to be found in that fact that I have emphasized language."
20. Ebeling, "Wort Gottes und Hermeneutik," 333, 338ff.; Ebeling, "Die Frage nach dem historischen Jesus und das Problem der Christologie," in *Wort und Glaube*, 300–18, here 306ff; Ebeling, "Theologische Erwägungen über das Gewissen," in *Wort und Glaube*, 429–46, here 431ff.
21. G. Ebeling, *Theologie und Verkündigung. Ein Gespräch mit Rudolf Bultmann* (Tübingen: Mohr Siebeck,

recognized sufficiently the fundamental hermeneutical significance of the problem of sin, clearly recognized by Luther, for the analysis of the world- and self-understanding of human existence that is always mediated in language.[22]

With the hermeneutical turn toward language, Fuchs and Ebeling were not simply stressing the fact that we always find ourselves involved in events of tradition mediated by language, as was the case in the contemporary hermeneutics of Gadamer. The accent on language within hermeneutical theology was instead placed elsewhere (although Fuchs and Ebeling themselves placed it in different spots). In order to understand this, we must first briefly call to mind the fundamental difference between the hermeneutical approaches of Barth and Bultmann. Their efforts to understand theologically the understanding of the understanding of God were guided by differing interpretations of the genitive "understanding of God."

For Bultmann, this had to do with *our understanding of God*, and thus was to be developed *from human self-understanding*.[23] Among the phenomena of our experienced world—the phenomena we can understand—God is not to be found. If, therefore, talk about the understanding of God is not to be meaningless, in light of the two options of understanding or self-understanding, it must be an understanding in the mode of our self-understanding. If there is to be any understanding of God at all, then the self-understanding that is always present within knowing anything, the self-knowledge of the human, is the key to understanding God—that is, to how God is understood by us and must be understood. If theology begins from this point, then the problematic of sin must be accorded a fundamental hermeneutical relevance inasmuch as there is no human self-understanding, and thus no understanding of God developed from it,

---

1962), 51ff., 77ff., 115–16, 122ff, and passim. Cf. H. C. Knuth, *Verstehen und Erfahrung. Hermeneutische Beiträge zur empirischen Theologie* (Hannover: Lutherhaus, 1986), 63ff.

22. Trowitzsch, *Verstehen und Freiheit*, 35ff. See, however, R. Bultmann, "Das Problem einer theologischen Exegese des neuen Testamentes," *Zwischen den Zeiten* 3 (1925): 334–57, here 353.

23. "If one wants to speak of God, one must apparently speak of oneself." R. Bultmann, "Welchen Sinn hat es, von Gott zu reden?," in *Glaube und Verstehen I*, 26–37, here 28. Cf. G. Ebeling, "Zum Verständnis von R. Bultmanns Aufsatz: 'Welchen Sinn hat es, von Gott zu reden?'" *Wort und Glaube II*, 343–71.

that is not affected by the (difference between) the creatureliness and sinfulness of human beings.[24]

With Barth, in contrast, everything is about how God understands us and Godself. This means that the understanding of God, and the human self-understanding and world-understanding that are determined by it, are to be developed starting with the divine self-understanding: to understand God means to so understand God as God understands Godself. But what does this mean? And how can we know about the divine self-understanding?

Barth answered both questions by referring to God's self-revelation in Jesus Christ. If one understands the total event of the life and death of Jesus (the Jesus-event) in light of the resurrection-confession (Jesus is the Christ) as *the self-interpretation or self-exegesis of God's saving will for creation*—and that is a basic decision that has far-reaching hermeneutical consequences[25]—then the logic of self-exegesis leads us to say that God will only be truly understood as God, if God's nature, in and of itself, is the same as that which God here for others exegetes and discloses. That is to say, the Jesus-event only makes God truly understandable as God if God so exegetes Godself therein as God understands Godself as God. Accordingly, for the second question, this means that human beings cannot know the divine self-understanding based on any inherent competence for interpretation that would allow them to interpret the Jesus-event as the self-exegesis of God. If that were the case, the question about the truthfulness of this interpretation would always remain open, so that one could not claim to know God's self-understanding. For Barth, that is possible only if God here truly makes God understandable as God for human beings, that is, as the one who precisely so and in no different way makes Godself understandable as God to anybody. He calls this the *self-revelation of God*, that is, the event in which God makes understandable for humans the self-revealing self-interpretation which God as God is (the Trinity), by

---

24. See also W. Schultz, "Die Grundlagen der Hermeneutik Schleiermachers, ihre Auswirkungen und ihre Grenzen," *ZThK* 50 (1953): 158–84, especially 174ff., 179ff.
25. The basic hermeneutical decision is to understand the Jesus event, and thus God, humanity, and the world, in the light of the resurrection-confession.

disclosing *something quite distinct* in human history (Jesus) *as something quite distinct* in God's relationship to that history (Christ) *through something quite distinct* that God Godself is (the Spirit).

From this point, God's divine self-understanding can be developed theologically (as Christology and Pneumatology) in such a way that one can justifiably speak of a human understanding of the divine self-understanding, and not just of an interpretation of the Jesus-event *as* God's self-revelation that is, at best, possible and, in any event, highly unlikely. In the fellowship of Father, Son, and Spirit, God has always understood Godself as overflowing love to those who are different; in the revelatory event of the cross and resurrection of Jesus, God concretely exegetes this self-understanding for us. It is not human self-understanding, but rather divine self-exegesis that is thus the key to the understanding of God—that is to say, to how God wants to be understood, and must be understood, in order to be truly understood as God.

Against the background of the proposals from Bultmann and Barth, the hermeneutical theology of the era after Bultmann represented an attempt to develop all theological questions as a unified whole within the framework of a *hermeneutics of self-interpretation*, whose point was the priority in principle of *the self-interpretation of that which we can interpret over all interpretation by us*. This fundamental hermeneutical orientation was justified with arguments of the following sort: if to interpret means that an *interpreter* expressly interprets something (*interpretandum*) for someone (*addressee* or *recipient*) as something (*interpretans*), then in the case of a self-interpretation, the *interpreter* and the *intepretandum* coincide, while this is not the case in interpretation by another. Now we cannot interpret what is not disclosed to us in some way, and we cannot adequately interpret anything that has not disclosed itself to us in some way. However, everything is disclosed to us either through others or through itself. It follows then that nothing is a possible *interpretandum* for us except what appears in the form of an already-completed interpretation: we can only interpret the already interpreted. Even when, in the event of self-disclosure, nothing appears without immediately hiding itself, it still appears *as something* and thus has an interpretative structure. Every *interpretandum* possible for us is thus itself to be conceived as the differential relationship of *interpretandum* and *interpetans*, and thus has the structure of either interpretation or self-*interpretation*. If, however, it is not the act of interpretation, in which we interpret something as something, that constitutes the hermeneutically differentiated relationship of *interpretandum* and *interpretans*, but rather that every *interpretandum* itself is so structured, then, hermeneutically, the process of self-interpretation has fundamental ontological relevance. For we can only interpret (actuality) what can be interpreted (possibility), that is, being and its divine ground, so far as it is disclosed to us. However, we can interpret only that which has already been interpreted by others or by itself. Since others, too, can only interpret what has already been interpreted, all interpretation and self-interpretation must ultimately be traced back to the self-interpretation of what can be interpreted, in the precise sense that, without self-interpretation, there would not be interpretation, that which is interpreted, or anything that could be interpreted.

From the standpoint of this hermeneutics of self-interpretation (which can only be developed theologically in a coherent way), it is a retreat behind the problematic of the situation under consideration if one seeks to resolve the problem of interpretation in terms of the key distinction of language/subject (interpreter) within the framework of a hermeneutics of interpersonal communication rather than in terms of the more primary distinction of language/being (what can be interpreted) within the framework of a theologically based hermeneutics of the linguistic self-manifestation of God as the divine ground of all being. This also has theological reasons. As Bultmann has shown, a theology that seeks to ground itself in objective saving facts or in a particular history of salvation is forced into epistemological and theological impasses: it is not able to identify its starting point in any generally acceptable way, that is, within the horizon of human history, but can present it only in mythological ways. Therefore, instead of focusing on salvation history, Bultmann attempted to concentrate on the life-illuminating *salvation-event* of the Christian kerygma and the *faith* corresponding to it.[26] Hermeneutical theology goes one step further in that it specifies this salvation-event more precisely as a *speech-event*.[27] Just as Bultmann transforms the theological focus on *salvation history* into a focus on *salvation-event* by substituting "event" for "history," so the following generation transforms the focus on *salvation-event* into a focus on *word-event* (Ebeling) or *language-event* (Fuchs, Jüngel) by replacing "salvation" with "word" or "language." Thus, it is no longer existence and history, but rather language, that becomes the fundamental frame of explication for theological reflection. But how is "language" understood here?

---

26. Cf. R. Bultmann, "Heilsgeschehen und Geschichte. Zu Oscar Cullmann, *Christus und die Zeit*," ThLZ 73 (1948): 659–66, here 665.
27. Cf. J. M. Robinson, "Die Hermeneutik seit Karl Barth," in *Die Neue Hermeneutik*, ed. J. M. Robinson and J. B. Cobb (Zürich/Stuttgart: Zwingli, 1965), 13–108, here 83–84.

5

The Hermeneutical Way of Thinking: Language as Word-Event

Bultmann largely remained with Heidegger's existential-ontological analysis from the 1920s. Later developments in Heidegger's thought, which took place after his return to Freiburg and the alienation that resulted from their differing responses to the rise of Nazism, were not reflected in Bultmann's theology.

1. Language as the Self-Interpretation of Being

The generation of Bultmann's students was different, as they were clearly influenced by the linguistic reflections of the later Heidegger (as in the case of Fuchs) and Gadamer's effective-history hermeneutics of tradition (as in the case of Ebeling). For them, language is not simply the human means of speaking about all that is possible and real, but also the medium in which and through which Being itself so interprets itself that we can interpret it, speak about it, and recognize it. Language, wrote Ernst Fuchs, "allows Being to become 'present' in time, makes it into an event."[1] "The ground in which language takes root is Being," for being "is the necessary condition for something to be *addressable* 'as' something, for that which exists to be addressable 'as' that which exists."[2] This is not because Being is, as it were, silently speaking to us, but because everything that exists is always disclosed to us already through language—the language spoken by actual human beings. Thus, just as one cannot think of Being without language, one cannot think of language without humans who make use of language and perceive Being as it exegetes or interprets itself linguistically. "Where the call of Being is heard and accepted, there is the human. Humanity," as J. M. Robinson sums it up, "is the loudspeaker of the silent ringing of Being."[3] Humanity is the place in which Being interprets itself in language and where its interpretation is noted.

This altered understanding of the relationship of language and Being (not that we speak about Being, but rather that Being brings itself to speech in our use of language) implies an altered conception of phenomena. Phenomena are no longer simply the *interpretanda* of understanding subjects, *interpretanda* that lie before us and can be linguistically exegeted, interpreted, and understood by us. Instead, phenomena as such are projected onto language and interpretation and themselves possess an interpretative structure—in other words, they interpret themselves to us *as* something. Because this self-interpretation (that is, this interpreting of itself as something to someone) takes up the hermeneutical distinction between the *immediate interpretant* and the *final interpretant* as it occurs in exemplary fashion within language, hermeneutical theology always thinks of it in terms of language. *Language*, it says, agreeing with the thesis of the later Heidegger's critique of subjectivity, *is the self-interpretation of Being*. But it expands this further in that it also asserts the reverse. *Everything that possesses the structure of self-interpretation is language*; even the cow that licks dry her newborn calf and in this way recognizes it *as*

---

1. E. Fuchs, "Was ist ein Sprachereignis? Ein Brief," in *Zur Frage nach dem historischen Jesus* (Tübingen: Mohr Siebeck, 1960), 425.
2. Fuchs, "Das Problem der theologischen Hermeneutik," in *Gesammelte Aufsätze I*, 116–37, here 126–27.
3. Robinson, "Die Hermeneutik seit Karl Barth," in *Die Neue Hermeneutik*, ed. James M. Robinson and John B. Cobb (Zürich: Zwingli, 1965), 72.

her own, performs, according to Fuchs, a speech-event.[4] Accordingly, our understanding of phenomena is adequate only when it understands them as they interpret themselves to us, when, that is, our interpretation matches their self-interpretation. Such is the case when we follow the clues of their original self-interpretation in language and use them to correct our falsely objectifying interpretations of phenomena, interpretations that thus fall short of and twist the truth.

2. Authentic versus Inauthentic Uses of Language

This ontological and epistemological priority of language means that a pure phenomenology of existence is impossible. In contrast to Bultmann, hermeneutical theology does not seek to go behind language to some reality beyond language and its sometimes-misleading objectification of Being and human self-understanding. Instead, it seeks *within* language to distinguish the authentic self-interpretation of Being (which takes place in assertion and, above all, in address) from our inauthentic and inadequate interpretations.[5] The fundamental distinction to be observed in all hermeneutical analysis of language is thus not simply the distinction between language and Being, but more precisely the distinction *between authentic and inauthentic manifestations of Being in language*. Since we can never step out of the circle of language, the fundamental distinction between language and Being can never be addressed directly, but only *within language*. It is a distinction to be specified within language, and it is there defined by hermeneutical theology as the distinction between authentic and inauthentic uses of language.

But what are the criteria for such a distinction, and why does the distinction exist at all? Cannot all language be understood equally as the self-interpretation of Being? The answer to both questions lies in the doctrinal foundations of the hermeneutical approach of hermeneutical theology. On the one hand, this serves to emphasize

---

4. According to ibid., 84n159.
5. Jüngel has repeatedly addressed these two fundamental types of speech (assertion and address) and their differing perils. See E. Jüngel, "Der Gott entsprechende Mensch," in *Entsprechungen: Gott-Wahrheit-Mensch. Theologische Erörterungen* (Munich: Kaiser, 1980), 290–317, esp. 310ff.

that we can only use and misuse language insofar as we have first been addressed through it, or, more precisely, insofar as Being presents itself to us as already disclosed to us in language. In our technological culture, with its objectifying and instrumental grasp of reality and our resulting limited and inadequate usage of language, we have largely lost the ability to perceive the self-manifestation of Being in language and to give it our attention. Theologically, this insensitive and objectifying use of language is seen as an expression of our sin: the true self-interpretation of Being is misjudged, abridged, and perverted in the linguistic reality of our interpretation of Being and self. However, just as the sinner remains a creature and, even as sinner, exists because of the prior beneficence of the Creator, even so the reality of our language usage lives from the truth of Being that continuously interprets itself in our use of language.

The difference between authentic and inauthentic usage of language is measured, accordingly, by the degree to which it discloses the truth of our existence (*Sein*) and our factual reality: an authentic usage of language is one that interprets us as God interprets us, as sinful creatures in need of justification by God. Thus, the hermeneutical project of hermeneutical theology proves itself to be a theological project from the outset: the fundamental hermeneutical distinction between language and Being is defined as the distinction within language between authentic and inauthentic usage of language. The criterion for authentic usage is that language is used to interpret us as we truly are. The substantiation of this criterion and the explication of the content of "who we truly are" are provided by Christology, the doctrine of creation, the doctrine of sin, and the doctrine of justification. Only from this theological standpoint can authentic self-interpretation of Being be distinguished from inauthentic interpretations of Being by others. Doctrine—as will be demonstrated below—guides hermeneutical theology.

3. Language as Word-Event

Hermeneutical theology concentrates on the distinction in language between authentic self-interpretation of Being and inauthentic interpretations of Being by others. Thus, it does not deal primarily with the language-using human, but rather with the language used by humans or, more precisely, the human use of language. This implies a significant hermeneutical reorientation that can be clarified in reference to the issue of interpreting texts.

The hermeneutics of the post-Enlightenment period largely followed the romantic paradigm, in which understanding a text consisted of understanding what the text's author or authors wanted us to understand through it. Now, however, efforts to understand focus primarily on the meaning of the text and no longer on the intention of the text's author. This textual meaning is sought within the text itself, no longer in some historical or metaphysical reality behind the text. More precisely, the authentic meaning (*Sinn*) of a text is not (in contrast to the primary focus of Schleiermacher's hermeneutics) "what the author in pursuing a particular point of view intended to express through words, but instead, totally apart from any subjective intention, what [the text itself] wants to bring to expression."[6] Accordingly, to understand a text means to understand the topic addressed in the text. One understands this not by attending primarily or exclusively to the intentions of the author as they are expressed in her words, but rather to the surplus of meaning that appears in the text before and beyond all of the intentions pursued by the author.

This realignment of hermeneutical questioning, from the intention of the author to the meaning of the text, should not be misunderstood in a formalist or structuralist way, although, methodologically, a number of parallels could be named. Hermeneutical theology seeks

---

6. H. Franz, "Das Wesen des Textes," *ZThK* 59 (1962): 182–225, 204, who adds, "Admittedly this is a highly risky way of approaching a text, because it appears to open the gate wide for hearing all sorts of fantasies from a text." But this need not be the case. In order to understand the text as text, one must indeed probe "behind the mere intention of the author after what is intended by the underlying thing being addressed, of which the author of the text need not have at all been aware." But that best takes place when the interpretive question takes into account "that it is not first of all the author of a text that is addressed in some way or another, and then also has intentions, but rather that the text itself, as the one addressed, also addresses us" (204–5). That the text addresses us, and how it does so, is the decisive thing to keep in mind in any attempt to understand that wants to be hermeneutically true to the meaning of the text and not to the intention of the author.

the meaning of a text not in its structure, its composition, or the way it links various elements of meaning, but rather in its hermeneutical effect on its reader or hearer. It is concerned with the meaning disclosed by the text, not that constituted within the text. In order to understand this meaning, we must pay attention to how the text interprets us and not primarily to how we interpret, or might interpret, the text. The decisive hermeneutical procedure is not bringing the text into the interpreter's horizon of understanding and current self-understanding, but rather the "reconstitution of the self-understanding of the one who understands, on the basis of that which is to be understood."[7] Accordingly, hermeneutical theology is oriented toward a model of language that understands language not as a system of verbal signs for constructing meaning, but rather as spoken word or *word-event*, as a communicative event of speaking and hearing between persons. Language, as Ebeling puts it, is a "process of life," whose basic structure is "I say something to you."[8] The authentic meaning of a text is therefore not, as in structuralism, to be found in the semantic textuality of texts, but rather in the communicative event of address and answer, in which our humanity, and our true situation as humans, is brought to light and clarified.

This last point is important. Hermeneutical theology's conception of language differs from that of structuralism because it does not focus semantically on the *langue*, or language as a system, but rather pragmatically on the *parole*, or language as a process of speech-behaviors or speech-acts. It also differs from a poststructuralist hermeneutics of reception in which the hermeneutical interest shifts not just from the author to the text but from the text itself to the process of reading as a social institution; for biblical texts, then, it would shift to their ecclesiastical reception. Although it sets out from the situation of reading and hearing and assumes the conversational model of language, hermeneutical theology does not simply concentrate on the spoken word as such but on that word-event that

---

7. M. Trowitzsch, *Verstehen und Freiheit. Umrisse einer theologischen Kritik der hermeneutischen Urteilskraft* (Zürich: TVZ, 1981), 47 (italicized in the original).
8. G. Ebeling, *Einführung in theologische Sprachlehre* (Tübingen. Mohr Siebeck, 1971), 195, 201.

illuminates our existence and discloses truth within it. The authentic meaning of a text is its existence-illuminating function rather than being found simply in one of the various possible readings that are open to a reader or hearer in the syntactical and semantic structure of a text. Accordingly, the key hermeneutical distinction of hermeneutical theology is neither the distinction between authorial intent and the text's meaning nor that between the text's meaning and the reading of the text, but rather that between authentic and inauthentic meanings of a text. This distinction determines whether the text will be experienced as a word-event that discloses an understanding of self and world in which we come to see ourselves as we in truth—that is, *coram deo*—are.

4. Word-Event as a Fundamental Theological Category

Obviously, this is not simply the effect of the spoken word as such, but of a specific word addressed to us: the Word of God. In the end, hermeneutical theology's focus on conversation, on the situation of address and answer as the basic model of language, is motivated by its understanding of the Word of God. As our language is grounded in the word-event, so this is grounded in the event of the Word of God in creation, revelation, and redemption. This, in turn, is grounded in God's self, who is the original word-event, the structure of which is developed in the doctrine of the Trinity.

The category of word-event (used by Ebeling since 1955) thus becomes the fundamental model of thought for hermeneutical theology.[9] It is brought into play in all dimensions of theological reflection: the world, human existence, even God are thought of in terms of language, more precisely of word-events. Thus, a human being is defined as that being *with whom* God speaks and from whom God summons and enables an answer. The world is defined as the totality of that *about which* God speaks (to us). God is defined as the one *who* speaks with us. The distinction between God, world, and human consists

---

9. H. Knuth, *Verstehen und Erfahren. Hermeneutische Beiträge zur empirischen Theologie* (Hannover: Lutherhaus, 1986), 40.

precisely in this: God speaks before God is spoken to and before anything is spoken about God. Thus, God is to be understood as conversation, as the original word-event that the doctrine of the Trinity explicates. This systematic employment of the category of word-event results in an ontologically and theologically unified framework of explication that shapes hermeneutical theology in all its dimensions.

Methodologically, this means that humanity, world, and God are understood within the horizon of a self-interpretative event that arises from itself, in which that which becomes understandable for us makes itself understood. The priority gradient of activity and passivity in the interpretative event is thus reversed. It is not that we are the interpreters of all; first of all, we are interpreted. It is not that we interpret the world, God, and ourselves in some original or ultimate way, but rather that we are first and foremost ones who are interpreted and directed toward interpretations that are offered to us. Through our interpretative activities, we are always in the process of constructing our worlds of meaning; only thus can we live as human beings. But we can be active interpreters only because, and insofar as, we are first the locus in which that which freely interprets itself and makes itself understandable becomes understandable for us. Only as addressees of self-interpretation can we ourselves become interpreters and self-interpreters. The first is treated theologically under the heading of *faith* (justification), which has to do with the fundamental passivity of our lives before all our activity. The second is developed under the heading of the *life of faith* (sanctification), which has to do with the activity appropriate to this basis and within the horizon of this passivity.

Accordingly, all theology has, in fact, two primary tasks: the systematic explication of faith and the coherent interpretation of our reality as it is lived and experienced. The first task is more basic inasmuch as it provides the systematic categories and perspectives of meaning for carrying out the second task. Compared to other theological approaches, hermeneutical theology gains its consistency precisely because it pursues both tasks uniformly by means of the basic category of the self-interpreting word-event.

This can be seen initially in how it carries out the first task. The methodological starting point is the revelation-event of the Word of God, received in faith, borne witness to in Scripture, and always occurring anew within the congregation—the event in which God interprets Godself in Jesus Christ as love and is made understandable as such through the Holy Spirit. This self-interpretation is transmitted afresh to new people in the human word-event of the proclamation of the gospel (*verbum externum*). The self-manifestation of the Spirit within this proclamation makes clear that it is a divine, not merely a human, word-event (*verbum internum*). As an event in time and history, it corresponds to the original divine word-event in which the Father through the Spirit interprets Godself in the Son in such a way that the Son, in the Spirit, corresponds fully to the divine being of the Father. Together with the Spirit, therefore, the Son—in creation, revelation, and salvation—seeks to move everything that is not God to be a creaturely counterpart to God's love (*verbum aeternum*). Human interpretation of God as love, in faith in the words of the gospel, thus fully corresponds to the self-interpretation of God in the revelation of God's word in Jesus Christ, which, in turn, is the perfect historical counterpart to the original event of self-exegesis that God exists as Father, Son, and Spirit. The divine event of self-exegesis of Trinity (God), revelation (Jesus Christ), and faith (Spirit) thus forms an ontological connection of equivalence; this is reflected ontically in the creaturely context of existence either in the mode of contradiction to the divine word-event (sin) or correspondence with it (justification). While the sequence of events leads from the divine word-event of original self-exegesis in the Trinity through historical self-exegesis in revelation to existential self-exegesis in faith, the methodological and epistemological sequence of theological reflection and dogmatic interpretation of the divine self-exegesis is reversed. It begins with the Scripture that bears witness to faith, unfolds the meaning of the word-event to which Scripture bears witness in Christology and

Pneumatology, and explicates its basic realities and possibilities in the doctrine of the Trinity. This doctrine is thus conceived as a structural theory of the self-exegesis or self-interpretation of God so that the deepest objective basis of all word-events in the Trinity corresponds to the loftiest conceptual constructs of Trinitarian doctrine.[10]

While the systematic unity of hermeneutical theology, through its explication of faith in terms of the word-event category, has been well documented, its carrying out of the second task remains largely a postulate. To be sure, it offers the catchy formula of "experience with the experience" to our interpretation of our experienced reality in the light of faith.[11] It proposes to carry this out hermeneutically as a new understanding of all previous understandings through the lens of law and gospel in light of being interpreted by the Word of God. However, neither Ebeling nor Jüngel ever moved much beyond making proposals in this regard. Jüngel responded to his own call for a "more natural theology" as an "understanding of human world-understanding and self-understanding in light of the revelation of God" only on certain points or in a preliminary fashion; he came closest in his sermons.[12] And Ebeling's attempt to discover constant fundamental experiences and a uniform fundamental situation within the variety of our experiences often seemed arbitrary as a result of inadequately defined terminology and the ontological baggage that came with it.[13] In both cases, what was lacking was a theoretically clear explanation of the nature and possibility of dual meanings or (nonhierarchical[14]) multiple

---

10. U. Barth, "Zur Barth-Deutung Eberhard Jüngels," *Theologische Zeitschrift* 40 (1984): 296–320, 394–415, here 312.
11. Cf. E. Jüngel, *Erfahrungen mit der Erfahrung. Unterwegs bemerkt* (Stuttgart: Radius, 2008); G. Bader, "Erfahrung mit der Erfahrung," in *Wirkungen hermeneutischer Theologie, FS Gerhard Ebeling*, ed. H. F. Geisser/W. Mostert (Tübingen: Mohr Siebeck, 1983), 137–53.
12. E. Jüngel, "Das Dilemma der natürlichen Theologie und die Wahrheit ihres Problems. Überlegungen für ein Gespräch mit Wolfhart Pannenberg," in *Entsprechungen*, 158–77, 176; Jüngel, "Gott—um seiner selbst willen interessant. Plädoyer für eine natürlichere Theologie," in *Entsprechungen*, 193–97. H. Fischer, "Natürliche Theologie im Wandel," *ZThK* 80 (1983): 85–102, 100; J. B. Webster, *Eberhard Jüngel: An Introduction to His Theology* (Cambridge: Cambridge University Press, 1986), 118ff.
13. W. Härle and E. Herms, "Deutschsprachige protestantische Dogmatik nach 1945," *Verkündigung und Forschung* 27 (1982): 2–100 and *Verkündigung und Forschung* 28 (1983): 1–87, 17ff.
14. This is not about a hermeneutical implementation of the *gratia non tollit, sed perficit naturam* formula. Rather, it is about the hermeneutical and epistemological justification for *more than one true perspective* on human life, the world, and God, without letting things come to differing

meanings of events and facts in the world—that is, of their "natural" meaning given within our experience and their "more natural" or "more fundamental" meaning disclosed in experiencing the experience anew in the light of faith.[15]

A major reason for this inadequate performance of the second major task of theological reflection may be the problematic parallel construction of the two primary tasks of theology caused by the unrestricted usage of the word-event category. As theology, on the one hand, interprets Scripture, it also, on the other hand, interprets our experience. It is a consistent interpretation insofar as the two interpretations—that of Scripture and the word-event to which it bears witness and that of our experience in light of this word-event—are related, or, more precisely, insofar as the Scripture and the word-event that comes to speech through it are interpreted in such a way that we are interpreted by it and thereby led to an experience with our experience. But the parallel is misleading: Scripture and experience are not two different objects of a unified action of theological interpretation. They have vastly different internal structures, hermeneutically, and thus present vastly different interpretative challenges. Accordingly, they require different hermeneutical methods. To be sure, both Scripture and our experience have interpretative structure inasmuch as in both something is interpreted as something; theological reflection must take that into account and offer an explanation.[16] However, in contrast to Scripture, the experience of our world's reality cannot readily be made understandable as a self-interpretation. It is not a word-event in which the self-interpretation of another word-event is manifested and can

---

total perspectives simply existing side-by-side. This can only be achieved when the theological perspective makes the possibility of all the nontheological perspectives understandable: God is the necessary condition of the possibility to live with God or without God, in faith or in unfaith and, accordingly, also the necessary condition of the possibility of understanding the world, self, and God in a theological or nontheological way.

15. Webster, *Eberhard Jüngel*, 126ff. Jüngel's figure of speech should not be understood as a mere intensification of the natural, as though the natural, as such, were somehow ontologically deficient and its naturalness must be outdone in order to set aside its ontological shortcomings. Instead, it should be seen as an indication of the horizon within which the naturalness of the natural can first be accorded its full weight.

16. I. U. Dalferth, *Religiöse Rede von Gott* (Munich: Kaiser, 1981), 447–68.

be traced back hermeneutically. While Scripture lends itself to being grasped and interpreted as the witness of an event of interpretation, that is not so for our experience of the world. At first glance, nothing in our world-experience appears to possess interpretative structure in and of itself; thus, it does not properly lend itself to being interpreted as such. The world is not a word-event that brings itself to speech in our experience. We interpret it; it does not interpret itself. Theological reflection on Scripture, as the interpretation of something that itself has interpretative structure and indeed the structure of self-interpretation, thus has no direct parallel to theological reflection on our experience of the world as the interpretation of something that itself has no interpretative structure. When this nonetheless takes place in hermeneutical theology, it is the result of an imprecise usage of the category of word-event—one that is not restricted to the understanding of cultural artifacts such as writings, speeches, contracts, or other original texts—in all aspects of theological reflection.

It is just this comprehensive usage, however, that generates fundamental problems. On the one hand, this has to do with the hermeneutical construction of Being (*des Seins*) as a self-interpretative event in language: why should whatever exists, simply because it exists, be understood as an event of self-interpretation? On the other hand, it has to do with the identification or (at times) undifferentiated treatment of God and Being. Can and may God and Being be treated hermeneutically in identical ways? Must not the distinction between God and Being—namely, that God alone, not Being, is to be understood as an event of self-interpretation—be brought to expression? Being is the medium of divine self-interpretation but is not itself self-interpretation. And God is distinct from Being in that God, in the act of God's self-interpretation or self-exegesis, created both the media and the addressees of God's self-interpretative self-exegesis.

6

Toward a Critique of Hermeneutical Theology

The hermeneutical approach outlined emphasized the self-interpretation of being or the self-interpretation of God in language, either of which is to be distinguished in principle from all linguistic self-interpretations of persons and from their interpretation of being or God. This drew massive criticism: it was seen as inherently aporetic, based on a problematic combination of differing hermeneutical models, guided by an inadequate understanding of language, and failing to provide a methodology for reliably identifying such self-interpretations intersubjectively or for distinguishing between "true" and "false" interpretations and theological reconstructions in some verifiable way. Theological teaching and argument within hermeneutical theology were criticized for being primarily aesthetic, focusing on the harmonious unfolding of its theological intuitions but without conceptual controls of its basic decisions. It was accused of rising only incidentally, but not systematically, to contemporary problems and challenges, and then only insofar as these proved to be awkward or cumbersome within the structures of the accepted theological perspective, and it was blamed for being consummated largely within the categorical framework of prior theological traditions, primarily those represented by the names of Luther and Barth.

1. The Silencing of the Debate

The waning interest in hermeneutical theology in the closing decades of the twentieth century is often attributed to the fact that only inadequate answers were offered to these questions and objections. However, changing trends in the history of theology are seldom due simply to the sufficient or insufficient treatment of important issues. Instead, they can be traced mostly to other social, political, scholarly, and cultural challenges, to changing topics of theological interest, and—not to be underestimated—to the career-related need of a new generation of theologians to distinguish themselves from the generation of their teachers by posing new questions; after all, one has to do something different to set oneself apart from the prior generation. In the 1950s and 1960s, hermeneutical theology clearly belonged to the most up-to-date forms of Protestant theology because it sought to answer the challenges of an increasingly secular world. It is equally obvious that, after the end of the 1960s, other theological movements attracted the attention of church and society, and of theology itself.

This had to do neither with the satisfactory treatment of the questions addressed by hermeneutical theology nor with the refutation of the answers it gave to them. To be sure, there is hardly any doubt that the turn away from the theological traditions of Barth and Bultmann and the turn to other issues since the middle of the 1960s led to a noticeable silencing of hermeneutical debates in German Protestant theology. But when the facts are examined more closely, a different picture appears. In the 1970s and 1980s there was a lively discussion of hermeneutics in Germany—outside of theology, in literary studies and in philosophy. There was also a lively discussion of hermeneutics in theology—outside of Germany, in Scandinavia and the English-speaking world. There was a lively theological discussion of hermeneutics in Germany—outside of systematic theology, especially in the exegetical disciplines. In contrast, there was hardly any hermeneutical discussion worth mentioning in German-language systematic theology, and, where there was any, it took place without the participation of the hermeneutical theology that had once set the tone for systematics. The "significance and discussion of hermeneutics in theology, where it had once found its most important field of activity," Claus von Bormann observed in 1986, "has shrunk into near silence."[1] A variety of reasons have been offered for this change.

Some are of the opinion that the concerns of hermeneutics, as they shaped the discussions of systematic theology in the 1950s and 1960s, have become the common property of systematic theology as a whole, so that any special discussion of hermeneutics is superfluous. But that is hardly the case. Instead, one must say that the fathers of hermeneutical theology had only limited success in passing on to the next theological generation their view of hermeneutics as posing the most fundamental and pressing questions for systematic theology.

It is also not true that discussions about hermeneutical theology within systematic theology led to a clear result. Rather, they came to nothing and were broken off not because the questions had been cleared up, but because those discussing them became tired of the topic. If, however, the claim by hermeneutical theology's protagonists that hermeneutics is *the* fundamental theological discipline should be even partly on target, then the topic of hermeneutics cannot simply be dismissed as the fashionable theological topic of the postwar period. Rather, it should have remained on the agenda, even as interest turned to other topics. Such, however, was not the case. Either the topic's significance has been grossly undervalued in recent decades, or it was totally overvalued in the earlier period.

The notion is also questionable that any need for a special discussion of hermeneutics within systematic theology has been dispensed with because the posing of hermeneutical questions, since the 1970s, has

---

1. C. von Bormann, "Hermeneutik: I. Philosophisch-theologisch," *TRE* 15 (1986): 108–37, 130.

been taken up in other, more comprehensive, or more basic questions—such as in universal history, as Pannenberg believes;[2] in social ethics and political theology as with Dorothe Sölle, Moltmann, and Johann Baptist Metz; in linguistic or analytical studies as with Erhardt Güttgemanns, Werner Jeanrond, Dalferth, and Klaus von Stosch; in theoretical science as with Gerhard Sauter and Pannenberg; in reflection and cultural philosophy as in Ricoeur, Richard Rorty, and Taylor; in communicative actions and the critical development of the proposals of Karl-Otto Apel and Habermas by Helmut Peukert and Theodor Ahrens; in liberation theology's and feminism's hermeneutics of suspicion as in Gustavo Gutiérrez, Leonardo Boff, Jon Sobrino, Kuno Füssel, Elisabeth Schüssler Fiorenza, Luise Schottroff, and Rosemary Radford Ruether; in the turn back to Kant, Fichte, Schleiermacher, Hegel, or Ernst Troeltsch by Ulrich Barth, Falk Wagner, Eilert Herms, Jan Rohls, Thomas Pröpper, Hansjürgen Verweyen, and Friedrich Wilhelm Graf; in the hermeneutics of religion and culture of Wilhelm Gräb, Dietrich Korsch, and Jörg Lauster; in the "radical hermeneutics" that John Caputo, following Friedrich Nietzsche, Heidegger, Gadamer, and Jaques Derrida, has developed since the 1980s, and so forth. A variety of successive topics have thus claimed to inherit hermeneutical issues. However, every version of this inheritance thesis should be taken with a grain of salt—not only in light of the fundamental claims that hermeneutical theology once brought to the table, but also in light of the explicit and many-sided discussions of hermeneutics that have taken place in recent decades outside of systematic theology or of theology in general. The questions of hermeneutical theology have apparently not been so absorbed within other questions that it would be superfluous to raise them again independently.

This also applies regarding a fourth position, which contends that while there are indeed hermeneutical questions *within* theology, there is no hermeneutical question *of* theology. This position contends that the hermeneutical discussion today properly proceeds as an argument

---

2. W. Pannenberg, "Über historische und theologische Hermeneutik," in *Grundfragen systematischer Theologie* (Göttingen: Vandenhoek & Ruprecht, 1979), 123-58, esp. 132ff., 140, 148ff.; Pannenberg, "Hermeneutik und Universalgeschichte," in *Grundfragen*, 91-122, esp. 104, 120ff.

about the appropriate methods of interpretation within the individual theological disciplines, each with its specific issues, and no longer as the basic discussion of fundamental theological issues, as in the heyday of hermeneutical theology. If so, the lack of such a methodological discussion within recent systematic theology is, frankly, surprising. Instead, the question of a fundamental understanding of hermeneutics arises even more sharply, not only with hermeneutical theology but also, albeit in other ways, with Catholic theologians such as Lonergan, who not only asked about the methods of the individual theological disciplines but considered theology as a whole to be a method—the method of understanding what it means to understand, and thus to clarify the fundamental conditions and fundamental structures of all understanding.[3]

None of the proposed answers is so convincing as to make a more focused engagement with the questions raised about hermeneutical theology unnecessary. Its hermeneutical way of thought and its theological procedures raise fundamental ontological, epistemological, and methodological-hermeneutical issues.

2. Being as Self-Interpretation: The Ontology of Meaning in Hermeneutical Theology

The comprehensive and fundamental employment of the category of word-event implies a specific ontology that arises from turning away from conceiving this category in terms of material content (word-event as that authentic speech-event that discloses the truth of our reality and of our being, inasmuch as it so interprets us as we are interpreted by God) and turning toward its formal structure as sign-occurrence and interpretative event. Hermeneutical theology thus represents a rigorous realism of the word-event, which includes the clear priority of becoming over being, of possibility over actuality, of relationship over substance, and of meaning over being. Word-events

---

3. Cf. B. Lonergan, *Method in Theology* (London: Herder & Herder, 1973); D. Teevan, *Lonergan, Hermeneutics, and Theological Method* (Milwaukee: Marquette University Press, 2005); I. U. Dalferth, *Kombinatorische Theologie. Probleme theologischer Rationalität* (Freiburg: Herder, 1991).

cannot be reduced to any sort of more basic ontological entities, nor can they be analyzed as something other than word-events. They are events of meaning in which something (for instance, the world) through something (the proclamation of Jesus) for someone (Christians) becomes understandable as something (God's creation). The category of word-event allows no possibility of separating language as the "form" of that which comes to speech from the "content" that is brought to speech in this form. A word-event is not the manifestation of some reality that lies beyond this event; it is the real presence of that of which it speaks.[4] Word-events are not information processes, which refer to something other than themselves, but processes of the presentation and re-presentation of that of which they speak: they transform possible into actual being in the event of Being concretely interpreting itself.[5] In this sense, the reality of the world consists of concrete word-events. One cannot get behind them in order to find something more basic or more real. Fundamentally, reality possesses the character of word-events. In the end, it is not given phenomena that are real, but that which comes into being as a self-interpreting word-event. The following points should here be emphasized:

2.1 The Process of Meaning: The With-Structure of Meaning

All reality as a process of transforming possible into actual being has the basic structure exemplified by the word-event: "something interprets itself for someone as something." It thus has the structure of meaning: whatever is appears modally within the horizon of the

---

4. The Augustinian understanding of sacraments is unmistakable as a background. As the sacrament is a special case of a *signum* that not only refers to a *res* but in which the thing signified is itself present with the sign, so too is the word-event a sign-event that does not bring to speech something that is different from itself, but rather makes that of which it speaks really present. The category of word-event can be understood as a generalization and further development of this sacramental understanding of signs.
5. What is concrete is what occurs as a coherent unit of meaning in the process of reality's becoming. Word-events are concrete events of meaning in which something becomes understandable as something for someone. They are not susceptible to being analyzed in terms of more basic elements, such as "something," "someone," "understandable," or so forth; these points appear simultaneously in an event of meaning as "something-becomes-understandable-for-someone-as-something," as an inseparable structural unity which one cannot get behind.

possible as actual, and thus is perceived not only as being (*Sein*)—something that exists—but as meaning (*Sinn*)—something that exists in a certain meaningful or intelligible way. This applies both to individual events and to reality as a whole. Because meaning always may be understood in more than one way, reality as a whole possesses a surplus of meaning that is never exhausted by any one understanding. There is always more to understand than what one has understood. This is possible because reality is intrinsically plural; it is not limited only to one word-event or to some. No word-event occurs isolated and alone; instead, every word-event appears in the context of others that either take it up and develop it further or take its place and bring it to an end. As we can speak only because others have already spoken, just so every discourse creates the possibility of continuing a discourse in another way. In this pluriform reality of word-events linked one to another, the "with-structure" of Being as Meaning becomes apparent: Being takes concrete shape in word-events that constitute meaning, which become what they concretely are only in the context of, and as the development of, other word-events.

2.2 Media of Sense: The Through-Structure of Meaning

Every instance of reality is thus a hermeneutical event in which every entity within a wide horizon of possibilities is presented to another by something as something, and thereby disclosed as meaningful. This is possible only insofar as something comes into view *through* something for someone as something, that is, as something becomes understandable not only as being (something that is) but as meaning (something that is meaningful). Being becomes meaning where some actuality (something that is) is used as a medium in order to communicate something (actual or possible) as something (actual or possible). Nothing is a medium, per se, but everything that is actual can become a medium when it is used in an appropriate way. As Augustine recognized long ago, every *signum* is a *res* and every *res* can become a *signum* when it is appropriately used and understood (*uti*) and not simply perceived and inappropriately enjoyed (*frui*). For it is not the temporal sign that is to be enjoyed, but that toward which all signs finally point: the eternal truth of God. At any rate, a concrete actuality becomes a medium precisely by being employed in word-events that are directed toward entities that (can) understand them in order to communicate something as something to them. In all word-events, there is something more taking place than constituting meaning through the use of something actual as medium and signifier; in addition, through such usage the distinction between meaning and being is made, the distinction between what is communicated (meaning) and that through which it is communicated (being). As something is made understandable *through* something *as* something, concrete actuality becomes a medium for meaning, and thereby distinguishes meaning from being.

2.3 Self-Interpretation: The As-Structure of Meaning

Anything can become a medium in an event of meaning, and all events of meaning display the hermeneutical as-structure (something is interpreted *as* something). Reality, as a process of meaning, has hermeneutical structure. It takes place as the dynamic self-distinguishing of *interpretandum* and *interpretans*, of being and language, of thing and word, whose very point is that there is no *interpretandum* that is not itself structured as the dynamic relationship of *interpretandum* and *interpretans*. Reality is a hermeneutical process of the self-interpretation of Being. It knows no point of origin beyond this process in some yet-undisclosed realm of Being, but, instead, it is a process in which Being always comes into view only as an event having already interpreted itself and continuing to further interpret itself. This process takes place in a perpetual further interpretation of interpretations that have already taken place. Everything that was, is, and will be is a self-interpretive event, in which an interpretation that has already taken place is taken up by a new self-interpretation that develops the first or supplants it, refines it or corrects and dismantles it. This process of constructing and dismantling meaning leads to no intrinsically determinable end but rather toward an always more differentiated meaning and toward more diverse interpretations. In the course of the hermeneutical processing of already-completed self-interpretations, certain successive interpretations are developed. Moreover, through the same process, several prior interpretations may be abandoned or overhauled while, at the same time, more interpretive possibilities are generated than those actually realized. This can lead to a diffuse variety of interpretations, but need not do so. The opposite can also happen; the authentic self-interpretation of Being prevails against the inauthentic interpretations of it by others through a fuller development of the truth of its self-interpretation.

2.4 Event: The Temporality of Meaning

This event of the self-interpretation of being implies not only its hermeneutical as-structure, but also the temporality and historicality of its meaning. Without time, there is no event, and every self-interpretive event constitutes and processes meaning into history. Time and history are thus structural elements of reality itself as the process of the self-interpretation of being, not simply of our dealings with reality.

However, can there be a unified temporal horizon for the occurrence of the self-interpretive event of reality and the occurrence of our interpretation of this self-interpretive event? Can the two events temporally coincide so that the self-interpretation of reality takes place in the very act of our interpretation, and vice versa? Or does this lead into the aporia of the temporal coordination of two different temporal horizons, each of which is relative to the occurrence of a different interpretive event? At any rate, the time of the word-event and the time of our understanding of the word-event are not necessarily the same time; they can only *become* contemporaneous when the self-interpretation of the word-event takes place *at the very time of our understanding of this word-event*. Insofar as our understanding, however, is constitutively dependent on the precedence of the self-interpretation of the word-event for it to be possible at all, such becoming contemporaneous can never arise from our initiative, but only from the side of the word-event. We cannot make ourselves contemporary to it; it must make itself contemporary to us if there is to be a self-interpretation of the word-event *for us*.[6] This asymmetry between the self-interpretation of the word-event and our interpretation of it is decisive: even where the self-interpretation takes place in and through our interpretation, the self-interpretation of the word-event constitutes the condition of the possibility of our interpretation, not vice versa. We can discover, understand, and interpret the meaning of the word-event, but we do not constitute it through our understanding and interpretation. Reality's self-interpretation takes logical and temporal precedence over our interpretations of reality.

2.5 Understanding: The For-Structure of Meaning

However, interpretations and self-interpretations are *for someone*. A reality understood as a process of self-interpreting word-events implies recipients who can understand these interpretations. For this to be possible, they must be able or have the competence to understand (that is to say, possess the cognitive *structure of understanding*); only those who do may also develop the competence to understand and interpret themselves (that is, manifest the *structure of subjectivity* by becoming self-understanding subjects). Just as understanding something implies someone who can understand (structure of understanding), so self-understanding is possible only for those who apply the understanding they have self-referentially to themselves and thereby become subjects (structure of subjectivity). That is to say, the distinction between *interpretandum* and *interpretat* makes sense only for an understanding that can receive, understand, and interpret the as-structure of the self-interpretation of being. In order to be able to do so, it must exemplify the structure of understanding (*understanding something*) but not necessarily the structure of subjectivity (understanding itself or *self-understanding*). Thus, there are two

---

6. Cf. I. U. Dalferth, *Becoming Present: An Inquiry into the Christian Sense of the Presence of God* (Louvain: Peeters, 2006).

possible options for the ontology of hermeneutical theology; it has largely followed the latter.

First, one could conceive the understanding needed as a structural property of reality itself (intelligibility), and not of an understanding subject. The structure of understanding ("someone understands something as something") and of self-interpretation ("something interprets itself for someone as something") would then constitute the intelligibility of reality independent of any understanding subjectivity. It would be the condition for the possibility of a subjectivity that understands itself but not something conditioned by it. The self-interpretive process of being, as a specific intelligible reality within the horizon of the specific possibilities at any given time, would then be the necessary condition of both the reality and possibility of an understanding subjectivity, but not something produced or conditioned by it. Just as reflexivity is a structural property of a subject capable of self-experience because of it, self-interpretation is likewise a structural property of the reality that through it becomes intelligible and understandable for subjects, including the reality of the subject itself. As a result, both the symbolic apprehension of reality by subjects through acts of construal, interpretation, and appropriation and the reality so construed, interpreted and thus understood would possess the structure of interpretation and understanding (meaning and intelligibility) That is to say, reality's process of self-interpretation through time and history would be differentiated by the as-structure of intelligibility into *interpretandum* and *interpretans* in a fundamental way that cannot be dissolved into something more basic but, in principle, is insurmountable. Reality then would be intelligible precisely because this self-differentiating process of self-referential semiotic events occurs as the interpretation-of-themselves-for-someone and the understanding-of-themselves-as-something, and all of our understanding and interpretation could only reflect on that. And that would mean—against the modern resignation that the complexity of the world is always greater than the most complex thought we can think—that reality as such would always be more intelligible or understandable than we have yet understood, so that all our efforts to better understand ourselves and our world would be justified, in principle.[7]

Otherwise—and this is the option most favored by hermeneutical theology—one can tie the understanding that corresponds to the self-interpretation of being back to the understanding subject; that is, one can base it on the structure of subjectivity and not merely on the structure of understanding. The self-interpretation of individual word-events is thus conceived of as linked to the understanding of finite, creaturely subjects, while the self-interpretation of being in all the processes of reality is linked to the understanding of God. The primordial word-event, which is God, is at the same time the primordial understanding: God's being is God's self-interpretation and self-understanding as word-event. Our task of understanding, in our interpretive dealings with the world and with ourselves, is to conform ourselves as creatures to this understanding and to comprehend it to the best of our creaturely abilities. That the world, ourselves included, is always more understandable than we have yet understood is based in that fact that God has already understood it, and us, better than we can. It is not reality that interprets itself for us, but rather God who interprets God, the world, and us for us: the event of divine self-interpretation *is* what constitutes reality. Self-interpretation and understanding are therefore, in the strictest and truest sense, predicates of God: God is the one who by acting intelligibly in and through all created events makes Godself understandable in a way that helps us to a true understanding of self, world, and God.

Here, however, two fundamental questions arise: What is the *ontological relationship* of our experienced reality of the world to the Word of God in which everything is based? And what is the *epistemological relationship* of human word, experienced reality, and God's Word?

The first requires an answer from the theology of creation; the second an answer from Pneumatology. Simply establishing that such

---

7. D. Henrich, *Fluchtlinien. Philosophische Essays* (Frankfurt am Main: Suhrkamp, 1982), 125ff.

relationships exist can satisfy neither. They must also explicate their types and concrete structures, thus exposing the "how" of their existence, if establishing their existence is not to remain an empty exercise. It is precisely here that the proposals of hermeneutical theology have not been convincing. How are the varieties of creaturely word-events in nature and in culture related to the unity of the divine word-event in which they are based? Even when this unity is seen as one differentiated within itself (creation, revelation, salvation), this differentiation is clearly not the same as the plurality of self-interpretive events that are perceived in both natural and cultural reality. But precisely what relationship exists between the word-event of God, self-interpreted in this differentiated way, and the manifold phenomena of nature and culture? To what extent do these varied phenomena lend themselves to being interpreted at all, in a meaningful and convincing way, through the category of word-event? And how does God, in and through these phenomena, make Godself understandable to us? Referring to the categories of law and gospel, whether for correspondence or differentiation, does not provide an instrument of interpretation; at best, it provides a framework of interpretation worth considering. In and of themselves, law and gospel do not provide the interpretation required. Finally, in what relationship does the word-event of God, which constitutes reality as the event of the self-interpretation of Being, stand to the manifold word-events of our language in which, within reality, we communicate about reality and about ourselves? This question leads to a second problematic area for hermeneutical theology, which now requires our attention.

3. Self-Interpretation and Knowledge: On the Epistemology of Hermeneutical Theology

The explicative and interpretive use of the category of word-event in hermeneutical theology has specific epistemological consequences. The most important ones can be summarized under seven headings.

3.1 Act-Extensionality before Act-Intentionality

The adequate starting point for a knowledge of reality that is methodologically controlled is not an empirical or phenomenological description of our experience of the world, but rather a hermeneutical account of our understanding of language and of our understanding of the world manifested in our language. A critical explanation of our knowledge of reality is not to be based on our experience of the world, but of the word—that is, on a critical analysis of the self-interpretation of Being in our language and our linguistic tradition. It is here that we can find the phenomena that are to be "saved" from being replaced or suppressed by the theoretical constructs of science and scholarship.

The linguistic, historical, and cultural formation of our experience is so comprehensive that we cannot experience reality otherwise. For hermeneutical theology, however, in contrast to several other similarly argued positions, this is not primarily a fact of cultural anthropology or of cultural studies, but rather an implication of the insight that events of self-interpretation are the nature of reality itself, as has been argued. This conclusion rests not simply on that fact that all our knowledge and understanding is always passed on to us by others, but primarily on the insight that reality itself makes itself known in these processes. Thus, the ontological priority of the reality-constituting word-event also implies its epistemological priority. It interprets itself for us before we interpret it, and our interpretation must follow this self-interpretation. Jüngel called this a phenomenological-historical method, inasmuch as "the 'act-intentionality' of the understanding advancing *toward* the things themselves' anticipates an 'act-extensionality' coming *from* the things themselves that presupposes an inquiring and understanding mind. For thinking may ascend out of the conceptual horizon of human consciousness to the things themselves only insofar as the things themselves *have* already made an appearance as phenomena for human consciousness. For theology, this means insofar as they *have* come into language."[8]

Hermeneutical theology shares this turn away from the basic orientation of modern epistemology with a range of philosophical positions: from Heidegger, through Wittgenstein, Alfred North Whitehead, and Charles Hartshorne, up to Rorty, Hilary Putnam, Emmanuel Levinas, Derrida, Bernhard Waldenfels, and Jean-Luc Marion. Its specific insight, however, consists in conceiving the word-events that ontologically determine the fundamental aspects of reality as intrinsically interpretive themselves: they are *self-interpreting events* before and beyond all of the intentionality directed toward them by finite understanding subjects. The interpretive activities of these subjects are based entirely in a fundamental passiveness in regard to the prior activeness of the self-interpreting word-events. Thus, the decisive and fundamental epistemic issue for hermeneutical theology is not a critical analysis of our capabilities of knowing and understanding, but rather the claims on our knowledge and understanding by the self-disclosing word-event that are already directed toward us—by the "thing itself," so to speak. True understanding and knowing occur in the form of attentive hearing, seeing, and comprehending of that which has already been disclosed to us long before all our efforts toward knowing and understanding. That which we have to understand, above all (but not only) in the case of God whom we seek to understand, has, in principle, an (ontological and epistemological) priority so that it can never be comprehended once and for all by any receptive act on our part. God's being remains, as Jüngel puts it, always "in *coming*."[9]

3.2 Event as Occurrence

This precedence of passivity above all activity correlates with a transposition from the model of the event (*Ereignis*) to that of the occurrence (*Widerfahrnis*).[10] An occurrence is something that occurs

---

8. E. Jüngel, *Paulus und Jesus* (Tübingen: Mohr Siebeck, 1967), 5.
9. E. Jüngel, *Gott als Geheimnis der Welt. Zur Begründung der Theologie des Gekreuzigten im Streit zwischen Theismus und Atheismus* (Tübingen: Mohr Siebeck, 2001), 415.
10. For the following, see I. U. Dalferth, *Das Böse. Essay über die kulturelle Denkform des Unbegreiflichen* (Tübingen: Mohr Siebeck, 2006), A.2.

passively, without one's own initiative, and is usually unexpected. Thus, an occurrence is not something that simply confirms and continues a pattern of life and experience; rather, it impacts a life so that it becomes different, so that all that it does or does not do, in its what and in its how, in its character and in its being, is affected by this occurrence and significantly determined by it.[11]

In phenomenology, the category of event was intended from the beginning to convey this passive-pathic character of occurrences. This is shown in Rosenzweig's use of "occurred event" in *The Star of Redemption* (1918-1919), no less than in Heidegger's use of the event category from the 1930s onward, which was closely linked with the turn that had become necessary, following the failed project of fundamental ontology in *Being and Time* (1927), toward his later thinking on the history of Being.[12] The event that *gives* being and time is not, as such, phenomenologically accessible, but can be grasped only indirectly through its resonances and continuing effects. This is demonstrated clearly in the already-published volumes and those yet forthcoming of the collected works that are dedicated to the topic of event.[13] This analysis of event in the later work of Heidegger was

11. B. Waldenfels led the way in researching this phenomenon, with his studies of the structures of pathos and responsiveness. See *Ordnung im Zwielicht* (Frankfurt am Main: Suhrkamp, 1987); *Der Stachel des Fremden* (Frankfurt am Main: Suhrkamp, 1990); *Antwortregister* (Frankfurt am Main: Suhrkamp, 1994); *Grenzen der Normalisierung. Studien zur Phänomenologie des Fremden 2* (Frankfurt am Main: Suhrkamp, 1998); *Sinnschwellen. Studien zur Phänomenologie des Fremden 3* (Frankfurt am Main: Suhrkamp, 1999); *Bruchlinien der Erfahrung. Phänomenologie, Psychoanalyse, Phänomenotechnik* (Frankfurt am Main: Suhrkamp, 2002); "Die Macht der Ereignisse," in *Ereignis auf Französisch*, ed. M. Rölli (Munich: Fink, 2004), 447-58; *Phänomenologie der Aufmerksamkeit* (Frankfurt am Main: Suhrkamp, 2004); and *Schattenrisse der Moral* (Frankfurt am Main: Suhrkamp, 2006). On the fundamental nature of passive experience in and beyond the dimensions of the practical and epistemic, see especially *Bruchlinien der Erfahrung*, 54-60. On responsiveness, see *Schattenrisse der Moral*, 106: "Responsiveness means, *I myself begin, not with myself but elsewhere*. In other words, *I go into that from which I have come out*. The evidence of this basic feature that shapes all of our behavior is not to be found in either goal-directed or rule-directed behavior, as in nearly every other proposal in contemporary practical philosophy. Instead it goes back to events in which I and others certainly took part, but not as their author." I call such events *occurrences* (*Widerfahrnisse*).
12. See the following works by M. Heidegger: "Zum Einblick in die Notwendigkeit der Kehre" (1964), in *Vom Rätsel des Begriffs* (FS F.-W. v. Herrmann), ed. P.-L. Coriando (Berlin: Duncker & Humblot, 1999), 1-3; *Beiträge zur Philosophie (Vom Ereignis) (1936-1938)*, GA 65 (Frankfurt am Main: V. Klostermann, 1994); *Besinnung (1938/39)*, GA 66 (Frankfurt am Main: V. Klostermann, 1997); and *Die Geschichte des Seyns*, GA 69 (Frankfurt am Main: V. Klostermann, 1998).
13. The published volumes are M. Heidegger, *Beiträge zur Philosophie*; *Besinnung*; *Über den Anfang* (1941) (Frankfurt am Main: V. Klostermann, 2005); Heidegger, *Brief über den "Humanismus"* (1946), in *Wegmarken*, GA 9 (Frankfurt am Main: V. Klostermann, 1996), 313-64; Heidegger, "Zeit und Sein" (1962), in *Zur Sache des Denkens* (Tübingen: Niemeyer, 1988), 1-26; Heidegger, "Der Satz der

taken up in French-speaking phenomenology by various thinkers such as Levinas, Derrida, Jean-François Lyotard, Gilles Deleuze, and Alain Badiou in their own ways.[14] While, for Badiou, past events can only be comprehended by pursuing their consequences and considering them, Levinas employs the term *trace* to speak of something that refers indirectly to that which cannot in and of itself be grasped as a phenomenon and the presence of which cannot be readily defined: the in-breaking of the other into a life.[15] It retains its alterity precisely because this in-breaking cannot be described phenomenologically as present, but only considered indirectly on the basis of its "traces" as the presence of its "non-presence."[16] Derrida also proceeds from this present trace of what is absent in his presence-critical negative phenomenology of gift, of sacrifice, of promise, of hospitality, and of the event, although with Derrida the term *event* appears to have less the connotation of a retrospective-responsive stance toward what has occurred and more of an ethical or political stance toward what should or ought to occur.[17] In any case, the term *event* is not only a fundamental category of the experience of time but the key term, phenomenologically and ontologically, for the in-breaking of the new, the unique, the unforeseen, the extraordinary, and the not-to-be-expected in life and in history.[18] This in-breaking is experienced,

---

Identität" (1957), in *Identität und Differenz* (Stuttgart: Klett-Cotta, 1999), 9–30. Cf. Fr.-W. von Herrmann, *Wege ins Ereignis. Zu Heideggers »Beiträgen zur Philosophie«* (Frankfurt am Main: V. Klostermann, 1994); P. Trawny, *Martin Heidegger* (Frankfurt am Main: Campus, 2003); and R. Wansing, "Im Denken erfahren. Ereignis und Geschichte bei Heidegger," in *Ereignis auf Französisch. Von Bergson bis Deleuze*, ed. M. Rölli (Munich: Wilhelm Fink, 2004), 81–102. The forthcoming volumes include M. Heidegger, *Das Ereignis* (1941/42), GA 71; and Heidegger, *Zum Ereignis-Denken*, GA 73.

14. Cf. M. Rölli, ed., *Ereignis auf Französisch. Von Bergson bis Deleuze* (Munich: Wilhelm Fink, 2004). A. Badiou, *L'être et l'événement* (Paris: Seuil, 1988). Cf. J. Barker, *Alain Badiou: A Critical Introduction* (London: Pluto, 2002); and P. Zeillinger, "Badiou und Paulus. Das Ereignis als Norm?" *IWK-Mitteilungen* 61 (2006): 6–12.

15. On Badiou, cf. P. Hallward, *Badiou: A Subject to Truth* (Minneapolis: University of Minnesota Press, 2003), 115: "An event is something that can be said to exist (or rather, to have existed) only insofar as it somehow inspires subjects to wager on its existence (EE [= Badiou, L'être et l'événement] 214)."

16. See P. Zeillinger, "Phänomenologie des Nicht-Phänomenalen. Spur und Inversion des Seins bei Emmanuel Levinas," in *Phänomenologische Aufbrüche*, ed. M. Blaumauer /W. Fasching/M. Flatscher (Frankfurt am Main: Peter Lang, 2005), 161–79.

17. Cf. J. Derrida, *Eine gewissen unmögliche Möglichkeit, vom Ereignis zu sprechen* (1997), trans. S. Lüdemann (Berlin: Merve, 2003).

individually or collectively, as an interruption of one's life-shaping activities, structures, and arrangements. For those affected, therefore, it has primarily the nature of something experienced passively, *something that befalls them* (*Widerfahrnis*). On the one hand, such in-breaking disturbs the already-existing patterns of life, activity, and order, interrupts them, or even demolishes or dismantles them, bringing them to an end. At the same time, its active passivity may provoke the building and budding of new structures, arrangements, and activities—a new departure, a new beginning.

From this double perspective, occurrences can fall into one of two fundamental types: those that arise in the course of a life that somehow affect or guide it (life-shaping occurrences) and those that initiate a course in life that did not exist before (life-shaking or, better, life-grounding occurrences). Life-shaping occurrences happen *in a life* and alter it from being a certain way to being somewhat different. Life-grounding occurrences, on the other hand, occur *to a life* and are the basis of its transition from nonbeing to being, or from being to nonbeing. Life-shaping occurrences can take many forms and have very different characteristics. They may be pleasant or unpleasant, joyful or sad, helpful or damaging; they may make a life boring or interesting, happy or unhappy. Life-grounding occurrences, however, have either a life-giving or a life-ending character. They nurture new life and protect it, or they bring an existing life to an end, resulting in its death. This in no way means that there are two different types of life-grounding occurrences, each aimed at an opposite effect, but rather that that which establishes a life takes place *or does not take place*. Just as a life-grounding occurrence establishes and protects a life, its failure to occur (or its no longer occurring) leads to the end of a life.

Life-shaping occurrences may have differing significance, with some shaping a life only marginally or incidentally while others have measurable and deep effects. Losing your wallet is one thing, losing your job is something else, and losing a loved one or one's own life

18. Cf. N. Müller-Schöll, ed., *Ereignis. Eine fundamentale Kategorie der Zeiterfahrung. Anspruch und Aporien* (Bielefeld: Transcript, 2003).

is something else again. In all cases, however, a condition for the possibility of an occurrence is that one is alive; someone who is not alive can undergo (*widerfahren*) nothing. This is different in the case of life-grounding occurrences. They are the condition for the possibility of there being a life that can undergo something. One should not think only of those occurrences without which a life could not begin, but also of those without which a life could not be maintained and continued. Life-grounding occurrences do not appear in life as tangible phenomena alongside or among others, but as the condition for the possibility of subjective (*Erlebnis*) or empirical experiences (*Erfahrung*) of phenomena. Without them, there would not be the life that they ground. In every moment of a life, therefore, they are presupposed and present in an unthematized way: in the temporal mode of the past as the immemorial origins of one's own life (I exist even though I might not have existed) and in the temporal mode of the present as its fathomless rootedness in Being (I still exist even though I could stop doing so at any moment). To be mindful of life-shaping occurrences and to appreciate their existential significance is to live with awareness. In contrast, to become mindful of life-grounding occurrences and to be guided by them is to be transformed from mere inauthentic existence into true and authentic life. It is to become aware of the contingency of one's own being and of the significance of the seemingly trivial fact that one (still) is, although one might (long ago) have not existed or might no longer exist.

What befalls one in life is revealed in how one actually responds to being thus affected. Occurrences cannot be observed as such; they can be defined only on the basis of the retrospective perspective of those who undergo them as that which makes them become those they become through them. When someone receives an unexpected inheritance, when someone is loved by the person whom he or she loves, when someone despite all care and precaution falls ill, when someone has something important stolen or has an accident, that person undergoes something that makes them someone whom they would not, by their own volition, have become—someone who not only can respond to such an occurrence, but actually does respond to it, because every subsequent behavior represents a position taken in response to that occurrence.[19]

Occurrences, thus, are not merely events that impact someone casually and induce other events. To be sure, the occurrence that befalls someone may be so described from a third-person perspective, but then one is ignoring what is seen and how it is perceived from the first-person perspective of the person impacted. Without someone impacted, there is no occurrence. This also applies when that which befalls someone else (actual event) is perceived by me (epistemic event) and described as an occurrence for the other person. The actual and the epistemic events may, but need not, coincide. An infection is an occurrence for the one who gets sick, even if she herself is not (yet) aware of it and only the doctor can determine it. One need not personally be aware of undergoing an occurrence, but it would be no occurrence if it were impossible to become aware of it, and one could not describe it as an occurrence if no one was aware of it.

For life-shaping occurrences, what is decisive is not simply that they happen but that they are subjectively experienced (*erlebt*), that is, that they are (or can be) perceived and understood, without the experience coinciding with the occurrence. What impacts me—an occurrence (*Widerfahrnis*)—and how I experience it—a subjective experience (*Erlebnis*)—can and must be distinguished methodologically, although they happen simultaneously. An occurrence that is not experienced is only one more event in a series of events, but it is not an occurrence.[20] An experience that is not the correlate of an occurrence points to no reality beyond itself; it is not an experience *of something*. Since not

---

19. One is not an heir because one accepts an inheritance; only someone who is already an heir can accept or decline an inheritance. And even when one does neither the one nor the other, one is still taking a position regarding what one has become because it amounts to not acceding to the inheritance.
20. This is true of life-shaping occurrences. For life-grounding occurrences, however, one must say that without them, there would be no one to whom something life-shaping could occur or who could experience it. Whoever is not alive cannot experience anything. No one lives without experiencing, but the fact that one does live does not depend on what or how one experiences. To be alive is the necessary condition for the possibility of experience, but this condition is not itself a case of what it makes possible.

every event is an occurrence and not every experience is corollary to an occurrence, one must not only distinguish between events and occurrences but also between occurrences and experiences. The first distinction highlights the difference between the perspective of someone who is not affected by the event (a third-person perspective) and someone who is affected (a first-person perspective) when it comes to describing an event. The second distinction highlights a difference within the first-person perspective of those affected, the difference between *what* affects them and *how* it affects them.

While events (in the sense of an observable sequence) always lead to a string of other events, occurrences lead to subjective experiences and through them to empirical experiences (*Erfahrungen*) in which that which has occurred, in light of how it was subjectively experienced, can be represented semiotically in a certain way and, with the help of a conventional system of signs, be communicated to others in a way that is accessible to them. In experiencing, what occurs becomes clear, but only in the way it is subjectively experienced. Experiences, therefore, may always be described as events. However, they always have a symbolic structure, which, unlike the bare events themselves, allows one to ask about their meaning inasmuch as that which has occurred, which was subjectively experienced in a certain way (subjective meaning), is symbolically presented in a certain way (objective meaning). These experiences are indeed always experiences of something that has occurred and has been subjectively experienced, but that in no way means they must be pleasant or unpleasant, gratifying or annoying, or (morally) good or bad. As everyday, legal, or scientific descriptions of such events demonstrate, it is quite possible to describe accidents, illnesses, inheritances, or romantic relationships without ever addressing their significance (their meaning) for those affected. If, however, they are described as gratifying or annoying, morally good or evil, then what has occurred has been so experienced by the one affected or so judged by an observer. That which is described or judged in this manner may be the occurrence itself (the illness or the inheritance). It may also be that which is experienced in and through this occurrence (for example, the shock, the pain, and the fear, or the joy, the surprise, and the happiness). Or it may be what is caused by the occurrence or what results from it (the loss of employment or financial independence). Whatever the case, the categories of pleasant or unpleasant, gratifying or annoying, even the moral categories of good and evil, belong to the appropriated experience, not to the occurrence that occasioned these experiences. Terms like gratifying or annoying and good or evil do not apply to that which happens to someone but to how they experience what happens to them. They are not characteristics of the events that befall someone but of the experience of those occurrences.

3.3 Self-Interpretation and Conceptual Construction

By emphasizing the priority of passivity over all activity on the part of the understanding subject, and by grounding this priority in the prior self-interpretation of word-events or speech-events, hermeneutical theology made a decisive turn in regard to the modern emphasis on the human subject and the inevitability of constructing reality within the horizon of its dealings with the world. However, despite this correct and important emphasis on the priority of phenomenal disclosure before any subjective reconstruction, the pendulum sometimes swings too far to the other side. The issue of the conceptual coining and symbolic construction of all our knowledge, including our theological knowledge, is minimized in a problematic way.[21] Perceiving, understanding, knowing, and thinking are more than just an obedient acceptance of phenomena, an attentive reproduction of already

---

21. U. Barth, "Zur Barth-Deutung Eberhard Jüngels," *Theologische Zeitschrift* 40 (1984): 413ff. It is here that the debate about the necessity of a critical "hermeneutics of suspicion" has a justified point of departure. Cf. P. Ricoeur, *Die Interpretation: ein Versuch über Freud* (1965) (Frankfurt am Main: Suhrkamp, 1974); Ricoeur, "Philosophische und theologische Hermeneutik," in *Metapher. Zur Hermeneutik religiöser Sprache*, Mit einer Einführung von Pierre Gisel, ed. P. Ricoeur and E. Jüngel (Munich: Kaiser, 1974), 24–45; D. Stewart, "The Hermeneutics of Suspicion," *Journal of Literature and Theology* 3 (1989): 296–307; E. White, "Between Suspicion and Hope: Paul Ricoeur's Vital Hermeneutic," *Journal of Literature and Theology* 5 (1991): 311–321; B. Leiter, "The Hermeneutics of Suspicion: Recovering Marx, Nietzsche, and Freud," in *The Future for Philosophy*, ed. B. Leiter (Oxford: Oxford University Press, 2004), 74–105; K. Wenzel, *Glaube in Vermittlung. Theologische Hermeneutik nach Paul Ricoeur* (Freiburg: Herder, 2008); and R. Felski, "After Suspicion," *Profession*, 2009, 28–35.

disclosed meaning. Thinking is not simply a correspondence in the medium of thought to the self-interpretation of being; understanding is not primarily a receptive process, but rather a critical and creative symbolic process. In understanding, we generate the meaning of the world in which we live through living in a particular way.[22] We construct it through our perceiving, learning, knowing, and understanding in the manifold practices of our life. It is just this constant construal that is the starting point for the parting of the ways between everyday life experience and the formation of scientific theories, as well as for the (never-absolute but always relative) distinction between life practice and science, between life as lived and explanatory theory.

The constructed character of all our understanding—of the world, self, and God—cannot be limited to our reconstruction of the prior self-interpretation of world, self, and God that has already taken place. Construction and *reconstruction* can only be differentiated when one is able to provide criteria for distinguishing between the meaning proffered to understanding and the meaning constructed by understanding. Limiting the theoretical or theological explication to a mere reconstruction assumes that we can distinguish the self-disclosure and self-interpretation of reality (and, mutatis mutandis, the self-interpretation of God) from the reconstructing interpretation of it by an understanding subject. As hermeneutical theology has not been able to provide such criteria, either in general or for the specific case of the self-interpretation of God, it has been accused of dogmatically advocating an epistemological realism of the phenomenal self-interpretation of Being or of God that is beyond any critical epistemological control.

---

22. Phenomenologically, "world" does not mean a "big thing," nor does it mean the totality of all possible and actual events, but rather a manner of living. Humans live in a "worldly" way when they live according to the cultural habits present in their community; they live "spiritually" when they live according to the guidelines of their religious community; they live in an "everyday" manner when they carry out their lives in the mode that is held to be normal and self-evident in their place and time; they live in an "alternative" way when they intentionally (try to) set themselves apart from these norms so as to make clear that they are not self-evident; and so on and so forth. In each case, an understanding of the world is linked to the mode of life, an understanding that can be explicated as the world-conception of each manner of life.

But the matter is more complicated; it must be described differently in regard to the understanding of Being than in regard to the understanding of God. To be sure, recourse to the self-disclosure or self-interpretation of Being or of God, which precedes all of our interpretations, does not take care of the epistemological question. Self-interpretation can only be spoken of seriously if that which interprets itself not only interprets itself *for someone* but also, in so doing, interprets itself *as itself*. That can only happen if it interprets itself *for others* as it is interpreted *for itself*. This appears to make sense in the case of God, but not in the case of Being. Talk of the self-interpretation of Being would then mean that Being interprets itself in reality as self-interpreted—that is, as not interpreted by others. However, if the idea of self-interpretation is construed in this sense as absolute self-interpretation (that is, as self-interpretation-not-interpreted-by-others), then the point of the very distinction between interpretation by others and self-interpretation cannot be clearly grasped without clarifying the reference of absolute self-interpretation to interpretation by others. The decisive questions then become in which sense self-interpretation is interpretation and how self-interpretation is to be distinguished from a true interpretation by another. So long as these questions remain unanswered, talk of the self-interpretation of Being appears, in reality, to be little more than a figure of speech for a true interpretation of Being, suggesting an epistemological standard without actually providing one.

When it comes to the self-interpretation of God, things may be different. The notion that God interprets Godself for us as God is interpreted for Godself can be precisely grasped in terms of Trinitarian theology. Prior to our understanding of God in faith and its theological interpretation, God interprets Godself for us as our God (divine self-revelation) inasmuch as God discloses in Jesus Christ (Word) and through the Spirit (self-interpretative event) who and what God is for us (self-giving love) in such a way that it can and does lead to faith in God as utterly trustworthy because God discloses the divine heart of love to us. This event of self-revelation is the self-interpretation of

God in a strict sense inasmuch as God here so interprets Godself for others in time (through the temporal *logos*-event of Jesus Christ and the Spirit in the communication of the gospel) as God is interpreted for Godself in eternity (in the eternal *logos*-event of the Son and the Spirit in the life of the Trinity): as creative and self-giving love for creation. This is possible inasmuch as God in God's self-revelation through Word (Jesus Christ as *verbum personale*, the gospel as *verbum praedicatum*) and Spirit (*creator spiritus, testimonium sancti spiritus internum*) makes Godself understandable for others as God is eternally understandable to Godself as Father, Son (*verbum aeternum*), and Spirit. The event of God's self-revelation for us is the temporal iteration for us of the event of God's eternal self-revelation for Godself. The doctrine of the Trinity spells this out, as it construes revelation as the self-revelation of God, understands self-revelation as the temporal iteration of the eternal self-interpretation of God, and bases the structural correspondence between God's self-interpretation for us and for God in the ongoing event of the triune being of God.

Thus, in the case of God, in contrast to the case of Being, we can in principle understand what it would mean to say that God so interprets Godself for others as God is interpreted for Godself. God inherently possesses the interpretative structure of a word-event and therefore can be thought of as a self-mediating event of meaning. However, this still leaves the question unanswered regarding the criteria by which this divine self-interpretation can be distinguished from the constructs of Trinitarian theology in such a way that the theological constructs are shown to be *re*constructions that can be tested against the reality that precedes them. Does the sign *Trinity* stand for that which is to be theologically interpreted (*interpretandum*) or for a (possible) theological interpretation (*interpretans*) of that which in the practice of faith is referred to as "God"? Is God's self-interpretation Trinitarian so that only the concepts of a Trinitarian theology could be adequate? Or is God's self-interpretation interpreted in a Trinitarian way by (several strands of) Christian theology, although it could be interpreted otherwise? Is Trinitarian theology the reconstruction of the prior

Trinitarian reality of God? Or is it a temporally conditioned construct of divine reality that could and must be replaced by other, non-Trinitarian constructs should these prove to be less open to misunderstanding? And what are the criteria by which one could judge between the two theses of construct or reconstruction?

Trinitarian doctrine itself cannot be such a criterion because it, in each of its various forms, is a theological construct that is to be judged by this criterion. The hermeneutical thesis, that Trinitarian doctrine represents a human theological interpretation of the prior self-interpretation of God, remains merely a dogmatic assertion so long as no criteria are provided for critically distinguishing the constructions of Trinitarian theology from the self-revelation of God. Within hermeneutical theology, this question of criteria is answered with reference to Scripture. The primary context for verifying the statements of Trinitarian theology is not the divine self-revelation as such but the witness of Scripture that God, through the Spirit, has disclosed Godself in Jesus Christ. The claims of Trinitarian theology are to be tested not against God but against Scripture.

To be sure, this only serves to relocate the problem. For it is not the texts of Scripture as such that are the sought-for criterion; rather, the criterion is their understanding as witness to God's self-revelation. This understanding itself, however, is a matter of theological contention. Hermeneutical theology does not settle the dispute between considering theological assertions to be constructs or reconstructions by reference to an undisputed criterion, but rather through entering into the disputes regarding the interpretation of Scripture. The hermeneutical problem is thus "resolved" by linking it to another hermeneutical problem.

3.4 Unity and Diversity in Self-Interpretation

J. B. Webster has called attention to a further problem, albeit without sufficiently recognizing the difference between the case of Being and the case of God.[23] Emphasizing the self-interpretation of being in reality as the basic hermeneutical fact, and locating all problems of knowing and understanding in the insufficient correspondence of our interpretation to this self-interpretation, ignores the fact that reality discloses itself in manifold ways, never unambiguously with only one meaning. As Jüngel repeatedly emphasized, reality is experienced ambivalently and even understanding that appears self-evident can be improved upon. Even if one begins epistemologically from the self-interpretive structure of Being in reality, this in no way implies or guarantees the unity, uniformity, or unique accuracy of this interpretation. If the self-disclosing word-event is to be understood as fundamental and not as the coming to speech of some reality lying beyond this event, then the form of speech *as which* it comes to speech is precisely *that which* comes to speech. Jüngel explicitly drew this conclusion regarding the kingdom of God, which comes "to speech in parable as parable, in demand as demand, in threatening word as threatening word."[24] This insight must be applied consistently in the epistemological consequences of this approach: everything is that and only that *as which it comes to speech on its own*.

However—as Heidegger in *Being and Time* saw correctly—nothing appears as it is without simultaneously concealing what it is, and nothing comes to speech as it is without simultaneously distorting what it is. As a rule, it is not *as* truth but *sub contrario* that truth makes its appearance, so it cannot be discussed *as* truth without critically distinguishing it from its manner of appearing: no interpretation of truth without a prior deconstruction of its distortions. The same is true in the case of language. That which comes to speech as it interprets itself must be critically brought off against its perversions and distortions in order to be brought to speech. No phenomenon can be perceived by us as it shows itself from itself, unless it is critically and explicitly extracted from its distortions that reveal how it does *not* show itself. And no word-event is understood by us in the way it makes itself understandable, unless its self-interpretation is critically distinguished from those interpretations that do not interpret it as

---

23. J. Webster, *Eberhard Jüngel: An Introduction to His Theology* (Cambridge: Cambridge University Press, 1986), 60–61.
24. E. Jüngel, *Paulus und Jesus* (Tübingen: Mohr Siebeck, 1967), 292.

it interprets itself, or that interpret it as it does not interpret itself. This is why phenomenology and theology are needed. Without critical phenomenology and its deconstruction of misleading theoretical constructions, there is no understanding of how phenomena themselves disclose themselves, and without critical theology and its deconstruction of misleading theological constructions, there is no understanding of how word-events themselves bring themselves to speech. The function of this deconstructive critique is not to state the "right" or "authentic" understanding, but precisely the opposite—to raise questions about, and to dismantle and deconstruct, false or questionable understandings in order to free up space for the correct understanding to appear.

Yet another problem arises. Since we are always confronted with a variety of things that come to speech and various ways in which something comes to speech, it is not self-evident that it is one and the same thing that brings itself to speech within this variety and in these varied ways. This is clearly true for the kingdom of God, which comes to speech in a variety of linguistic forms: as parable, demand, threatening word, and the like. What is the justification for seeing precisely the kingdom of God coming to speech in this variety of forms? It is also true in a more comprehensive sense for hermeneutical theology's entire understanding of Being and reality. The unity of reality and the uniformity of the original self-interpretation of being, which hermeneutical theology at least implicitly assumes, is an assumption of its approach that has not been sufficiently accounted for.

3.5 Reconstruction versus Prescription

This also explains why hermeneutical theology tends to carry out its theological discussions in prescriptive, rather than descriptive, language.[25] Instead of analysis, at critical points one repeatedly finds an appeal that seeks to make a certain view of the matter intersubjectively

---

25. Cf. Webster, *Eberhard Jüngel*, 50 (with reference to the analysis of Thomas in *Gott als Geheimnis der Welt*, 322ff.); Barth, "Zur Barth-Deutung Eberhard Jüngels," 413–14.

plausible. With an emphatic appeal to the matter itself and by rhetorically portraying the "disjunctive completeness of the alternatives and the unavoidability that thus results," it does not say what is and how it is, but rather what and how it *really* is and how it accordingly must be understood it if it is to be rightly understood.[26] Normative concepts of faith, the human, God, reality, thought, theology, and so forth thus take the place of descriptive analysis. These normative concepts and the appeal to understanding wrapped up with them result from specific decisions about contents, the appropriateness of which is justified by reference to the self-interpretation of the subject matter itself that is under consideration. However, no criteria are offered for making such identifications or for distinguishing them from the possibly false interpretations of others. As a result, these decisions in fact appear to be little more than the subjective and arbitrary preferences of a given theologian. For example, faith is understood in such and such a way; this is presented as its proper understanding; the justification for this view is that this is how faith brings itself to understanding, as can be seen from the relevant texts from Scripture and their best theological interpretations from Luther up through Barth. In the end, however, it is precisely this assumed self-interpretation of faith that remains fully without any epistemological controls.

This has led to the obvious and repeated accusation of decisionism. To this, hermeneutical theology has responded by referring to the evidence of the subject matter of theology, shown in the specific way in which faith has come to speech in history, as the Scripture and its tradition of interpretation in the church demonstrate, and on whose power of self-interpretation we must also rely on in the future because there is simply no alternative. While this explains the frequently noted theological conservatism and (by no means uncritical) traditionalism of hermeneutical theology, it does not, in itself, constitute an answer to the question at hand. Even the Scriptures demonstrate only how faith came to speech and the variety of ways in which it came to speech.

26. Barth, "Zur Barth-Deutung Eberhard Jüngels," 413.

That faith has so brought itself to speech and, therefore, is thus to be brought to speech is a dogmatic thesis that must be justified in some way other than by simple recourse to the facticity of Scripture and its history of interpretation.

There is no simple or straightforward account of faith to be found in Scripture. This cannot even be ignored by the hermeneutical project of a grammar of faith based on the contingency of the particular way in which faith has come to speech. In the manner of Hermann Diem's criticism of Bultmann, it does not seek to raise up a pure kerygma behind the biblical texts.[27] Instead, in line with the theological maxim that all human knowing has to be true to how humans are known by God, it accepts the biblical interpretation of faith as the fundamental datum of all theological reception and reconstruction. Still, it cannot overlook the fact that the Scripture brings faith to speech in a variety of more or less adequate ways. This factual and qualitative variety of the biblical speech on faith, which hermeneutical theology has always acknowledged, requires critical thinking. This, however, is impossible without conceptual clarification of the theological or dogmatic content of the term *faith*. According to the realistic self-understanding of hermeneutical theology, if this dogmatic concept of faith wants to be more than a mere arbitrary definition, it must conceptualize and encapsulate the self-interpretation of faith by critically distinguishing it from misleading and inadequate interpretations by others. This, however, requires that the self-interpretation of faith first be identified within the language of faith by distinguishing it from other interpretations in the texts of Scripture. Unfortunately, hermeneutical theology has provided no convincing criteria for making such a distinction. The problem has certainly been recognized, but it has not been solved.

The second component of the answer sketched above, however, points toward the core insight of hermeneutical theology from which a solution to the problem might be developed. This is the conviction

---

27. H. Diem, *Theologie als kirchliche Wissenschaft*, vol 2: *Dogmatik* (Munich: Kaiser, 1960), 60–75, 72; Diem, "Zur Problematik theologischer Wahrheitsfindung," *ThLZ* 95 (1970): 161–72.

that, in the end, it is not theology that is to decide what is correct faith or a correct understanding of faith. Rather, its efforts of critical reflection remain directed toward an occurrence that always takes place freely. Its contingent occurrence and factual identity cannot be controlled by believers or determined by theologians. Humans are not masters of the occurrences that affect them, nor of the rules that these occurrences follow (if they follow rules at all). At all times, humans can only react in responsive ways to something that has happened to them by relating to that which precedes them. The occurrences by which humans orient their living, understanding, and thinking are not accessible other than in this responsive mode. They themselves and others are indeed participants in them, but simply as those impacted and involved, as those who are recipients, not as authors or originators. The identity of what is to be explained theologically is not to be found in some definable content, but rather only in the repeated, freely occurring amen with which humans acknowledge that what has been made known to them in the communication of the gospel is the truth about their lives, an acknowledgment that is never forced but is compelled by the inner conviction that "I can do no other."

3.6 Self-Interpretation and Truth

All of these issues come to a head in the question of truth.[28] On the basis of the epistemological model of Being-Language-Thinking, held together by the concepts of self-interpretation and correspondence, hermeneutical theology was in a position to develop a conception of truth that critically diverged from the traditional adequation model of truth. Reflective thinking is adequate, or true, when its interpretation of reality corresponds to reality's self-interpretation. Truth thus is still understood as a relation of correspondence. However, this

---

28. On this issue, see I. U. Dalferth and P. Stoellger, "Wahrheit, Glaube und Theologie. Zur theologischen Rezeption zeitgenössischer wahrheitstheoretischer Diskussionen," *Theologische Rundschau* 66 (2001): 36–102; Dalferth and Stoellger, "Perspektive und Wahrheit. Einleitende Hinweise auf eine klärungsbedürftige Problemgeschichte," in *Wahrheit in Perspektiven. Probleme einer offenen Konstellation*, ed. Dalferth and Stoellger (Tübingen: Mohr Siebeck, 2004), 1–28; and I. U. Dalferth, "Religion und Wahrheit," in Dalferth and Stoellger, *Wahrheit in Perspektiven*, 195–232.

correspondence consists not in the agreement of the judgment of understanding (*intellectus*) with the reality given to it (*res*), but rather (one may say) with the prior "self-judgment" of being within reality. The real problem of truth is located neither in the relationship of thought and language nor in the relationship of being and language, but rather within being itself or, more precisely, in the self-disclosure of being's meaning in the mode of authentic self-interpretation. For if being is conceived as a word-event, it is not merely an object of interpretation but itself possesses the structure of self-interpretation: "something or someone interprets itself as something for someone."

But when is such a self-interpretation authentic or true? Apparently, when the matter in question interprets itself as it is. This, however, either leads us in a circle or into an infinite regress. For either the matter is then indeed that as which it interprets itself or it is something that itself possesses self-interpretative structure—that is, something that interprets itself as something. In the former case, the matter is identical with its self-interpretation; in the latter, with the self-interpretation of its self-interpretation. In either case, truth is so closely identified with the self-interpretation that it effectively dissolves the hermeneutical as-structure. Since a self-interpretation is ipso facto true, the distinction between the matter itself and its self-interpretation is epistemologically invalid; it is exactly that which it presents itself to be. Thus, when the problem of truth is taken back to the level of the self-interpretation of being, it is reduced to the becoming present of something for someone. This is what Jüngel called the "arrival," "advent," or "interruption of the continuity of our life" that leads to its "enhancement" or "intensification," that is, to the opening of possibilities that were not there before.[29] But then, whether intentionally or not, the question of truth as commonly understood is not even raised, much less answered. To be sure, unless something becomes present for us, we have no reason or occasion to pose the *question* of its truth and, possibly, answer it. Without becoming present

---

29. E. Jüngel, "The Truth of Life. Observations on Truth as the Interruption of the Continuity of Life," in *Creation, Christ and Culture: Studies in Honour of T. F. Torrance*, ed. R. W. Mackinney (Edinburgh: T&T Clark, 1976), 231–36.

for us, the matter in question and its possibilities would not be part of our life and thus no object for our *question* of truth. However, just because there is no *question* of truth without an interruption of the continuity of life does not mean that this interruption constitutes *truth*. And just because our life is enhanced when something previously unknown becomes present in it does not mean that such intensification is to be equated with truth. If that is what "truth" is to mean here, then the problem of truth as commonly understood still exists, and is by no means answered.

Transferring the problem of truth to the level of the self-interpretation of being in language does not absolve us from answering the question of truth at the level of our interpretation of this self-interpretation. Even at that level, the question of truth is not answered by identifying the self-interpretation as truth, since nothing can become present for us without becoming present *as something*. How, then, is the self-interpretation of something that becomes present for us as something (and, as such, is declared true) to be distinguished from its interpretation, that is, from being interpreted by us as something (and, as such, may possibly be false)? Apparently, for a verifiable way of engaging with our experience and understanding, we require criteria for identifying the self-interpretation of being, declared ipso facto to be true, as distinct from all problematic interpretation by us. Without such criteria, a theology that reflects on faith as it comes to speech can have no knowledge and no conceptual clarity. If self-interpretation as such is seen as an event of truth, which is beyond the distinction between true or false interpretation, it either becomes indistinguishable from a true interpretation or takes on a character different in principle from that of interpretation, which can be true or false. As the one cannot be distinguished from the other, when it comes to clarifying the question of truth, nothing is gained through recourse to self-interpretation that is ipso facto true. At no point can we know which interpretation deserves to be called self-interpretation and thus must be considered true.

Therefore, one might well conclude that hermeneutical theology, in a misconceived realist attitude, downplays the critical epistemological question of truth by identifying truth with an event of self-interpretation that has no conceptual controls, is insufficiently distinguished from its interpretation by us, and thus provides no viable authority for guiding our theological thinking, in effect granting that authority to the conventional traditions of theological thought. As with all thinking, theological thinking can only be appropriate, that is, be controlled by the subject matter of faith, when it orients itself through a clear conception of that matter. Appeal to the self-interpretation of the subject matter of faith cannot replace the efforts toward clear theological concepts. Of course, hermeneutical theology is aware of this as well. Still, its justified realist concern, that the subject matter must control the theological concepts and not vice versa, cannot avoid the fact that any theological access to this matter is always conceptually determined. Even the realist hermeneutics and epistemology of hermeneutical theology have theological, and that means conceptual, underpinnings, inasmuch as their access to the subject matter of faith is guided by a prior concept that it owes to the church's life of faith and its theological reflection in the dogmatic tradition. In hermeneutical theology, the doctrine of justification plays exactly this role. However, precisely because this doctrine has to do with the event of faith, which is clearly distinct from it yet which it claims to adequately address, the question arises: How can its appropriateness be theologically decided? Merely to postulate the control of theological concepts by the subject matter itself leads, in effect, to its control by other theological concepts. The very distinction between subject matter and (theological) concept is drawn within the horizon of theological concepts and thus is a theological construct and not a predetermined difference. This means, however, that the original distinction, the fundamental epistemological difference between self-interpretation and other-interpretation, is functionally meaningless. Moreover, it reveals that, if the subject matter can be brought into play in a specific conceptual form that helps to clarify the issue and not obfuscate it, the appeal to the subject matter itself is only a theological argument and not a refusal to argue.

3.7 Self-Interpretation and Copresence

This leads to a final point. The epistemological problems of hermeneutical theology result from two methodological decisions whose consequences have not been sufficiently thought through. Epistemologically, a privileged position is given, on the one hand, to a particular means of gaining knowledge—that of *communication*—and, on the other, to a particular situation of gaining knowledge—that of *communicating persons copresent with one another*, in which each presents herself to the others and each understands the others as they present themselves. This privileging of communication over against perception, and of communication between those present about what is present over against communication between those who are absent or communication between those present about something that is absent, follows from hermeneutical theology's emphasis on the word-event and on the conversational model of language. This explains its higher valuation of self-interpretation over against interpretation and also clarifies its anti-Cartesian version of the problem of certainty through its emphasis on the event of the *verbum externum* that creates certainty in and through comfort and challenge. It explains its identification of the questions of validity and truth in the event of self-interpretation. And it elucidates its specific conception of the problem of verification as that which makes us true, rather than that which we must demonstrate to be true.

In contrast, classical epistemology derives its inventory of problems directly from the situation of *perception* and from *communication about that which is absent*. Accordingly, it comes to other solutions for the questions of validity, certainty, and verification, and seeks logically assured and unquestionable foundations for our knowing and understanding, foundations among which an appeal to the *verbum externum* can never belong because it always remains subject to doubt.

The two approaches, however, do have one thing in common: each seeks to apply its basic approach monistically to all problems of knowing and thus neglects a problem-based differentiation of epistemological questions. This desire for uniformity, coming at the expense of a nuanced variety, leads in both cases to problematic shortcomings. Whereas the one side comes down to a metaphysics of reflection that is hardly capable of making sense of how people actually understand each other in the event of direct communication, the other side comes down to a metaphysics of copresence that strains to make conversation the model of all knowing and at the same time undervalues conceptual precision and its critical control in the process of understanding, even in the situation of copresence. This essential monism of hermeneutical theology is also to be found at its core, in its hermeneutical basis.

7

On Hermeneutical Theology's Hermeneutical Approach

The universal, comprehensive, and exclusive employment of the word-event model is also the basis for the characteristic and fundamental hermeneutical orientation of hermeneutical theology. Its primary goal is to understand the understanding of God and to understand everything else in the light of this understanding.

1. From Occurred Proclamation to Occurring Proclamation

It sought to reach this goal by way of a consequential exegesis of the experience of faith as witnessed in Scripture, and of all other experiences in light of this experience of faith. The intent was that faith would understand God, the world, and us as we, the world, and God are understood by God. That which is to be understood (God, God's self-interpretation in revelation, and the world in light of this revelation), the means by which it becomes understood (proclamation, Scripture, the apprehension of faith, and faith's apprehension of our apprehended experience of the world), and the realization of this understanding (faith, the life of faith, and theology)—all were construed as word-events. These were linked through relationships of correlation and referred to one another, both within each of these levels and in the relationship of the levels to each other. So the understanding of God that hermeneutical theology sought to understand was the divine word-event that is borne witness to in the word-event of Scripture, that had eschatologically interpreted itself in Jesus Christ and in faith in Christ, and that also constantly interprets itself anew. Because this word-event and the faith that corresponds to it are not directly accessible to theological reflection, but only as mediated through human witness—fundamentally through the witness of Scripture—the work of hermeneutical theology is carried out primarily in exegetical efforts with biblical texts. However, it is not the text as text that is its interest, but that which comes to speech in and through the text. What is to be emphasized in these texts is the witness in human word-events to the divine word-event. As Ebeling suggests, by interpreting these texts with regard to that word-event, the "occurred proclamation" can become "occurring proclamation" again.[1]

At first glance, this agenda for systematic theology as "consequential exegesis" (Jüngel) appears clear and lucid. It operated, however, with a problematic combination of different hermeneutical models in its dealings with the biblical texts, with the meaning of these texts, and with their subject matter, all of which were conceived of as word-events. Thus, hermeneutical theology engaged the biblical *texts* exegetically through the classical methods of a modern hermeneutics of works, which sought to understand the texts intentionally, by the communicative intent of their authors within their original situation. In contrast, it sought to ascertain the theological *meaning* of these texts nonintentionally, from the texts themselves, and from the manner of their reception in faith. Finally, it dogmatically interpreted the meaning ascertained thus in a realistic/referential way as a

---

1. G. Ebeling, "Wort Gottes und Hermeneutik," in *Wort und Glaube* (Tübingen: Mohr Siebeck, 1967), 347–48.

manifestation of the *subject matter* of the texts, that is, of the divine word-event, which itself, again within the framework of the intentionalist paradigm, was construed as God's address to us.

2. Incompatible Hermeneutic Methods

More precisely, within these three dimensions, four different hermeneutical methods are employed, some from literary, textual hermeneutics and some from conversational hermeneutics; some belonging to the intentionalist paradigm and some belonging to the nonintentionalist paradigm. Hermeneutical theology employs (1) explicitly historical-critical methods in dealing with the biblical texts. It ascertains (2) their theologically relevant meaning through methods of literary criticism. It employs (3) an analysis-of-reception method in interpreting their theological usage. And, finally, it reconstructs (4) the subject matter of the text dogmatically as an event of address, within the framework of the intentionalist paradigm.

The first approach is typical for an intentionalist paradigm of literary, textual hermeneutics (of classic or romantic provenance) in asking about the thoughts and intentions of the authors and about the historical *Sitz im Leben* of texts. The second moves toward the nonintentionalist paradigm of formalist or structuralist literary criticism, which seeks the meaning of a literary work in the linking of its elements of meaning, in the formal character of its composition, and in the universal application of thoughts expressed in it. The third approach comes close to the poststructuralist methods of reception analysis, in which the hermeneutical interest shifts not just from the author to the text but also from the text itself to its reception by, and its impact on, its readers and hearers. Finally, the fourth approach follows the intentionalist paradigm, not of textual hermeneutics but of conversational hermeneutics, inasmuch as it focuses not on communication between parties who are absent but between parties who are present in a situation of personal copresence.

It is one thing to ask about the intention of the author or about the original meaning of the text in the situation where it was created, but it is something else to discuss the theological meaning of the text. It is something else again to concentrate on the forms of its reception and the manner of its impact. And it is yet something else to interpret its theological meaning realistically, within the framework of a hermeneutics of copresence.

3. Combination of Textual Hermeneutics and Hermeneutics of Subject Matter

Hermeneutical theology seeks to overcome the obvious difficulties that arise through the combination of these different approaches by, in essence, distinguishing between a *textual hermeneutics*, guided by the key distinction between language and the one who speaks it, and a *hermeneutics of subject matter*, guided by the key distinction between language and being. The former has to do with texts as products and processes of interpersonal communication events. The latter has to do with the subject matter that comes to speech in, with, and beneath these texts. Decisive for the basic hermeneutical approach of hermeneutical theology is the linking of these two hermeneutical issues, both horizontally and vertically: only thus does this approach attain a *theological* hermeneutics of biblical texts. As a result, the depth dimension of its theological textual hermeneutics is the subject matter of faith, which brings itself to speech in the biblical texts; this is what hermeneutical theology is truly interested in understanding. From the perspective of a hermeneutics of works, hermeneutical theology thus focuses on communication between parties who are absent. However, from the perspective of a hermeneutics of matter, it conceives the problem of understanding as it arises in communication between parties who are present. In this way, it seeks to attain a critical principle for theological engagement with the biblical texts, one that allows it to inquire critically about the distinction between authentic self-interpretation and inauthentic interpretation by others of the matter of faith that is brought to word in them. Accordingly, the basic problem of this hermeneutical approach is to develop these two divergent hermeneutical perspectives, which focus on differing situations of communication, and combine them into a methodologically usable program of interpretation. It attempts to do this through the following operations:

Its first step toward linking the two perspectives, within the hermeneutics of works perspective, is *to replace the author's intent with the divine word-event.* The biblical texts are not primarily shaped by the intentions of their authors; instead, they are shaped by the word-event that comes to speech in them by means of and through the authors' intentions. Historical theology's usage of the historical-critical method thus differs from the manner in which it is used by neo-Protestantism: it does not inquire about the intentions of the biblical authors nor about the conventions of an author's *Sitz im Leben*, but rather about the word-event that comes to speech in them and to which they bear witness. (For this reason, Ebeling extols it as particularly appropriate for a theology of the Reformation.)[2]

Its second step, within the perspective of the hermeneutics of subject matter, is *to identify this word-event with the subject matter of the biblical texts.* It thus assumes that this underlying word-event, or its structure, is so imprinted in the meaning-structure of the texts that a careful analysis of their linguistic structures can ascertain the theological scope of the word-event manifesting itself in them. This scope need not coincide with the intention of the author, and can be found even in texts such as the Psalms where no direct or clear authorial intent underlies the text. That biblical texts, as Ebeling says, must be interpreted "with reference to the word-event" presupposes, however, that this word-event is already known and need not first be ascertained from the texts.[3] It does not need to be discovered in the texts because the divine word-event has already made itself present in the proclamation of the gospel. The meaning of biblical texts can thus be discovered (hermeneutics of texts) when they are interpreted in light of the message of the gospel that reveals itself in proclamation (hermeneutics of subject matter).

---

2. G. Ebeling, "Die Bedeutung der historisch-kritischen Methode für die protestantische Theologie und Kirche," in Ebeling, *Wort und Glaube*, 1–49.
3. Ebeling, "Wort Gottes und Hermeneutik," 348.

Hermeneutical theology thus assumes, third, *structural parallels between the perspectives of a hermeneutics of subject matter and that of a hermeneutics of texts*. In other words, it assumes that the pragmatic structure of the *word-event* ("I say something to you") has so imprinted itself in the biblical texts that it compels a pragmatic reading of the text, one that draws the reader or hearer into the conversation. These texts reveal their meaning, then, when the word-event expressing itself in them interprets those it addresses: as sinners in need of justification, as those having a part in God's salvation. Therefore, the distinctive feature of a theological reading of biblical texts is distinguishing (at the level of a hermeneutics of subject matter) law and gospel as categories of the Word of God. When the biblical texts are interpreted from this point of view, they are interpreted as the word-event imprinted within them interprets us.

Finally, in the hermeneutics of subject matter perspective, hermeneutical theology develops the theological meaning of the word-event that manifests itself in and through the biblical texts *within the horizon of the key distinction between law and gospel, in consequential exegesis*—that is, in exegesis directed toward the lives of contemporary human beings. Continuing the theological intentions of Bultmann, it seeks, by systematically working out of the structure, content, and character of the divine word-event that shapes the biblical texts, to offer contemporary people a true understanding of themselves and of their world—or, more precisely, to make such an understanding possible. Such self-understanding and world-understanding is true when it corresponds to the divine word-event. The systematic efforts of hermeneutical theology, therefore, have the goal of introducing anew, through the interpretation of biblical texts as occurred proclamation, an occurring proclamation in which God's self-interpreting word-event takes place again and again, as law and gospel.

4. Unresolved Problems

Each of these four operational steps raises problems. The major problem of the first step is that the transposition from author's intent to word-event within the text-hermeneutical perspective does not really escape the intentionalist paradigm. The word-event, which takes the functional place of authorial intent in this model, is itself interpreted in intentionalist fashion, within the hermeneutics of subject matter perspective, as the self-interpretation of God for us. In other words, God is not really understood as the original word-event, whose structure of meaning is truly fundamental in the sense that it owes its existence to no intention standing behind it, not even a divine intention. Instead, God is understood in personal terms, as the original speaker who interprets Godself in God's Word, thus making God's intentions concerning Godself and God's creation known. Thus, the word-event model, in the hermeneutics of subject matter perspective, is tied to the model of personal speech—in fact, to a *personal speech model of copresent communication.* By focusing on the key distinction between language and being (as the difference between authentic self-interpretation of Being presented in language and inauthentic interpretation by others) instead of the key text-hermeneutical distinction between language and speaker, hermeneutical theology wants to replace the latter with the former. Hermeneutical theology's hermeneutical approach sets itself apart from the issues of a horizontal hermeneutics of texts and conversations between humans precisely by directing its primary attention toward the issues of a vertical hermeneutics of self-interpretation, namely toward the process of the self-explication of Being in language. Yet this special characteristic of its fundamental hermeneutical orientation is lost when it construes the issues of the vertical situation as analogous to the horizontal hermeneutics of communication modeled on communicating, copresent partners. It thus ceases to be an alternative proposal, in fact dissolving the fundamental difference between hermeneutics of texts and hermeneutics of subject matter, and ends up being just a special case among all the usual hermeneutical approaches.

The major problem of the second step is that it assumes the autonomy of texts when seeking the meaning of texts; in practice, this means turning away from the procedures of the historical-critical method. As the early exegetical work of Jüngel clearly demonstrates, with its focus on structural issues such as chiasm, parallelism, contrasts, and equivalents, this leads to a more structuralist reading of biblical texts.[4] There is, however, a significant difference, arising from the fact that hermeneutical theology ascribes a *referential meaning* to the texts' thus-ascertained structures of meaning: they refer to an underlying word-event to which they owe their existence and which manifests itself in them.[5] In contrast to structuralist approaches, hermeneutical theology represents a strictly realistic reading of the biblical texts. The texts do not simply unfold a universe of meaning; they also speak of a word-event that exists in reality, independent from them.

The major problem of the third step is that it combines literary hermeneutics (referring to texts) and theological hermeneutics (referring to the Word of God) in such a way that theological categories (law and gospel) become the categories of adequate textual interpretation. On the one hand, the structure of the subject matter of the text is thus transferred over to an appropriate engagement with the texts themselves. On the other hand, both the (divine) subject matter and the (human) texts that deal with it are construed as word-events. The texts are (human) word-events or the result of such events; the matter discussed in them is a (different, namely divine) word-event; and both word-events are thought to be linked in the meaning-dimension of the texts. But why should that which the text discusses have the same hermeneutical type and structure as the text itself? Why should the word-event model through which the text is understood

---

4. E. Jüngel, "Das Gesetz zwischen Adam und Christus. Eine theologische Studie zu Röm 5,12–21," in *Unterwegs zur Sache. Theologische Bemerkungen* (Munich: Kaiser, 1972), 145–72; Jüngel, "Ein paulinischer Chiasmus. Zum Verständnis der Vorstellung vom Gericht nach den Werken in Röm 2,2–11," in *Unterwegs zur Sache*, 173–78. See also his reconstruction of the Pauline doctrine of justification in *Paulus und Jesus* (Tübingen: Mohr Siebeck, 1967), 17–70, and the structural-semantic analysis of parallels by E. Güttgemanns, "'Gottesgerechtigkeit' und strukturale Semantik. Linguistische Analyse zu δικαιοσύνη θεοῦ," in Güttgemanns, *studia linguistica neotestamentica* (Munich: Kaiser, 1971), 59–98, 82ff.
5. On this issue, see M. Devitt and K. Sterelney, *Language and Reality: An Introduction to the Philosophy of Language* (Oxford: Blackwell, 1987), 215ff.

also apply to the subject matter of the text? Or looked at from the opposite angle: why should the theological understanding of this subject matter as law and gospel also provide the standards for an appropriate literary understanding of the text?

Finally, the main problem of the fourth step is that hermeneutical theology, in its doctrinal reconstruction of the divine word-event disclosed through hermeneutics of subject matter, operates with a model—(past) word-event, text, (present) word-event—that imputes the transtemporal identity of God's Word to the words. The eschatological word-event that manifests itself in the biblical texts and imprints itself within them repeats itself identically in different situations and at different points in history. But how is this possible? What do these different incidences of the divine word-event have in common?

5. Commonality in Diversity

Hermeneutical theology has essentially answered this question in three different ways.

The first answer refers to the *existential structure of our human situation*. For Bultmann, the divine word-event that takes place in the proclamation of the gospel also discloses common anthropological—or existential—fundamental structures of human existence in this world. It unmasks us as sinners in need of justification and proclaims faith in Jesus Christ and a life of love and hope made possible by faith as the fulfillment of the truth of human existence *coram deo*.

The second answer refers to the *structure of appropriation* of the divine word-event *within the hearer's or recipient's situation*. According to Ebeling, the human way of life possesses common structures of appropriation or ontological deep structures (the fundamental situation of humanity) into which the Word of God speaks directly. Under the central themes of law and gospel, in a life characterized by creatureliness and sin, these structures can be seen as the threefold *coram*-structures of human existence—before God, before the world, and before oneself—that shape every concrete situation of life as a fundamental existential situation.

The third answer concentrates on the *christological and pneumatological structures of the word-event itself*. What the different occurrences of the divine word-event have in common, according to Fuchs and Jüngel, is neither primarily the existential structures of those it addresses nor the structure of appropriation of the situation in which it occurs, but rather its christological content (Jesus Christ as the self-communicating love of God) and the pneumatological character of this occasion (the self-manifestation of Jesus Christ as God's love, by the Spirit, in the word of the gospel).

Each of these answers brings with it specific difficulties. Do the fundamental, anthropological possibilities of existence disclosed by the gospel, of which Bultmann speaks, really exist? What do they consist of? What exactly are the deep structures of our appropriation of existence to which Ebeling appeals? What theological significance do they have? And precisely what is the common christological content of the eschatological word-event, and how is it to be developed in theologically appropriate ways?

Furthermore, all three attempted answers are confronted with a common problem. They all understand the divine word-event in a personalist way, following the intentionalist paradigm, as God's action in words. God is the author (or speaker) of this word-event, then and now; this is the ultimate basis for claiming that the divine word-events, then and now, are identical. This fact has two significant theological implications.

First, despite its criticism of the so-called axiom of God's unchangeableness or apathy, all versions of hermeneutical theology uphold a strict theory of unchangeableness when it comes to God's saving intent and God's faithfulness. Only if this intent is unchanging—only if God is faithful—can it maintain its hermeneutical claim that the past and present divine word-events are identical.

Second, according to this personalist understanding, we can understand the divine word-event that is the theme of the biblical texts, that is propagated through proclamation, and that both precedes these texts and follows after them only if we understand the intention(s) of God that make(s) them what they are. The Christian conviction is that God has disclosed this intention in Jesus' life, death, and resurrection, disclosed it as God's saving will to draw all human beings, despite their sin, into a living fellowship of mutual love with God. Christology and soteriology, as formulations of this saving will of God, thus have a foundational theological function within hermeneutical theology. They are the standpoint from which both the biblical texts and our experience of the world is interpreted. Therefore, the fundamental task of hermeneutical theology must be, first of all, a coherent and conceptually consistent development of Christology and soteriology as the summation of the will of God revealed in Jesus Christ. It must also develop a coherent and conceptually consistent Pneumatology as the basis of its fundamental claim that Jesus Christ is, indeed, the eschatological word-event that fully and finally revealed God's saving intent.

6. The Theological Problem of the Category of Word-Event

No convincing solution is apparent for either of these tasks, and this is largely due to basic problems with the category of word-event when employed as the fundamental theological category. Within hermeneutical theology, this category serves as the fundamental concept for the formation of theological theories, a concept that is not amenable to explication by yet more basic concepts and is thus universally applicable. In the reconstruction of faith, this succeeds fairly well. It is less successful when it comes to interpreting our experience of reality in the light of faith. For example, no serious attempt was ever made to use this category for theologically interpreting the approach to the world disclosed by contemporary natural sciences, or to engage with these sciences in a relationship of constructive criticism. One would have expected that, however, if there was to be any serious talk of a more natural theology. There certainly have been numerous opportunities. Think only of how both fields clearly demonstrate a way of thinking that shifts the focus from substance to relationship, from being to becoming, and from reality to possibility. Or think of the hardly researched connections between the categories of *word-event* and *information*, both of which intrinsically mean epistemic and communicative events and each of which, as used in its contemporary context, tends to take the place of traditional ontological categories.

Because hermeneutical theology understands the category of word-event within the framework of a model of copresent, personal communication, it has not explored such issues more deeply. Despite what the term suggests, word-events are not understood theologically as something that happens on the model of empirical events. They are understood instead on the phenomenological model of occurrences. There are reasons for this. Events—in the empirical and historical sense—stand within a causal and temporal nexus of other events. This is the very reason Bultmann rejected the notion that salvation events could be localized as a special salvation history within the horizon of other events (even though it could not take place without such historical events). Furthermore, events (*Ereignisse*) are distinguished from actions (*Handlungen*) by the fact that events are determined by causality, not by intention or convention. It was assumed that word-events, in contrast, must be determined by divine intentions if they were to be capable of enlightening people about God's being and will. Now, there are two basic types of intention-guided activities: actions and speech-acts. In the first model, God is thought of as the *Original Actor* and the world as God's field of action (Pannenberg thinks along these lines). According to the second model, God is understood as the *Original Speaker* and the world is thought of as God's text (Ebeling thinks along these lines). Hermeneutical theology in essence opted for this second model. However, in binding its word-event category to the intentionalist framework of the speech-act model, and in conceiving the fundamental hermeneutical situation of faith as an asymmetrical interaction between the divine speaker and the human hearer, it created a series of nearly insurmountable problems for itself.

For one thing, it remained—at least with reference to Ebeling—trapped within a conception that understood God as a transcendent subject facing humankind, without ever interpreting this relationship of transcendence in any fundamental way through the category of word-event.[6] To be sure, God was interpreted as *deus revelatus* and *deus absconditus* in the light of the word-event perspective, differentiated as law and gospel. But God was not understood *as* word-event. Instead, within the framework of a doctrine of God focused on prayer, God was understood as that personal subject who, in contrast to us, enters into relationship with every human imaginable.[7] However, with this personal conception of God, what had been won hermeneutically at the level of understanding the Word of God was lost at the level of understanding God.

Furthermore, hermeneutical theology was not able to win from its hermeneutical approach any manageable hermeneutical method because the *prior* of this divine speaker's self-interpretation is beyond our grasp. This hermeneutical theory of the priority of self-interpretation before all interpretations by others is incapable of arbitrating any conflict of interpretations or of understandings, whether the conflict arises in the interpretation of Scripture or of experience. Thus, there is no way of discriminating, other than in some arbitrary way, between true and false interpretations of Scripture or true and false understandings of experience or of reality.[8] The *prior* of divine self-interpretation above all human interpretation remains an essential regulative idea, but it cannot be carried over into a hermeneutical method.

Finally—and these things go together—hermeneutical theology concentrated first and foremost on explicating the saving intent, as witnessed in Scripture, of the divine speaker who ordained all word-

---

6. R. Lorenz, *Die unvollendete Befreiung vom Nominalismus. Martin Luther und die Grenzen hermeneutischer Theologie bei Gerhard Ebeling* (Gütersloh: Gütersloher Verlagshaus, 1973), 342.
7. Ebeling, *Dogmatik des christlichen Glaubens I* (Tübingen: Mohr Siebeck, 1987), 224ff.
8. Cf. W. Schenk, "Hermeneutik III. Neues Testament," TRE 15 (1986): 144–50, 147–48, 145ff.; L. Danneberg and H.-H. Müller, "Wissenschaftstheorie, Hermeneutik, Literaturwissenschaft. Anmerkungen zu einem unterbliebenen und Beiträge zu einem künftigen Dialog über die Methodologie des Verstehens," *DVflG* 58 (1984): 177–237.

events and interpreted Godself in the events of revelation and faith. Little attention was given to developing the cosmological implications of this saving intent or to interpreting our experienced reality in its light. Hermeneutical theology thus failed to bring its view of the world—as created through the divine word that intends our well-being—into a fruitful relationship (that is, in an enlightening way) with the contemporary experience of the world and its scientific developments. If hermeneutical theology's contention that the reality of the world should be seen as a world-text created by the saving will of God is not to prove empty, it must also bring it to bear in the face of a world-reality that comes to experience in a totally different way. In other words, it must theologically locate the problems of evil and sin within cosmological (societal, political, cultural, scientific, and the like) dimensions. That it has not done so convincingly is one of the main reasons hermeneutical theology since the 1960s has been supplanted by other theological approaches with stronger social and ethical accents and is why the discussion of this theological approach has been silenced (as discussed above).[9]

The aporia of hermeneutical theology can be summarized in the following alternatives: Either (1) it represents a hermeneutical approach that, while theologically useful, does not truly set itself apart hermeneutically from other theological approaches that are in a position to provide clearer methodological conclusions and guidance. This is because it relies on the model it adopted from *the hermeneutics of copresent communication between persons* to address only the God-world or God-human relationships. Or (2) it represents an approach that is hermeneutically independent and does not proceed from the problems of interhuman communication, but then appears to be theologically

---

9. Among others representing this point of view, C. Gremmels and W. Herrmann, "Hermeneutik und Gesellschaftstheorie (Theologie, Hermeneutik und Gesellschaft)," in *Hermeneutik als Kriterium für Wissenschaftlichkeit? Der Standort der Hermeneutik im gegenwärtigen Wissenschaftskanon*, ed. U. Gerber (Loccum: Ev. Akademie Loccum, 1972), 48–65, speak explicitly of a "collapse of the hermeneutical text-model" (63ff). I have sketched how the task of a theological hermeneutics of evil might be undertaken in my book, *Malum. Theologische Hermeneutik des Bösen* (Tübingen: Mohr Siebeck, 2008). See also I. U. Dalferth, *Das Böse. Essay über die Denkform des Unbegreiflichen* (Tübingen: Mohr Siebeck, 2006); and Dalferth, *Leiden und Böses. Vom schwierigen Umgang mit Widersinnigem* (Leipzig: EVA, 2006).

unproductive since it is required to renounce a personal conception of the notion of God. It thus would not be capable of understanding the word-event between God and humankind according to the model of linguistic interaction between different persons. If this diagnosis is apt, there is hardly any reason to be surprised by the silencing of the discussion about hermeneutical theology and its theological hermeneutics. Insofar as this approach is theologically interesting, it offers no true hermeneutical alternatives; insofar as it might offer such alternatives, it presents more theological problems than it promises to solve.

8

Hermeneutical Theology as Radical Theology

The aporia stated at the end of the last chapter is not the final word about hermeneutical theology. There is a way out of the dilemma if hermeneutical theology remembers its roots and develops itself rigorously as a radical theology. Bear in mind that hermeneutical theology, as was mentioned at the beginning, is not a unified whole. While Bultmann's hermeneutical approach concentrated first on human understanding and self-understanding and then on the understanding of God that could be developed on that basis, hermeneutical theology after Bultmann had a different focus. Picking up themes from Barth and Luther, it focused first on divine understanding and self-understanding and only then on our understanding and interpretation of the divine, which is distorted and limited by sin. Moreover, its primary representatives, Ebeling and Jüngel, went about this task in markedly different ways. Put simply, Ebeling began from the standpoint of Luther and Schleiermacher as recovered and deepened by Bultmann, while attempting to also incorporate some of the insights of Barth. Jüngel, on the other hand, did just the opposite, incorporating insights of Bultmann, Schleiermacher, and Luther into a perspective largely derived from Barth.

1. Divergences in Hermeneutical Theology

The resulting divergences are substantial. I offer only a few examples. Ebeling sought the explanatory framework for theological hermeneutics in the doctrines of sin and conscience and, hence, in a theological anthropology.[1] In contrast, Jüngel sought his in Christology and, hence, in a Trinitarian doctrine of God.[2]

As a result, when it comes to theological method, Ebeling gave a place of privilege to the dialectic between God and God, and also between God and human, that comes to a head in the distinction between law and gospel.[3] He sought to recover valid points of analogy between God and humankind in this way.[4] Jüngel, meanwhile, set out in the opposite direction, beginning from the parallels specified in Christology between God and God and thus also between God and humankind, and then sketching the points of difference within them from the law-gospel dialectic.[5]

This shows up concretely, for example, in their anthropologies. In order to do justice to the dialectical tension of humanity between being sinners and creatures, Ebeling accorded a fundamental anthropological

---

1. G. Ebeling, "Wort Gottes und Hermeneutik," in *Wort und Glaube* (Tübingen: Mohr Siebeck, 1967), 348; Eberling, "Erwägungen zur Lehre vom Gesetz, Wort und Glaube," in *Wort und Glaube*, 255–93, 289–90; Eberling, "Elementare Besinnung auf verantwortliches Reden von Gott," in *Wort und Glaube*, 349–71, 364ff; "Weltliches Reden von Gott," in *Wort und Glaube*, 372–80, 374–75, 378–79; Eberling, "Glaube und Unglaube im Streit um die Wirklichkeit," in *Wort und Glaube*, 393–406, 404–5; Eberling, "Theologische Erwägungen über das Gewissen," in *Wort und Glaube*, 429–46, 429ff.; Eberling, "Das Problem des Bösen als Prüfstein der Anthropologie," *Wort und Glaube III* (Tübingen: Mohr Siebeck, 1975), 205–24.
2. E. Jüngel, *Gottes Sein ist im Werden. Verantwortliche Rede vom Sein Gottes bei Karl Barth. Eine Paraphrase*, 4th ed. (Tübingen: Mohr Siebeck, 1998), 12.15ff.
3. G. Ebeling, "Existenz zwischen Gott und Gott," in *Wort und Glaube II* (Tübingen: Mohr Siebeck, 1969), 257–86, 281ff.
4. G. Ebeling, "Karl Barths Ringen mit Luther," in *Lutherstudien III* (Tübingen: Mohr Siebeck, 1985), 428–573, esp. 540ff.
5. E. Jüngel, "Evangelium und Gesetz. Zugleich zum Verhältnis von Dogmatik und Ethik," in *Barth-Studien* (Gütersloh: Gütersloher Verlagshaus, 1982), 180–209; Jüngel, *Gott als Geheimnis der Welt. Zur Begründung der Theologie des Gekreuzigten im Streit zwischen Theismus und Atheismus* (Tübingen: Mohr Siebeck, 2001), 472ff., 509ff.

relevance to the dialectic of law and gospel.[6] In contrast, Jüngel accorded a comparable relevance to the parallels between God and humankind, as specified in Christology.[7]

Accordingly, when it comes to the doctrine of God, for Jüngel the doctrine of the Trinity functioned as the material foundation for theology as a whole, and for theological hermeneutics in particular, because it explored God's being as a being interpreting itself as itself for us.[8] For Ebeling, however, the doctrine of the Trinity presented the sum of appropriate discourse about God. It was the result of theological hermeneutics brought to definition, but it was not the factual basis of a theological hermeneutic of the Christian confession that God lives as love.[9]

The ontology implicit in all of this was similarly divergent. For Jüngel, this involved a transposition from the category of actuality to that of possibility, developed within the fundamental idea of correspondence, defined in christological and Trinitarian ways.[10] For Ebeling, however, it involved a transposition from the category of substance to that of relationship within the fundamental idea, shaped by the dialectic of law and gospel, of the threefold *coram* relationships of human existence: *coram deo, coram mundo,* and *coram seipso*.[11]

Finally, the hermeneutical projects advocated by the two theologians placed different accents on the notion of "experience with experience." Jüngel thought of experience as an interpretation of the world that could be and needed to be deepened as it was interpreted anew in light of the self-interpretation of God, while Ebeling always understood it as reality being interpreted in a certain way, an

---

6. G. Ebeling, *Luther. Einführung in sein Denken* (Tübingen: Mohr Siebeck, 1964), chs. 7–9.
7. E. Jüngel, "Der Gott entsprechende Mensch," in *Entsprechungen: Gott-Wahrheit-Mensch. Theologische Erörterungen* (Munich: Kaiser, 1980), 290–317, 304ff.
8. Jüngel, *Gottes Sein ist im Werden*, 14ff; Jüngel, *Gott als Geheimnis der Welt*, 19–25.
9. G. Ebeling, *Dogmatik des christlichen Glaubens III* (Tübingen: Mohr Siebeck, 1979), 42, 531ff., 540, 543ff.
10. E. Jüngel, "Die Welt als Möglichkeit und Wirklichkeit. Zum ontologischen Ansatz der Rechtfertigungslehre," in *Unterwegs zur Sache. Theologische Bemerkungen* (Munich: Kaiser, 1972), 206–33.
11. G. Ebeling, *Dogmatik des christlichen Glaubens I* (Tübingen: Mohr Siebeck, 1987), 14, 346ff.

interpretation that needed to be corrected and verified in the light of faith.[12]

2. Word-Event and Language-Event

Despite the divergences sketched here in broad strokes, there is also much in common. These commonalities have to do, first, with their focus on the hermeneutical model of language as an alternative to Bultmann's concentration on existence and history and, second, with their theological understanding of language as word-event (*Wortgeschehen*) or language-event (*Sprachereignis*).

Both terms point toward the creative activity of God's Word in concrete situations of life and are, therefore, *theological categories*. This is true even though they are closely linked to the shifting focus of linguistic philosophy and hermeneutics from *langue* and *langage* to *parole* as the starting point for reflection on language—that is, from a formal system of language or from linguistic capability in general to the concrete situatedness and specificity of human speech. Language, as Ebeling put it, is a "life-process" whose basic structure is, "I say something to you."[13] As we saw earlier, this is not merely the theological version of a pragmatic hermeneutics of reception, shifting the interest not just from the author to the text but also to the process of reading as a social institution—for biblical texts, therefore, to their reception by the church. The category of word-event (Ebeling) or of language-event (Fuchs and Jüngel) was never merely a linguistic category, never simply a shift from a semantic to a pragmatic conception of language. The category was understood as an appropriation and further development of Luther's understanding of the Word of God, Barth's treatment of the occurrence of the Word of God, Gogarten's dialectic of occurred and occurring revelation, and Heidegger's analysis of the event of existing Being as a way of clarifying

---

12. Jüngel, *Gott als Geheimnis der Welt*, 40ff., 381, 517-18. G. Ebeling, "Die Klage über das Erfahrungsdefizit der Theologie," in *Wort und Glaube III* (Tübingen: Mohr Siebeck, 1975), 3-28, 22-23; Ebeling, "Das Verständnis von Heil in säkularisierter Zeit," in *Wort und Glaube III*, 349-361, 357ff.
13. G. Ebeling, *Einführung in theologische Sprachlehre* (Tübingen. Mohr Siebeck, 1971), 195, 201.

Bultmann's category of salvation history. As such, it was primarily a theological category from the beginning, referring to the event of the Word of God in human life. It emphasized that our speaking is grounded in being spoken to, that our interpretation rests on being interpreted, and that our understanding is based on being understood by God.[14]

Similarly, the theological use of the category of word-event or language-event also implies a theological or christological understanding of language (for Fuchs and Jüngel) or a sacramental understanding of language (for Ebeling).[15] Language is "primordial language of God"; it is the form in which God's self-interpretation takes place within the medium of our being or, more precisely, within the medium of our interpretation of our being.[16] We participate in this event of linguistic self-interpretation through our own handling of language: either we contradict this self-interpretation event as a result of misunderstanding or a total failure to understand that is caused by sin, or we reflect it an agreement made possible by faith.

That is also the meaning of Fuchs's programmatic dictum, "Understanding is based in agreement," that is, in our affirmative understanding of the understanding of God and God's creation that has been disclosed to us by God.[17] True understanding is when we interpret and seek to understand God, the world, and ourselves as we, our world, and God have been interpreted and understood by God. Both Fuchs and Barth stressed that this was the genuine theological meaning of the hermeneutical circle.[18] Hence, Fuchs rightly insisted, against Bultmann, that his talk about a language-event not be trivialized.[19] Minimizing this topic would miss precisely the decisive

---

14. Ebeling, "Wort Gottes und Hermeneutik," 340ff.
15. E. Fuchs, *Hermeneutik* (Tübingen: Mohr Siebeck, 1970), 71–72, 78ff. Jüngel, *Gottes Sein ist im Werden*, 13n1. Ebeling, *Einführung in theologische Sprachlehre*, 53, 115, 210 passim.
16. E. Fuchs, "Das Christusverständnis bei Paulus und im Johannesevangelium," in *Jesus Christus. Das Christusverständnis im Wandel der Zeiten*, in Marburger Theologische Studien 1, ed. H. Grass and W. G. Kümmel (Marburg: N. G. Elwert, 1963), 11–20, 17.
17. E. Fuchs, *Marburger Hermeneutik* (Tübingen: Mohr Siebeck, 1968), 239.
18. E. Fuchs, "Kanon und Kerygma," in *Wagnis des Glaubens. Aufsätze und Vorträge*, ed. E. Grötzinger (Neukirchen: Neukirchener Verlag, 1979), 21–41, 38. K. Barth, *Rudolf Bultmann. Ein Versuch, ihn zu verstehen* (Zurich: Evangelischer Verlag, 1964), 60.
19. E. Fuchs, "Was ist ein Sprachereignis. Ein Brief," in *Zur Frage nach dem historischen Jesus* (Tübingen:

theological point of using this category: that our speaking is based in being spoken to, that our interpreting depends on being interpreted, and that our understanding is based on being understood by God. In short, for hermeneutical theology there is an intrinsic and indissoluble connection, one that cannot be ignored, between what it terms a word-event or language-event on one side and God and the Word of God on the other.[20]

Hence, even in our handling of texts, the decisive hermeneutical question is not how *we* (can) interpret them, but rather how *they*, through this process, interpret *us*. In our handling of texts, what is disclosed about ourselves?

Accordingly, hermeneutical theology does not concentrate simply on the spoken word as such, but on the word-event that illuminates human existence and reveals its truth. The authentic meaning of a text is this existence-illuminating function, not simply the different possible readings that a text offers. In theological terms, existence-illuminating means clarifying the reader's or hearer's concrete situation *coram deo*, thus elucidating his or her existence as a sinner or a justified sinner.

The key hermeneutical distinction of hermeneutical theology is neither the distinction between authorial intent and the text's meaning, nor that between the text's meaning and the reading of the text, but rather that between the *authentic* and the *inauthentic meaning* of a text. Does a text, in concrete practice, become a word-event that discloses to human beings an understanding of self, world, and God in which all are understood as they in truth—that is, *coram deo*—are? The primacy of this theological point is shown by Ebeling's efforts to use the category of word-event to elucidate the *fundamental situation* of humankind before God, not simply one or another of the many life-situations of human beings with one another. It is demonstrated also

---

Mohr Siebeck, 1960), 424ff; Fuchs, *Glaube und Erfahrung. Zum christologischen Problem im Neuen Testament* (Tübingen: Mohr Siebeck, 1965), 4–5; Fuchs, "Alte und neue Hermeneutik," in *Gesammelte Aufsätze III*, 193–230, 212; Fuchs, "Antwort auf die amerikanischen Beiträge," in *Die neue Hermeneutik*, ed. J. M. Robinson and J. B. Cobb (Zurich: Zwingli, 1965), 299–311, 300.

20. Ebeling, "Wort Gottes und Hermeneutik," 340ff.

in Jüngel's insistence that a language-event's surplus of meaning is not simply semantic but ontological, that it truly opens up more and different possibilities than had already been present in the actuality at hand.

3. Hermeneutics of God's Word

Both Ebeling and Jüngel sought a theological understanding of the impact of God's Word in human life. For Ebeling, this entailed examining the actual fundamental situation of human life *coram deo*, and exploring this situation in terms of relational ontology through use of the three *coram* relationships (*coram deo, coram mundo*, and *coram seipso*). Jüngel concentrated on the creative event that constituted the situation as one of always-new possibilities of life. Starting from this constitutive event, he explored the human self-understanding, world-understanding, and God-understanding that makes a human being who he or she is. Despite these significant differences in their lines of investigation, both the ontology of actuality found in Ebeling's hermeneutics of faith and the ontology of possibility found in Jüngel's hermeneutics of God had to do, at their core, with understanding the life-giving impact of God's Word in the lives of human beings.

In both approaches, the hermeneutical theory did not determine the understanding of the understanding of God. Instead, the understanding of the understanding of God determined the hermeneutical theory. In this sense, "hermeneutics in theology [is] nothing other than the 'doctrine of the Word of God' (G. Ebeling) or the grammar of faith."[21] The metaphor of God's word is thus not understood metaphysically but existentially and ontologically (Ebeling) or in christological and Trinitarian ways (Jüngel). For Ebeling, God's word, "seen in its character as word is totally normal, let us say it calmly, a natural, oral word taking place between two people." The difference between God's word and human words only becomes apparent "if the word-event among humans is a misused and corrupted

---

21. E. Fuchs, "Was ist existentiale Interpretation?," in *Zum hermeneutischen Problem in der Theologie. Die existentiale Interpretation* (Tübingen: Mohr Siebeck, 1959), 107–15, 115.

word-event or one that is healthy, pure and fulfilled," if it is "a corrupting and killing word or a healing and life-giving word."[22] According to Ebeling, the proper function of human language is to disclose the truth of our existence with one another. This is brought about by the divine Word "that makes humans human by making them people of faith."[23] Ebeling can therefore describe human existence as a word-event "that has its origin in the Word of God and, by responding to this Word, makes space for the correct and healthy use of words."[24] He sees our language as a "response to" and a "variegated echo of the inquiry of God"; he sees our world, that is, "the reality approaching us, coming as it always does in language," as "the call and inquiry of God even when not understood."[25] Everything that is, what we are and what we say, owes its existence to the primordial word-event in which God opened a conversation with us and ever opens it anew. Just as our language is based in word-events, these word-events are based in the event of God's Word in creation, revelation, and redemption; this event, in turn, is grounded in God, who is the original word-event, the structure of which is summed up in the doctrine of the Trinity.

4. Theological Event-Hermeneutics

It is just this point, however, that Ebeling and Jüngel understand in markedly different ways. Both set out from the occurrence (*Sichereignen*) of God in the event of God's Word, in which God makes Godself present as God in and through the processes of human communication. Ebeling, however, develops this communicative divine event by means of a hermeneutics of works; Jüngel, in contrast, by a hermeneutics of events.

For Jüngel, God is the foundational event, the event that makes itself understandable to others as God and, in so doing, allows others to exist at all. This foundational event unfolds in Trinitarian fashion. As a self-interpreting event having the structure "something interprets

---

22. Ebeling, "Wort Gottes und Hermeneutik," 341.
23. Ibid., 344.
24. Ibid., 343.
25. G. Ebeling, *Das Wesen des christlichen Glaubens* (Tübingen: Mohr Siebeck, 1959), 255.

itself through another thing as something understandable for others (or for itself)," God is the mystery of the world, without which the development of a self-understanding human subjectivity would not be possible. This structure is the basis for the reality, even the possibility, of an understanding subjectivity, but it does not, in itself, explain the human capability of symbolizing the reality disclosed in experience. World-experience is not based on self-experience, although it would not be possible without self-experience: "That 'I experience' must be able to accompany all my experiencing." Instead, both world-experience and self-experience are made possible by an experience of the God who communicates Godself, an experience that, in fact, constitutes its recipients, making them capable not only of experience (creation) but also of an "experience with experience" (new creation).[26] Only from this point of view are they able to distinguish, in a theologically relevant way, between self (*homo iustificandus*) and world (creation).

From this perspective, the metaphor that reality begins to speak takes on concrete meaning. It is not just the symbolic apprehension of reality, through subjects' acts of construal and interpretation, that possesses the hermeneutical structures of interpretation and understanding. The reality thus construed and interpreted also possesses those structures itself. Whenever we construe reality, we construe something that has already been construed. Reality is the creaturely manifestation of the unfathomable and inexhaustible self-interpretation of God, who makes Godself understandable for others by interpreting Godself for others as God interprets Godself for God. God interprets Godself in *creation*, which God shapes as the sum of the means God uses to communicate God's self-interpretation to humankind. And God interprets Godself in *Jesus Christ*, where God uses very specific created means (the human Jesus, the history of Israel) to make Godself understandable as God truly is, even for those who know nothing of God and who have no desire to understand themselves and their world on the basis of God.

---

26. See E. Jüngel, *Erfahrungen mit der Erfahrung. Unterwegs bemerkt* (Stuttgart: Radius, 2008), 9–10.

This hermeneutics-of-events perspective, as developed by Jüngel, has two significant consequences. First, not only does the world have meaning, but it always has more meaning than we could ever grasp. In contrast to modernity's resignation to the fact that the complexity of our world is always greater than the most complex thoughts we could ever think, this view means that the world, in all its actuality and possibility, is always more understandable than we have yet understood.[27] Thus, all our efforts toward a better understanding of self and world are, in principle, justified.

Second, even God is understood, fundamentally, as an event of self-interpretation, an event that cannot be traced back to anything else and cannot be understood better in any other way. God is the unfathomable and inexhaustible *making-self-understandable-as-itself-through-something-different* that makes it possible for others to understand themselves. Since this event of divine self-interpretation, as such, is an event of truth (because God simply cannot make Godself known in any other way than as God truly is), this event also creates the possibility for others to understand themselves as they truly are, in light of this event of divine self-interpretation. God is, therefore, not to be thought of within the categories of person, subject, or actor, but rather in the category of event; more precisely, in that of the making-Godself-understandable-as-God truth-event or *speech-event*. There is no going behind this necessary, or even more-than-necessary, self-interpreting reality. Instead, there is only an ever-deeper probing into its inexhaustible mystery, a mystery generating ever new possibilities, a mystery that is not at all beyond understanding but instead is an open and self-disclosing mystery.

5. Hermeneutics of Divine Subjectivity

Ebeling places the accent elsewhere. In his hermeneutics-of-works perspective, he does not take a self-interpreting foundational event as his theological starting point. Instead, as a matter of principle, he

---

27. D. Henrich, *Fluchtlinien. Philosophische Essays* (Frankfurt am Main: Suhrkamp, 1982), 125ff.

links the understanding that correlates with self-interpretation back to the understanding subject: *whenever something becomes understandable, there has to be someone for whom it becomes understandable.* Thus, the self-interpretation of individual word-events is linked to the understanding of finite, creaturely subjects. In contrast, the self-interpretation of the process of reality as a whole is linked to the understanding of God.

This has two consequences. On the one hand, it says that the primordial word-event, which is God's own self, is also the primordial act of understanding. The task, therefore, of human understanding in our interpretive dealing with the world and with ourselves is to reflect this divine understanding and to emulate it to the best of our creaturely abilities. That the world, including ourselves, is always more understandable than we have yet understood is based on the fact that God has already understood it and us better than we can. It is not that reality interprets itself for us, but rather that *God* interprets Godself, the world, and ourselves for us. Reality is nothing other than this divine event of interpretation. Self-interpretation and understanding are thus, in the strictest and truest sense, predicates of God, and it is God, in and through all the activities of interpretation and self-interpretation, who helps us to a true understanding of self, world, and God.

On the other hand, this means that God, in the end, is thought of very traditionally, as an acting subject who intentionally interprets Godself for us as God. God is not understood as the original word-event, whose structure of meaning is truly fundamental in the sense that it owes its existence to no intention standing behind it, not even to a divine intention, but rather makes persons and intentions possible in the first place. Instead, God is understood in personal terms, as the original speaker who interprets Godself in God's Word, thus making God's intentions regarding God and God's creation known.

Because Ebeling understands word-events in a works-hermeneutics perspective, he sees them as determined by divine intentions. Otherwise, they could shed no light for us about God's being and will. He accepts the aporia in order to link the word-event model, from a theological perspective, back to a model of personal speech. In fact, he links it to a speech model of copresent communication between subjects or persons ("I say something to you") that threatens to remove it entirely from the category of word-event. Accordingly, Ebeling's version of hermeneutical theology remains tied to an image of God that understands God as a transcendent subject encountering humankind.[28] The hermeneutical insight into God's Word as word-event thus bears no fruit when it comes to the understanding of God itself.

6. Hermeneutical Theology Today?

The insights and problems of hermeneutical theology coalesce around its understanding of God. This is what determines how everything else—the world, humanity, life, Scripture, faith, and church—will be understood. Such a focus on the understanding of God is crucial for any serious theology. For hermeneutical theology, however, this means that its focus is on an understanding of God as a symbolic event within human life disclosing itself as God: God is understood as the fundamental event through which God concretely interprets Godself as God within the symbolic processes of the world. It is thus that God becomes understandable, rather than something that cannot be understood.

Nevertheless, hermeneutical theology today must explore new paths if it wants to make a useful contribution to contemporary debates, from the neurobiology of religious experience and the multimedia construction of our reality through to the future of the church in Europe and other parts of the world.[29] As a form of Protestant theology, hermeneutical theology, even today, cannot dispense with a concentration on understanding the work of the Word of God as Reformation theology did. Still, this fundamental orientation can be

---

28. R. Lorenz, *Die unvollendete Befreiung vom Nominalismus. Martin Luther und die Grenzen hermeneutischer Theologie bei Gerhard Ebeling* (Gütersloh: Gütersloher Verlagshaus, 1973), 342.
29. Cf. M. Petzold, "Die Theologie des Wortes im Zeitalter der neuen Medien," in *Hermeneutik und Ästhetik. Die Theologie des Wortes im multimedialen Zeitalter*, ed. U. H. J. Körtner (Neukirchen-Vluyn: Neukirchener Verlag, 2001), 57–97; B. Beuscher, "WinWord. Die Sprachlichkeit des Evangeliums und das Nadelöhr der Medien. Eine semiotische Orientierungsskizze," in Körtner, *Hermeneutik und Ästhetik*, 98–133.

more productively developed within an event-hermeneutical perspective than within a works-hermeneutical or subject-hermeneutical approach. This perspective understands God as a self-interpreting foundational event that brings a world into being, by means of which it can make (and in specific symbolic events contingently does make) itself understandable for others through others as God. It is just this that allows these others and their world to ceaselessly and continuously become more than they have ever been before. This God, as the creative reality of the possibility of all possibilities, exists eternally as the basis of all worldly reality and goes unfathomably far beyond it.

Such an understanding of the understanding of God, which proceeds from God's ever-greater understandability in the face of all that is not understandable, makes hermeneutical theology today not only possible, but also necessary. To explore what this might entail, let us return for a closer examination of a period that played a decisive role in the prehistory of hermeneutical theology, to those few years of the brief, but intense and momentous, encounter between Bultmann and Heidegger in Marburg.[30]

---

30. Cf. A. Großmann, "Zwischen Phänomenologie und Theologie: Heideggers, Marburger Religionsgespräch' mit Rudolf Bultmann," *Zeitschrift für Theologie und Kirche* 95 (1998): 37–62.

9

Radicalizing Modernity

1. Live Forward, Understand Backward

When Georg Wünsch was asked to write the article "Heidegger" for the second edition of the encyclopedia *Die Religion in Geschichte und Gegenwart*, he turned to Rudolf Bultmann for advice. On December 29, 1927, Bultmann wrote to Heidegger about this project. Two days later, Heidegger responded:

> I find the article on 'H.' rather amusing, since I am just beginning to crawl. Other than as a list of motifs that have been, so to speak, pulled together, the matter would be hard to present. Regarding content, all one could say is that my work aims at radicalizing ancient ontology while at the same time seeking a universal development of that ontology for the field of history. These issues are based in correctly understanding "subject" as the "human being" so that this approach, along with the radicalization, gives the genuine motifs of German Idealism their due. Augustine, Luther, and Kierkegaard are philosophically important for developing a radical understanding of Being, while Dilthey is important for the interpretation of the "historical world." Aristotle and scholasticism is significant for the strict formulation of certain ontological problems. All of that lies within a methodology guided by the idea of a scientific philosophy, as established by Husserl. The investigations of Heinrich Rickert and Emil Lask regarding logic and theoretical science are also not without influence. My work

has neither ideological nor theological intentions. To be sure, there are approaches and aims within it that offer an ontological foundation for Christian theology as a scholarly discipline.[1]

Heidegger here, characteristically, describes his philosophical intentions as a *radicalizing* of ancient ontology and as the quest for a *radical* understanding of Being, building on Augustine, Luther, and Kierkegaard. But he also concludes the sketch of his philosophical development with the topic that had especially moved the two friends during their time together in Marburg: critically clarifying the self-understanding of Christian theology as a scholarly discipline. On this issue, the theologian, five years older than his colleague, had an interest every bit as intense as that of the philosopher who had been teaching at Marburg since 1923. For the former, of course, it had to do with the particular characteristics of theology; for the latter, with philosophy. In the critical conversations between the two during the 1920s, a concept begins to appear that I call "radical theology." This designation is not a term they used, but it does pick up Heidegger's terminology of radicalism from the 1920s.[2] In what follows, the concept of theology that is intended by this designation will be explored further through an analysis of Bultmann's approach and the way it was developed within hermeneutical theology. Such engagement with the thought of Heidegger and Bultmann would be pure monument-polishing, and thus no task for the intellect, if it were only about looking backward and not about striding forward.

1. "Martin Heidegger an Rudolf Bultmann, 31. 12. 1927," in R. Bultmann and M. Heidegger, *Rudolf Bultmann, Martin Heidegger, Briefwechsel 1925-1975*, ed. A. Großmann and C. Landmesser, intro. Eberhard Jüngel (Frankfurt am Main: V. Klostermann; Tübingen: Mohr Siebeck, 2009), 47–49, 47–48. O. Pöggeler, *Philosophie und hermeneutische Theologie. Heidegger, Bultmann und die Folgen* (Munich: W. Fink, 2009), offers a historically reliable presentation, rich in examples and biographical details from the available sources, both of Heidegger's path toward his proposal of a hermeneutical phenomenology in the 1920s and of the continuing influence of his philosophy on the development of hermeneutical theology. However, Pöggeler is more interested in the general relationship between philosophy and theology, and in the topic of "theology as hermeneutics" (294ff.), which he presents in doxographic detail, than in a hermeneutical theology of the sort defined at the beginning, a hermeneutical theology whose intensification might lead to a radical alternative to conventional theologies.
2. It is, therefore, *not* to be understood in the sense of the *radical theology* of the 1960s and its echoes up through the present, which advocated exactly the opposite concept, a "God-is-dead" theology focused totally on the issues raised by modernity.

They both would agree. One can only understand life backward, but it must always be lived forward, as they both had learned from Kierkegaard.[3] Looking backward offers orientation for life, and orientation is necessary if one is to move forward.[4] There is usually not much to see ahead of us; therefore, we must take our bearings by looking back toward things of the past, as they appear in the present, in the light of what is to come.

This is not always possible. Not everything that was is still important today. It is not the past, per se, that calls for understanding. Instead, what is coming requires us to understand the past—not everything about it, but much; not once and for all, but ever again; and not as a repetition of the old, but as an advance toward the new. Anyone who lives with awareness, guided by an orientation toward life, must come to grips with the past, even though the past can never be understood completely and can be understood only by each person appropriating it in his or her own way.

The driving force in all of this is only partly one's own wants and interests. Why do we want what we want? Why are our interests interesting? The answer, in many important cases, is that one simply cannot do otherwise. This is not because it is inherently impossible; it is because one cannot escape the necessity of understanding the past if one seeks to live with awareness in the face of what is happening in the present. One cannot live with awareness exclusively in the present, even if one wanted to. It is not possible because there is no present without a relationship to the past and to the future, and there is no Being in time without the present being determined anew, over and over again. Anyone wanting to escape from understanding the past loses both access to the present and a critical glimpse of the future. Not everything that might happen in the future is desirable and worth seeking. Without taking our bearings backward, we cannot live forward toward a goal. The past, however, can never be understood

---

3. S. Kierkegaard, *Die Tagebücher*, vol. 1 (Düsseldorf: Eugen Diederichs Verlag, 1962), 318 (IV A 164).
4. It is not life, as such, that is intrinsically hermeneutical, but the life-orientation. It is only because there is no conscious process of life without such a life-orientation that one can and must speak of life having hermeneutical structure.

with finality. It must always be understood afresh, so long as one is living forward. Whatever comes alters our perspective on the past and, hence, our view of the present. As a result, anyone who does not understand things in repeatedly new ways actually understands little at all.

Even Bultmann and Heidegger cannot be understood unless we think differently today, in light of what is approaching us, about how they attempted to think in their time. Hermeneutically, there is no direct way back to them; there is only the effort to think—with them or against them—about what is called for today theologically and philosophically.

2. Radical versus Modern Theology

Among the important themes, now as well as then, is their shared conviction that the end of modernity required something more than a modern theology: a completely radical theology instead. The time had run out for a theology that dressed itself in modernity, that thought to avoid quarrels about God by withdrawing to the supposedly less controversial field of religion(s), and that, in the contest for supremacy with religious studies, pursued a crafty both/and strategy as it sought to cater to the scholarly developments of the era. From our current point of view, we might add that there was even less need for a postmodern theology that derives its raison d'être above all else from negating the fundamental approach of modern theology.[5] To put it trenchantly, in order to secure the equality of everybody, modernism tended—despite (or perhaps because of) its insight into the sociohistoric individualization of all aspects of life in modern society—to subordinate every individual to concepts and thus to make the individual into a particular of some generality or commonality. Postmodernism—which developed alongside modernism, not simply after it—did just the opposite. With equal one-sidedness, it emphasized difference instead of identity and commonality in order to guard the

---

5. Cf. K. J. Vanhoozer, ed., *The Cambridge Companion to Postmodern Theology* (Cambridge: Cambridge University Press, 2003).

otherness of the other (and, simultaneously, one's own uniqueness), and it supported, against the generalizing and unifying tendencies of modernism, the individual's right to difference, peculiarity, eccentricity, contrariness, and otherness. In the name of autonomous self-determination, the theology of modernism abandoned recourse to God as a heteronomous determination by others. God was replaced by the softer and less offensive topic of religion. Since postmodernism could or can imagine "God" only as the threatening and violent figure of the monotheistic lawgiver, it calls for converting theology to a description of the undemanding variety of gods that human beings create out of their own desires or their boredom with life. It calls also for replacing what was once known as religion with the variety of spiritualities, which everyone is free to explore or not, according to their own needs and preferences. European modernism, in its efforts to secure the common good in the name of justice, equality, and solidarity, tended to make everything individual into a particular of something general. The protest of postmodernism, in the name of the freedom and creativity of the individual, claimed both the right to be different from the common and the necessity of plurality in the face of all the powers of unification. The ways they mirror one another are obvious.

Both would be left behind, therefore, when Heidegger and Bultmann, in their different ways, proposed a *radical theology* that recognized, in the face of both modernism and its postmodern countermovement, that the "path by way of religion" leads to a dead end, both methodologically and substantively, when it is pluralized and individualized in a postmodern manner as the path by way of the variety of spiritualities.[6] This is true not only because the term *religion*,

---

6. C.-D. Osthövener, "Weltvertrauen und Gottvertrauen. Theologische Bemerkungen zu dem humanen Phänomen des Vertrauens," in *Phänomenologie und Theologie*, ed. Th. Söding and K. Held (Freiburg: Herder, 2009), 106–20, 112. Just how closely modernism and postmodernism approach one another theologically, when seen from this point of view, is demonstrated by A. v. Scheliha, "Dogmatik, "ihre Zeit in Gedanken gefasst"? Die dogmatische Aufgabe zwischen historischer Kritik und christologischer Gegenwartsdeutung." In *Systematische Theologie heute. Zur Selbstverständigung einer Disziplin*. Edited by Hermann Deuser, and Dietrich Korsch. Gütersloh: Gütersloher Verlagshaus 2004, 60–84. It is no surprise that the "dogmatic self-description of modern Christianity," seen from this perspective, shrinks to "reformulating the religious ideas of

under the pressure of critical differentiation, threatens to dissolve into either nothing or everything (which also applies to the term spirituality) but also because what is theologically at stake is an either/or without compromise.[7]

This is the exact opposite of what has been said about theology again and again up to the present. For example, according to Wilhelm Gräb, theology in the modern era must be conducted as the hermeneutics of religion if it is not to be diverted into charismatic irrationality or religious fundamentalism, and this presupposes "the transformation of biblical theology into a theology of religion."[8] This approach sets out from the "religious relationship of humanity," which, however, is not "accessible other than in its cultural and symbolic forms."[9] For "religion is to be found wherever humans relate to the experiences of transcendence or the in-breaking of contingency by interpreting them."[10] To interpret these interpretations is what Gräb holds to be the business of theology. However, such an approach blurs the distinction not only between aesthetic experience and religious experience but

---

Christianity in light of their historical impact and of their yet-unfulfilled existential relevance" (82). Instead of an eschatological event radically changing the world, which sheds a new light on everything, Christian faith is belittled as the ensemble of religious ideas belonging to an evaporating handful of free Protestants, who can put these ideas to use, as needed, in the project of their individual "identity-management." But we no longer live in the late nineteenth century. What may have sounded advanced at that time, now, in the twenty-first century, sounds at best like a belated and tinkling echo from a time long past.

7. Cf. J. Waardenburg, *Religionen und Religion*, new ed. (Berlin: de Gruyter, 1996); K. Hock, *Einführung in die Religionswissenschaft* (Darmstadt: WBG, 2002); Tand, Fitzgerald, *The Ideology of Religious Studies* (Oxford: Oxford University Press, 2000).
8. W. Gräb, "Massenmedien—Religion—Hermeneutik," in *Hermeneutik der Religion*, ed. I. U. Dalferth and P. Stoeggler (Tübingen: Mohr Siebeck, 2007), 215–29, 215. From the extensive literature on this hermeneutics of religion school of thought within modern Protestantism, see also C. Albrecht, *Historische Kulturwissenschaft neuzeitlicher Christentumspraxis. Klassische Protestantismustheorien in ihrer Bedeutung für das Selbstverständnis der Praktischen Theologie* (Tübingen: Mohr Siebeck, 2000); C. Danz, *Gott und die menschliche Freiheit. Studien zum Gottesbegriff in der Neuzeit* (Neukirchen-Vluyn: Neukirchener Verlag, 2005); Danz, *Wirken Gottes. Zur Geschichte eines theologischen Grundbegriffs* (Neukirchen-Vluyn: Neukirchener Verlag, 2007), esp. 167–217; J. Lauster, *Religion als Lebensdeutung. Theologische Hermeneutik heute* (Darmstadt: Wissenschaftliche Buchgesellschaft, 2005); I. Mädler, *Transfigurationen. Materielle Kultur in praktisch-theologischer Perspektive* (Gütersloh: Gütersloher Verlagshaus, 2006); and W. Gräb and B. Weyel, eds., *Handbuch Praktische Theologie* (Gütersloh: Gütersloher Verlagshaus, 2007). Gräb, "Massenmedien," 216.
9. Ibid. 216–17.
10. Ibid., 217. Cf. U. Barth, "Was ist Religion? Sinndeutung zwischen Erfahrung und Letztbegründung," in *Religion in der Moderne* (Tübingen: Mohr Siebeck, 2003), 3–27; and U. Barth, "Theoriedimensionen des Religionsbegriffs. Die Binnenrelevanz der sogenannten Außenperspektive," in *Religion in der Moderne*, 29–87.

also between theology and the philosophy of religion or the hermeneutics of religion.[11] What is of interest here are not the distinctions, but the commonalities. In a similar way, one hears from the Catholic side that "theology's capability for communication and dialog today" requires "not only an emphasis on protecting the distinction between theology and philosophy, but also a constructively critical conversation with contemporary philosophical thinking, especially where—as in the philosophy of Emmanuel Levinas, for example—Biblical tradition is given a voice."[12]

There are certainly reasons to engage theologically with Levinas and with other schools of thought in contemporary philosophy and theology.[13] But exactly why dialogue with positions that deign to give biblical thought a right to speak should be a special credential for "theology's capability for communication and dialog" remains a puzzle. It leads one to suspect that we are dealing here with an understanding of philosophy and theology from which both Heidegger and Bultmann, with good reason, distanced themselves. The question is not if theology should enter into conversation with philosophy. The questions instead are these: From what theological positions and with what sort of self-understanding does theology seek such a conversation? Does it understand itself as one version of the social-scientific study of religion, competing on the same field as religious studies, hermeneutics of religion, and philosophy of religion? Or does it present itself as *theo*-logy, which finds its central themes in the topic of God, not in the question of religion? That the two must be systematically distinguished was an emphasis, after the First World War, not only for Heidegger, Bultmann, Barth, and Gogarten, but also for Tillich, even though he made the distinction somewhat differently. For Tillich, theology's shift from focusing on God to focusing on

---

11. Gräb, "Massenmedien," 219f.
12. H. H. Henrix, Review of *Das Wort wurde messianischer Mensch. Die Theologie Karl Barths und die Theologie des Johannesprologs* by Jochen Denker, *Theologische Revue* 105 (2009): 223–27, here 227.
13. Cf. L. B. Puntel, *Sein und Gott—ein systematischer Ansatz in Auseinandersetzung mit M. Heidegger, É. Lévinas und J.-L. Marion* (Tübingen: Mohr Siebeck, 2010).

religion was highly problematic; he summarized his concerns about such focus on religion in four objections:

> 1. It makes the certainty of God relative to the certainty of "I." 2. It makes God relative to the world. 3. It makes religion relative to culture. 4. It makes revelation relative to the history of religions. In short, this approach makes the unconditional contingent upon the conditional; it itself becomes conditional, that is, is being destroyed.[14]

In the 1920s, there was a parting of the ways in German-language Protestant theology over the question of whether *God* or *religion* should be the focus of its attention. This split was not only between, on the one hand, the dialectical theologies of Barth, Thurneysen, or Brunner with their emphasis on the Word of God and, on the other, the tradition of a theology of culture such as that of Troeltsch, which advocated a modern theology guided by the history of religions; it was also between modern theology in this sense and the radical theology of Marburg.[15] As Claus-Dieter Osthövener puts it, "Modern theology," which is an approach that remains widespread within German Protestant theology, travels "the path by way of religion. It discusses religion as a human form of life, as a form of the human conception of self and the world, while linking this discussion to the fundamental symbolic worlds of the Christian tradition, within which the idea of God plays a very important role."[16] God thus becomes a secondary theme of religion and, as such, a "project of reason"—a necessary implication of religious self-consciousness as Ulrich Barth, following in the steps

---

14. P. Tillich, "Die Überwindung des Religionsbegriffs in der Religionsphilosophie (1922)," in *Main Works = Hauptwerke*, vol. 4 (Berlin: de Gruyter, 1987), 73–90, 74. It is enlightening to compare Tillich's view of modern developments in theology and the philosophy of religion with the reconstruction offered by E. Jüngel in *God as the Mystery of the World: On the Foundation of the Theology of the Crucified One in the Dispute between Theism and Atheism*, trans. Darell L. Guder (Eugene, OR: Wipf & Stock, 2009).
15. On dialectical theologies, cf. H. G. Göckeritz, ed., *Friedrich Gogartens Briefwechsel mit Karl Barth, Eduard Thurneysen und Emil Brunner*, intro. H. G. Göckeritz (Tübingen: Mohr Siebeck, 2009), especially the detailed introduction, "Zwei Wege zwischen den Zeiten" 1–145. D. Korsch, *Dialektische Theologie nach Karl Barth* (Tübingen: Mohr Siebeck, 1996), also addresses the issue in constructive fashion.
16. Cf. W. Schluchter and W. Graf, eds., *Asketischer Protestantismus und der "Geist" des modernen Kapitalismus* (Tübingen: Mohr Siebeck, 2005). C.-D. Osthövener, "Weltvertrauen und Gottvertrauen. Theologische Bemerkungen zu dem humanen Phänomen des Vertrauens," in *Phänomenologie und Theologie*, ed. Th. Söding and K. Held (Freiburg: Herder, 2009), 106–20, 112.

of Fichte and Schleiermacher, argues.[17] But with this type of modern theology, one does not escape the objections of traditional and contemporary criticism of religion, as Osthövener knows.[18] Instead, theology takes on the additional difficulty of distinguishing itself in some theological way from the inquiry into the symbolic worlds of religions in the humanistic and scientific study of religion and the "human conception of self and the world" expressed therein. In fact, one cannot seriously expect any clear distinction between theology and the humanistic or scientific study of religion from this approach. Accordingly, such an engagement with religious studies in its various disciplines and forms takes the shape of either (a) the self-withdrawal of theology to become merely a special branch of religious studies, the study of Christianity, or (b) a bidding war in which modern theology seeks to present itself as a better theory of Christianity or as a better form of religious and cultural studies altogether.

An attempt to overcome the aporetic alternative between a cultural-hermeneutical theology of religion and a dialectical theology of the Word of God has been proposed by Dietrich Korsch, taking as its key idea an understanding of interpretation based in a theory of subjectivity.[19] According to Korsch, the specific contribution of religious formation in a culture consists in radicalizing the distinction "between oneself and the ground which carries all interpretations" by "inquiring about this ground of interpretation, and thereby also putting into question the styles of interpretation that are to be distinguished esthetically."[20] For all its sensibilities for differences, however, this leads us again into a uniformly conceptualized comprehensive scheme that completely levels the distinction between the old life and the new, epistemologically, ontologically, and theologically. Human life takes place through acts of interpretation, and all acts of interpretation take the "steadfast connection of humans

---

17. U. Barth, *Gott als Projekt der Vernunft* (Tübingen: Mohr Siebeck, 2005).
18. Cf. Osthövener, "Weltvertrauen," 108–9.
19. D. Korsch, *Religionsbegriff und Gottesglaube. Dialektische Theologie als Hermeneutik der Religion* (Tübingen: Mohr Siebeck, 2005).
20. Ibid., 317.

with God ... into account," a connection that is defined theologically as the dialectical "compatibility of God and humanity as an interconnection of free self-determination."[21] However, when the dialectic of divine and human freedom is defined in this way, everything rests on free self-determination in a relationship of reciprocity. This ascribes equal priority to the interpretive activity of both parties and their active self-formation through self-determination. It fails to acknowledge, on the human side, the always more basic passivity that corresponds to the primordial creative in-breaking of the other and the new, an in-breaking that means something fundamentally new has begun, not just the continuation of former things. If dialectic is to be employed here, it must be conceived in such a way that the continuity and unity of the freely self-determining God does not necessarily imply a corresponding continuity and unity on the part of the freely self-determining human. Instead, it must allow us to think of radical *discontinuities* between the old life and the new. It is not dialectic, but paradox, that is the language of a theology that takes such discontinuities seriously, that does not paint over the far-reaching differences with a gloss of continuity, synthesis, and unity, as modern theology with its orientation to religion tends to do.[22]

3. Working Radically Outward from the Most Extreme Position

Heidegger did just the opposite. "The only way we can shake things up is if we work radically starting from the most extreme positions," he implored Bultmann in 1927. The most extreme positions are never those of a philosophical theology of culture or a theological philosophy of culture intent on mediation. These are far more likely to represent the aporias of the philosophy and theology of modernity, as Kierkegaard had already pointed out in his untiring criticism of Hegel's world-historical synthesis of things that are not synthesizable.[23] These

---

21. Ibid., 326, 327.
22. On th point of paradox rather than dialectic, Milbank is to be agreed with, over against Zizek. See S. Zizek and J. Milbank, *The Monstrosity of Christ: Paradox or Dialectic?* (Cambridge, MA: MIT Press, 2009).

aporia, as Heidegger clearly saw, could only be overcome by radical thinking from extreme positions.

While this was not Bultmann's terminology, in substance he shared the same opinion. To be sure, he largely avoided the terminology of radicalism adopted by Heidegger, who campaigned "for the formation of a radical understanding of Being" and a "radicalization" of the understanding of subjectivity in German Idealism, who sought a "radical conception of metaphysics," and so forth.[24] But Bultmann made his turn toward radical theology clear, as was more his way, in *content*. A prime example is his essay "The Concept of Revelation in the New Testament," which he originally wanted to publish together with Heidegger's lecture "Phenomenology and Philosophy."[25] After the withdrawal of that lecture, Bultmann decided to let his essay "go its own way."[26] Only a theology that reflects on revelation without compromise, he clearly argued, is truly theology. Revelation, however, is an event, the act of God valid *for me* and *directed to me*, which can "not be ascertained through historical observation," but only explored through faith, through risky response to the "address of ordinary humans to us."[27] Only a theology that is practiced in radical fashion is capable of reflecting on these matters, a theology clearly scholarly in its methods but in subject matter devoted totally to faith, faith that is "no human posture of the soul, no human conviction, but instead a response to being addressed."[28]

Philosophically, Bultmann was in full agreement with Heidegger that the Marburg neo-Kantianism offered no helpful perspective.[29]

---

23. Cf. S. Kierkegaard, *Philosophische Brocken. De omnibus dubitandum est*, trans. E. Hirsch, *Gesammelte Werke*, vol. 10 (Düsseldorf: Eugen Diederichs Verlag, 1960); Kierkegaard, *Abschliessende Unwissenschaftliche Nachschrift*, in *Gesammelte Werke*, vol. 16 (Gütersloh: Gütersloher Verlagshaus, 1982).
24. Bultmann and Heidegger, *Briefwechsel*, 48, 62.
25. R. Bultmann, "Der Begriff der Offenbarung im Neuen Testament," in *Glauben und Verstehen III* (Tübingen: Mohr Siebeck, 1960), 1–34.
26. Bultmann and Heidegger, *Briefwechsel* 82.
27. Bultmann, "Begriff der Offenbarung," 31.
28. Ibid. The generation of Bultmann's students also used the terminology of radicalism in this sense. See G. Ebeling, *Das Wesen des christlichen Glaubens* (Tübingen: Mohr Siebeck, 1961), passim.
29. On this point, see the work of M. Steinmann, *Die Offenheit des Sinns. Untersuchungen zu Sprache und Logik bei Martin Heidegger* (Tübingen: Mohr Siebeck, 2008), which stems from the DFG research project "Heidegger und der Neukantianismus," and my review thereof in *ThLZ* 134 (2009): 739–42.

Theologically, he also agreed with him that, as Heidegger wrote, "for the smoldering problems . . . even Barth [is] too light-weight an opponent."[30] Theology and philosophy could only do justice to their present tasks if, instead of thinking modernly or dogmatically, they thought radically and extremely—that is, neither falling behind the modern nor accommodating themselves to modernity, but keeping a critical distance from the zeitgeist, never hesitating to test the furthest limits of the thinkable and the sayable, in order to protect the worldliness of the world and the divinity of God. At those furthest limits, where the terminology and the classifications of the particular and the general led no further, limiting concepts and creative metaphors provided the points of orientation from which a new light might be shed on everything.

On this point, nothing has changed. Theology that is not radical but modern makes itself superfluous—and most quickly when it tries to be radically modern. Such a theology offers little to guide the way to the future. That is equally true of a theology that only engages the issues of modernity dogmatically with its evangelical alternative, or thinks it can avoid modernity altogether by retreating to a premodern *radical orthodoxy*.

What Heidegger and Bultmann set in motion during the 1920s in Marburg was something different. Alongside everything else that was begun in that decade, it forms a unique path that cannot be overlooked,

30. Bultmann and Heidegger, *Briefwechsel*, 25. Cf. the note Heidegger had already addressed to K. Löwith two years earlier, on August 24, 1925, about the intellectual situation at that time: "What still shows 'signs of life' is the Barth-Gogarten movement, which in Marburg is represented, carefully and independently, by Bultmann" (cited by Pöggeler, *Philosophie*, 210). At much the same time, however, he also stressed Bultmann's differences from Barthianism and Kierkegaardianism, from whose "fanfare," which was "gradually [becoming] terrifying," Bultmann did well to keep his distance (Letter to Löwith of July 30, 1925, see Pöggeler *Philosophie*, 210). He also stressed his own distance from theology: he would appear "in a very bad light as a philosopher" if he was defined by the position taken in his lecture, "Phenomenology and Theology" (M. Heidegger and E. Blochmann, *Briefwechsel 1918-1969* [Marbach am Neckar: Deutsche Schillergesellschaft, 1989], 24). "As a philosopher he had to show how philosophy related to the arts, to the sciences and to religion, but to religion in general, not just to Christian religion and theology" (Pöggeler, *Philosophie*, 57). That is the reason he did not want to publish this lecture together with Bultmann (Bultmann and Heidegger, *Briefwechsel*, 60.70) and why he consistently declined, as a philosopher, to contribute to the *Theologische Rundschau*. If he "appeared to be a co-editor of the *Theologische Rundschau*," it would only encouarge an "unclear blending of theology and philosophy" (Bultmann and Heidegger, *Briefwechsel*, 63). Nonetheless, although he never contributed a paper, he was listed from 1928 until 1944 as a staff member of the *Theologische Rundschau*.

one that is worth pursuing if we want to find our theological bearings today. So what is this radical thinking that they embarked on? What does the radical theology they developed look like? And what from this approach is relevant for the present and offers guidance for the future?

4. Radical Hermeneutics and Radical Theology

The early Heidegger's emphasis on radicalism is well-known and a repeated topic for his interpreters.[31] John Caputo has pursued this path with particular diligence. From the beginning, however, his interest in Heidegger was directed primarily to the question of Heidegger's closeness to mysticism and to mystical thought.[32] Heidegger owed his own project of a "radical hermeneutics" both to critiques of the Western metaphysics of presence and, above all, to a bias for the concrete processes of life, derived from the hermeneutics of facticity.[33] For Caputo, radical hermeneutics is "an attempt to stick with the original difficulty of life, and not to betray it with metaphysics."[34] "It is a radical thinking which is suspicious of the easy way out, which is especially suspicious that philosophy, which is meta-physics, is always doing just that.... Hermeneutics wants to describe the fix we are in,

---

31. Cf. J. Salis, "Radical Phenomenology and Fundamental Ontology," *Research in Phenomenology* 6 (1976): 139–50, and especially the extensive works of J. Caputo: "The Question of Being and Transcendental Phenomenology: Heidegger's Relationship to Husserl," *Research in Phenomenology* 7 (1977): 84–105; *Heidegger and Aquinas: An Essay on Overcoming Metaphysics* (New York: Fordham University Press, 1982); *Radical Hermeneutics: Repetition, Deconstruction, and the Hermeneutic Project* (Bloomington: Indiana University Press, 1987); *Demythologizing Heidegger* (Bloomington: Indiana University Press, 1993); *The Prayers and Tears of Jacques Derrida: Religion without Religion* (Bloomington: Indiana University Press, 1997); *More Radical Hermeneutics: On Not Knowing Who We Are* (Bloomington: Indiana University Press, 2000); *On Religion* (London: Routledge, 2001); *Philosophy and Theology* (Nashville, TN: Abingdon, 2006; *The Weakness of God: A Theology of the Event* (Bloomington: Indiana University Press, 2006); and *What Would Jesus Deconstruct? The Good News of Postmodernism for the Church* (Ada, MI: Baker Academic, 2007); as well as the volume he edited with G. Vattimo, *After the Death of God* (New York: Columbia University Press, 2007).
32. Cf. J. Caputo, *The Mystical Element in Heidegger's Thought*, rev. ed. (New York: Fordham University Press, 1986); and Caputo, *Heidegger and Aquinas*, esp. chs. 1, 2, and 8.
33. Caputo follows Derrida's sharpening of Heidegger's thesis: "The present is never present" (J. Derrida, *Dissemination* [Vienna: Passagen Verlag, 1995], 340), and does so for hermeneutical reasons, as D. Mersch, *Was sich zeigt. Materialität, Präsenz, Ereignis* (Munich: Wilhelm Fink Verlag, 2002), 367, precisely states: "Every labeling of an event 'as' event or of presence 'as' presence has already been divided by the as-structure and thus pushed away from itself; such 'signage' ... chronically arrives too late." See also J. Derrida, *Eine gewisse unmögliche Möglichkeit, vom Ereignis zu sprechen* (Berlin: Merve, 2003).
34. Caputo, *Radical Hermeneutics*, 1.

and it tries to be hard-hearted and to work 'from below.' It makes no claim to have won a transcendental high ground or to have a heavenly informer."[35]

It is not surprising that a radical hermeneutics approached in this way supports the traditions of negative theology, calls for an "Openness to the Mystery," and emphasizes the traditions of a "weak theology" and the "weakness of God."[36] That is not what I am about. Despite great sympathy for Caputo's project of a radical hermeneutics, I am not talking about radical hermeneutics but about *radical theology*. This radical theology is not erected on the foundation of a radical hermeneutics of being and thus does not end up, theologically, in a celebration of negative theology, the mystical tradition, and weak thinking. It is not about a postmodern and antimetaphysically motivated religious radicalization and mystical deepening of everyday life-experience, such as pursued by Caputo. Instead, it is about a radical change of standpoint and viewpoint, one that pulls everything—the everyday and the scholarly, the orthodox and the mystical, the weak and the strong, the philosophical and theological traditions—in a new direction and into a fundamentally different way of looking at things. It is not the mystical deepening of human life-experience that stands hermeneutically at the center of this project. Instead, it is a radical *theological* interpretation of the "experience with experience" that is characteristic of the life-process of Christian faith. The designation "radical theology," rather than "radical hermeneutics," has thus been chosen quite intentionally.

For some time, Caputo has been employing this same term more frequently. However, what he understands it to mean is

> the theological tradition that ensued after Hegel, down to the most lively among contemporary Hegelians, Slavoj Zizek, and his radical readings of Christianity. By radical theology I mean the tradition launched by Hegel's critique of classical "transcendence" as abstract and one-sided, as a form of "alienation" or "estrangement" in which the human spirit fails to

---

35. Ibid., 3.
36. Ibid., 268–94. Caputo, *The Weakness of God*, esp. ch. 4, "Omnipotence, Unconditionality, and the Weak Force of God."

recognize itself. . . . In radical theology, religion is not about a gift from a being outside the world and it does not have to do with supernatural forces or with interventions here below by a divine being from the sky. It is instead a way of speaking about the unfolding life of the creative human spirit, and about the world itself, in which the divine life is actualized or actually worked out. In its most radical form, the name of God is finally translated ("without remainder") into the world so that to understand "culture" or the "secular" we need to understand the "religion" of which it is the translation or repetition. The name of "God" in "religion" has become an "immanent," "secular" or "cultural" formation, with the result perhaps that in the end we need to displace oppositions like religious/secular and transcendent/immanent.[37]

Thus, radical theology is here understood fully within the tradition of the "radical theology" or "God is dead" theology of the 1960s (Vahanian, Altizer)[38] with its roots in Meister Eckhard and Hegel, and its current revival by Nancy,[39] Vattimo,[40] Deleuze,[41] and Zizek.[42]

In contrast, I understand "radical theology" neither as an antimodernist, orthodox glorification of premodernism (*radical orthodoxy*: Milbank) nor as a mystical deepening (through a hermeneutics of negation) of a secular perspective that is religiously deficient and tends to ignore the mystical dimension of life (*radical hermeneutics*: Caputo). I use the term to mean a radical shift in theological perspective, which differs from other perspectives not just in degree but in principle because it takes its orientation from the key distinction between God and the other (the world) that is based on the self-appearance of the presence of God. In this light, all inner-

---

37. "Radical Theology From Hegel to Zizek," Fall 2009, http://religion.syr.edu/caputo.html.
38. Cf. G. Vahanian, *The Death of God: The Culture of Our Post-Christian Era* (New York: George Braziller, 1961); Vahanian, *Wait without Idols* (New York: George Braziller, 1964); P. van Buren, *The Secular Meaning of the Gospel: Based on an Analysis of Its Language* (New York: Macmillan, 1963); T. Altizer and W. Hamilton, eds., *Radical Theology and the Death of God* (Harmondsworth: Penguin, 1968); Altizer, *The Gospel of Christian Atheism* (Philadelphia: Westminster, 1966); Altizer, *The Contemporary Jesus* (Albany: State University of New York Press, 1997); J. W. Montgomery, *The "Is God Dead?" Controversy* (Grand Rapids, MI: Zondervan, 1966); J. B. Cobb, ed., *The Theology of Altizer: Critique and Response* (Philadelphia: Westminster, 1970); and D. Cupitt, *Radical Theology Selected Essays* (Santa Rosa, CA: Polebridge, 2006).
39. J.-L. Nancy, *La déclosion*, Déconstruction du christianism 1 (Paris: La Cebra, 2005).
40. G. Vattimo, *Jenseits vom Subjekt*, ed. Peter Engelmann (Graz: Böhlau, 2005); G. Vattimo and R. Rorty, *Die Zukunft der Religion*, ed. S. Zabala (Frankfurt am Main: Suhrkamp, 2006).
41. Cf. P. Hallward, *Out of this World: Deleuze and the Philosophy of Creation* (London: Verso, 2006).
42. S. Zizek, *The Parallax View* (Cambridge, MA: MIT Press, 2006); Zizek and Milbank, *The Monstrosity of Christ*.

worldly differences become relative when compared to the genuine difference between worldly reality and divine creativity. Accordingly, the significant differences for life-orientation are not the distinction between secular and religious, but those between faith on one side and religion or religiosity on the other, between God on one side and infinitude (mysticism) or finitude (naturalism) on the other, and between secularity on one side and secularism or religious fundamentalism on the other. Secular life in this world is not somehow too little, so that it needs to be deepened in some mystical or religious way. Instead, it is *coram deo*, with or without religion, all that we have.[43] This life lacks nothing that is to be found primarily in a mystical deepening. Instead, it is precisely within this secular life that God becomes present as God and makes Godself understandable for us as fortuitous goodness, fully unexpected and fully undeserved.[44] The secularity of the world does not need to be religiously criticized or mystically corrected, but instead to be taken seriously by theology and understood appropriately. This secularity appears as both a consequence of faith and a challenge to faith. It is the fundamental character of the factual, historical life-experience where God discloses Godself to human beings as God so that they might understand themselves as God's creation and acknowledge God as their creator.

---

43. Cf. I. U. Dalferth, "Post-secular Society: Christianity and the Dialectics of the Secular," *Journal of the American Academy of Religion* 78 (2010): 317–45.
44. Cf. I. U. Dalferth, "Alles umsonst. Zur Kunst des Schenkens und den Grenzen der Gabe," in *Von der Ursprünglichkeit der Gabe. Jean-Luc Marios Phänomenologie in der Diskussion*, ed. M. Gabel/H. Joas (Freiburg: Alber, 2007), 159–91.

10

Phenomenology and Theology

1. Radical Thinking

In the very first semester of Heidegger's five years of teaching in Marburg, in 1923, he participated in Bultmann's seminar on the ethics of Paul. What began as a working relationship soon led to friendship. When Heidegger left for Freiburg in 1928, the two agreed to address each other using the informal *Du* rather than the formal *Sie*. Despite all the reciprocal fruitfulness of their relationship, the theologian clearly was and remained a theologian while the philosopher was and remained a philosopher. Bultmann did not understand philosophy simply as the handmaiden of theology, nor did Heidegger attempt to subsume theology within philosophy. Those were outmoded ways of thinking that, although advocating the essential unity and correlation between philosophy and theology, always displeased both. Now the differences held central attention, and this was what bound them together.

An objection often heard in support of idealistic schemes of unity is that one could only speak of differences if the difference grows out of some identifiable commonality: without an assumed commonality, there is no difference. As a general rule, this is false. There are empirical differences (such as between *mice* and *men*) that can only be explained against the backdrop of some categorical communality. There are categorical differences (such as between *objects* and *propositions*) that only make sense against the backdrop of a system of categories. And there are transcendental differences (such as between *one*, *good*, and *true*) that presuppose the distinction between categorical and transcendental determinations. Thus, it is true that a difference is always a difference *with respect to something*, but the respect in which one differs from another is not necessarily something both have in common. A difference between A and B does not in general assume a C that both share in the same way. As we know from the doctrine of analogy, just as A may be to C so B may be to C', and C and C' do not need to share a univocal commonality. Moreover, in the case of minds, persons, or cultural phenomena, A and B can also differentiate themselves from one another by recognizing a distinction between them and acknowledging the other as other. This is more than the mere construal of the other from my perspective: to safeguard her irreducible alterity, I must understand her to be different and to understand herself differently from how I understand her, and the same applies to her view of me. We cannot do this without symbolizing the other from our perspective, but we must do it in a way that allows for a difference in principle between her view of me and my view of myself, and my view of her and her view of herself. This is only possible if on both sides of the distinction the reference to the other as other is somehow present: I must understand myself *as distinct from the other*, and the other must understand himself or herself *as distinct from me*. But—and this is important here—we need not acknowledge something in common with respect to that point on which we differ.

This is precisely how Heidegger understood the relationship between philosophy and theology during those years. On March 29, 1927, he wrote to Bultmann:

> The only way to change things is by working radically from the most extreme positions. You from the theological side, positively and

ontically—although the ontological by no means disappears, but is treated in an unsystematic way and appears only with question marks—I from the philosophical side, ontologically and critically—although the ontic in the sense of the positivity of the Christian remains unsystematic and has its own question marks. To play around in the middle, without a firm foothold either here or there and without any concrete or comprehensive knowledge, results, at best, in confusion.[1]

The compound confusions of philosophy-theology were a horror not only for Bultmann, but also for Heidegger. They were both united in "protest against a murky mixture of theology and philosophy."[2]

2. Against the Mixing of Theology and Philosophy

Heidegger's letter should be read in the context of a lecture that he first gave in 1926 or 1927 in the *Kränzchen* in Marburg and then presented publicly on July 9, 1927, in Tübingen and on February 2, 1928, in Marburg. It was first published in French in 1969 and in German in 1970 under the title, *Phänomenologie und Theologie*.[3] Bultmann, however, was aware of it from the beginning; it mirrors, even in phrasing, his reflections on theology as a positive science, which appeared in the lectures he gave about theological encyclopedias starting in 1926.[4]

Despite Bultmann's entreaties, Heidegger did not publish this

---

1. This last remark may have been directed toward "Brunner, Grisebach and Tillich" with whom, Heidegger complained, he was often "thrown into the same kettle." Rudolph Bultmann and Martin Heidegger, *Rudolf Bultmann, Martin Heidegger, Briefwechsel 1925-1975* (Frankfurt am Main: V. Klostermann; Tübingen: Mohr Siebeck, 2009), 63-64. Bultmann confirmed this when, in a letter to Heidegger from October 10, 1928, he referred to "people like Tillich, Brunner and Lohnmeyer" who "are counted as philosophically knowledgeable theologians" or who like "Griesebach baffle the mind" because they propagate precisely the "unclear blend of theology and philosophy" that Heidegger opposed (Bultmann and Heidegger, *Briefwechsel*, 71).
2. Bultmann 29.10.1928, in Bultmann and Heidegger, *Briefwechsel*, 71.
3. M. Heidegger, *Phenomenology and* Theology, trans. James. G. Hart and John C. Maraldo, in *The Piety of Thinking: Essays by Martin Heidegger* (Bloomington: Indiana University Press, 1976), 5-21. The issue treated therein—the relationship between ontology and ontic being—was first addressed publicly by Heidegger's student, K. Löwith, "Phänomenologische Ontologie und protestantische Theologie," *ZThK* NF 11 (1930): 365-99 (reprinted in *Heidegger und die Theologie. Beginn und Fortgang der Diskussion*, ed. G. Noller (Munich: Kaiser, 1967), 95-124; O. Pöggeler, ed., *Heidegger. Perspektiven zur Deutung seines Werkes* (Königstein: Kiepenheuer & Witsch, 1984), 54-77. See also M. Jung, *Das Denken des Seins und der Glaube an Gott. Zum Verhältnis von Philosophie und Theologie bei M. Heidegger* (Würzburg: Königshausen & Neumann, 1990), 171-78; and T. Kleffmann, "Systematische Theologie—zwischen Philosophie und historischer Wissenschaft. Eine Auseinandersetzung mit Martin Heidegger," *NZSTh* 46 (2004), 207-25, esp. 217-25.
4. R. Bultmann, *Theologische Enzyklopädie*, ed. E. Jüngel and K. W. Müller (Tübingen: Mohr Siebeck, 1984). Cf. E. Jüngel, "Glauben und Verstehen. Zum Theologiebegriff Rudolf Bultmanns," in *Wertlose*

lecture. As he explained to Bultmann in a letter dated October 23, 1928, Heidegger had already that year in Freiburg come to the conclusion that in this lecture the boundaries between philosophy and theology "are not yet, in principle, sharply enough drawn. What still lacks sufficient treatment is the character of theology, which does, in a certain formal way, resemble philosophy, as it also deals with the whole, but onticly." Radically understood, however, "philosophy as ontology, on the whole, has a totally different ontic nature from a positive science."[5] This then had the consequence, as he wrote in a later letter to Bultmann, dated December 18, 1928, that "the problem of 'Philosophy and Science'" must be "thought through in completely new ways." And, he added, it had in the meantime become clear to him that his "posing of the questions in the lecture . . . in regard to theology as a science [was] not only too narrow, but unsustainable." The "positivism of theology, which I do believe to have captured, is somewhat different from those of the sciences. Theology stands apart from the sciences in an entirely different way than philosophy does."[6] When the lecture was finally published in Germany in 1970, Heidegger included with it a letter from March 3, 1964, that in many details, such as its view of the role of language, set different accents. And he dedicated the publication to Rudolf Bultmann "with friendly thoughts of the Marburg years from 1923 to 1928."[7]

In critical respects, Heidegger's primary concern in this lecture was to speak out against "the muddling of the borderlines between phenomenology and theology" by defining their relationship in such a way that the differences were maintained.[8] According to Heidegger, there could no more be a phenomenological theology than there could be a "phenomenological mathematics."[9] "Phenomenology is always

---

Wahrheit, Zur Identität und Relevanz des christlichen Glaubens. Theologische Erörterungen III (Munich: Kaiser, 1990), 31–36.
5. Heidegger, 23.10.1928, in Bultmann and Heidegger, *Briefwechsel*, 62.
6. Heidegger, 18.12.1928, in Bultmann and Heidegger, *Briefwechsel*, 87.
7. M. Heidegger, *Phänomenologie und Theologie* (Frankfurt am Main: Klostermann, 1970), 5.
8. M. Heidegger, *Sein und Zeit* (Tübingen: Max Niemeyer, 1967), 272 (410 in Stambaugh translation), as criticism of the work of H. G. Stoker, *Das Gewissen. Erscheinungsformen und Theorien* (Bonn: F. Cohen, 1925).
9. Heidegger, *Phenomenology and Theology*, 21 (*Phänomenologie und Theologie*, 32).

nothing other than the designation for the methods of ontology," and thus of philosophy. According to Heidegger's discussion in *Sein und Zeit*, the task of phenomenology was to "let what shows itself be seen from itself, just as it shows itself from itself."[10] However, what phenomenology in this sense was to let "be seen" was something "that does *not* show itself initially and for the most part, something that is *concealed*, in contrast to what initially and for the most part does show itself. But at the same time it is something that essentially belongs to what initially and for the most part shows itself."[11] "As far as content goes," according to Heidegger, "phenomenology is the science of the being of beings—ontology" and thus precisely not a science of this or that kind of being, such as "'theology' and the like."[12] Thus, there was a fundamental difference between theology and philosophy.

In his lecture "Phenomenology and Theology," Heidegger expressed this fundamental difference in the following thesis: "*Theology is a positive science, and as such, is absolutely different from philosophy.*"[13] Philosophy is an "ontological science," and as such precisely phenomenology, because it is "the founding disclosure . . . of Being"—the being of whatever is.[14] Theology, on the other hand, is an ontic or positive science, inasmuch as it "is the founding disclosure of whatever is given and in some way already disclosed."[15] This "given *positum*" for theology is not "Christianity as something that has come about historically, witnessed by the history of religion and culture and presently visible through its institutions, cults, communities, and groups as a widespread phenomenon in world history" because

---

10. Heidegger, *Sein und Zeit*, 34 (Stambaugh trans., 30).
11. Ibid., 35 (Stambaugh trans., 31).
12. Ibid., 37 (Stambaugh trans., 33); ibid., 34 (Stambaugh trans., 30).
13. Heidegger, *Phenomenology and Theology*, 6 (*Phänomenologie und Theologie*, 15). On the relationship of philosophy and theology in Heidegger's thought, see G. Noller, ed., *Heidegger und die Theologie. Beginn und Fortgang der Diskussion* (Munich: Kaiser, 1967); A. Gethmann-Seifert, *Das Verhältnis von Philosophie und Theologie im Denken Martin Heideggers* (Freiburg: K. Alber, 1974); A. Jaeger, *Gott. Nochmals Martin Heidegger* (Tübingen: Mohr Siebeck, 1978); J. D. Caputo, "Heidegger and Theology," in *The Cambridge Companion to Heidegger*, ed. Charles Guignon (Cambridge: Cambridge University Press, 1993), 270–88; P. Brkic, *Martin Heidegger und die Theologie. Ein Thema in dreifacher Fragestellung* (Mainz: Matthias-Grünewald-Verlag, 1994); and P. Capelle, *Philosophie et Théologie dans la pensée de Martin Heidegger* (Paris: Cerf, 2001).
14. Heidegger, *Phenomenology and Theology*, 6.
15. Ibid., 8.

theology itself "belongs to the history of Christianity" thus understood.[16] What "is given for theology (its *positum*)" according to Heidegger is rather "Christianness"—that is, "a mode of human existence which . . . arises not from Dasein or spontaneously through Dasein, but rather from that which is revealed in and with this mode of existence, from what is believed."[17] For Christian faith, this is "Christ, the crucified God."[18] Insofar as theology is directed toward this "given," it has a historical event as its field of concern: the "crucifixion" (with reference to Jesus) and faith in the crucified one (with reference to Christians).[19] As a "'part-taking' and 'having-part in' the event of the crucifixion, which is realized only in existence," such faith "is *given* only through faith," and thus is divine gift rather than human deed.[20] This gift is the event that "places one's entire human existence . . . before God."[21] The "existence struck by this revelation becomes aware of its forgetfulness of God. Thus . . . being placed before God means that existence is reoriented in and through the mercy of God grasped in faith."[22] Such reorientation or conversion takes place as a transformation of existence from "forgetfulness of God" to trusting in God, to "*the believing-understanding mode of existing in the history revealed, i.e., occurring, with the Crucified.*"[23] Inasmuch as the topic of theology is this transformation of existence, where existence means *existing* and "existing entails action, *praxis*," theology is not only "to the very core an historical science" but, as such, also "*in its essence . . . a practical science*," and thus "a unique sort of historical science in accord with the unique historicity involved in faith": the science of "the action of God on faith-full men."[24]

Now, God's action on humans is no more a "phenomenon" than Godself—however one may understand the term *phenomenon*.[25] All that

---

16. Ibid., 7–8.
17. Ibid., 9.
18. Ibid.
19. Ibid.
20. Ibid., 10.
21. Ibid.
22. Ibid.
23. Ibid..
24. Ibid., 14, 12, 14, 12, 14.

is perceptible as phenomena are faithful existence's "'part-taking' and 'having part in'" the "event which is revelation (= what is revealed) itself" that is the "occurrence of revelation" whose existential "appropriation" Christian faith is.[26] Insofar as theology considers this faith to be its object of study, it addresses the *modes of faithful existence in the practice of faith*. Echoing Kierkegaard, Heidegger characterizes this as a *process of appropriation*: the appropriation of revelation "which co-constitutes the Christian occurrence, that is, the mode of existence which specifies a factual Dasein's Christianness as a particular form of historicity."[27] However, that which is appropriated in faith and consummated in existence is something that is given, accessible, and understandable only by participating in this process of appropriation: "The occurrence of revelation, which is passed down to faith and which accordingly occurs through faithfulness itself, discloses itself only to faith" and occurs only as a reorientation of existence from self-centered "forgetfulness of God" to an openness to God lived in faith.[28] Theology, accordingly, is directed toward a "phenomenon" that is given only in the very enactment of *its practice* and *for those who practice it, even though*, as "God's action," it is at the same time not being

25. Cf. G. van der Leeuw, *Phänomenologie der Religion* (Tübingen: Mohr Siebeck, 1970): "We can consider religion as an ... understandable experience; or we can accept it as a no-longer-understandable revelation. An experience ... is a phenomenon. A revelation is not" (778). "Here we depart from the realm of appearances and inner experience. Faith does not show itself to us"(610). "With faith, a totally new element makes its entrance into religious life. Strictly speaking, it does not 'enter into' this life. In that case, it would be a phenomenon. Instead, it refers to life, first of all, as a judgment about that life, and then as its liberation" (610). "In religion, God is the agent in relation to humankind, and science can only speak of the actions of humans in relation to God; it has nothing to say about the actions of God" (3). Cf. M. Moxter, "Die Phänomene der Phänomenologie," in *Religion als Phänomen. Sozialwissenschaftliche, theologische und philosophische Erkundungen in der Lebenswelt*, ed. W.-E. Failing, H.-G. Heimbrock, and T. A. Lotz (Berlin: de Gruyter, 2001), 85–95.
26. Heidegger, *Phenomenology and Theology*, 10.
27. Ibid.
28. Ibid. Heidegger's argument here is completely aligned with Bultmann's. "Revelation is an event that destroys death," but, just like eternal life, it is *not a phenomenon of this life*." R. Bultmann, "Der Begriff der Offenbarung im Neuen Testament," in *Glauben und Verstehen III* (Tübingen: Mohr Siebeck, 1960), 15. It is "an event not *inside* human life, but comes *from outside* and therefore cannot be ascertained within human life" (15). It is not a "fact of the world" but instead "an act of God" (30). "It cannot," therefore "be discovered through historical observation" (31). It is understood only by faith, which, for its part, is "act, but never something acted" (30), is "no human inclination of the soul, no human conviction, but rather an answer to that address" (31) in which revelation comes to speech for me as the promise of the love of God. Even faith is thus not a phenomenon of life, but revelation, "because it exists only in this event and not otherwise" (31). Heidegger, *Phenomenology and Theology*, 10.

constituted by the faithful "I," thus escaping phenomenological reduction in Husserl's sense.

A phenomenological alternative appears in the later Heidegger's efforts toward a "phenomenology of the inconspicuous."[29] Even these attempts, however, do not alter the fact that the presence or absence of God as such is not manifested as a phenomenon, but only by means of other phenomena. It is thus always and only mediated through and by means of something else. That something else, however, *is* not a sign of God's presence or absence; rather, it *becomes* such a sign only when the phenomena in question are perceived within an appropriate horizon, and thus from a specific point of view, so that they can be understood, either concurrently or retrospectively, as something whereby the presence of God makes itself evident in, with, or through them. The theological distinction between the standpoint of faith and that of unfaith (as judged from the point of view of faith) is found precisely here. The standpoint of faith does not stand ready as a freely choosable option but can only be attained against the prevailing normality of unfaith. On the part of those without faith, this cannot happen through their own desire. On the part of those with faith, it no longer needs to happen because their point of view already presupposes this change. They are the first, however, to recognize that they can take no credit for this change but can only thank the one to whom their faith is directed: God. Thus they confess their faith: neither I myself nor any other human is to be given credit; God alone is to be thanked. Therefore, it is theologically correct to say that this altered point of view can be brought about by God alone, the one who is the exclusive object of faith. Faith is attached only to the one to whom it owes its existence. Thus, the point of view and the horizon that allow us to talk sensibly at all regarding the presence or absence of God is to be understood theologically as a shift of orientation, from unfaith to

---

29. Cf. M. Heidegger, *Seminar in Zähringen, Vier Seminare*, ed. C. Ochwaldt (Frankfurt am Main: V. Klostermann, 1977). To this may be added various proposals such as D. Janicaud, *La phénoménologie éclatée* (Combas: L'Eclat, 1997); Janicaud, *Le tournant théologique de la phénoménologie française* (Combas: L'Eclat, 1991); S. W. Laylcock and J. G. Hart, eds., *Essays in Phenomenological Theology* (Albany: State University of New York Press, 1986); and C. Welz, *Love's Transcendence and the Problem of Theodicy* (Tübingen: Mohr Siebeck, 2008), esp. 57ff.

faith, that is made possible and brought about by Godself. Accordingly, speaking of a "phenomenology of the inconspicuous" becomes meaningful not in the sense of something "inconspicuous" appearing in addition to or alongside the phenomena of normal life. Instead, it is just the opposite: from the newly won point of view, the phenomena of life can be opened up and understood afresh as signs of God's presence or absence.[30]

3. Enactment-Sense as Phenomenological Key

In emphasizing the enactment character of faith, Heidegger reached back to a methodological distinction made in his lecture "Introduction to the Phenomenology of Religion," given in the winter semester of 1920–1921, a distinction between the content-sense (*Gehaltssinn*, the "what" of the experience), the relational-sense (*Bezugssinn*, the "how" of the experience), and the enactment-sense (*Vollzugssinn*). The enactment-sense is "the manner in which the relational-sense (the primary relationship within an intentional action) is itself enacted."[31] Inasmuch as this always refers to a factual and historical life-experience as the basis and prerequisite of all phenomenological analysis, one that does not allow itself to be bracketed by an *epoché* without the risk of losing the phenomenon entirely, this notion makes it clear beyond doubt that Heidegger has already taken the decisive turn away from Husserl and the conceptions of transcendental subjectivity in neo-Kantianism.[32] The issue of the constitution of objects is abandoned in favor of the issue of their disclosedness; free variation as the methodology of phenomenology is thus replaced by the analysis of the locus of the disclosedness of phenomena, which—as in *Sein und Zeit*—is called the existential analytic of *Dasein*. Only by

---

30. Cf. Dalferth, *Becoming Present: An Inquiry into the Christian Sense of the Presence of God* (Louvain: Peeters, 2006), 130–31 passim; and Dalferth, ed., *The Presence and Absence of God* (Tübingen: Mohr Siebeck, 2009).
31. M. Jung, *Das Denken des Seins und der Glaube an Gott. Zum Verhältnis von Philosophie und Theologie bei Martin Heidegger* (Würzburg: Königshausen & Neumann, 1990), 46.
32. Cf. M. Steinmann, "Der frühe Heidegger und sein Verhältnis zum Neukantianismus," in *Heidegger und die Anfänge seines Denkens*, in *Heidegger-Jahrbuch 1*, ed. A. Denker (Freiburg: K. Alber, 2004), 259–93.

reenacting and comprehending factual life-experience will the understanding gain access to that which has already been disclosed and understood in this experience. With this emphasis on "enactment-based understanding," understanding is not only focused on the field of factual life-experience but also, in a fundamental and consequential way, linked to the perspective of the participants.[33] Only through participation does the "phenomenon" one seeks to understand become present and understandable, because only through participation is the horizon provided within which the thing in question can become visible, which is to say, "phenomenal."

Martin Höfner has aptly demonstrated that this is precisely the point of Heidegger's earlier phenomenology of religion. Starting with the *Phenomenology of Religious Life* (1920-1921), Heidegger insisted, in contrast to Ernst Cassirer, Ernst Troeltsch, and Rudolf Otto, that the perspective of the participant could not be circumvented when seeking to understand religion and faith.[34] Höfner also, rightly, points out the difficulties that come with Heidegger's approach.

First, he had to shift the key term of philosophy's engagement with theology from *God* to *religion*: God is not a possible topic for phenomenological analysis; only religion is. Consequently, all philosophical attempts to address the topic of God were criticized as ontotheological objectification, which Heidegger found already in Augustine's efforts to secure his factual life, by "seeking to ground it in God conceived as a metaphysical object."[35] Conversely, he understood his own phenomenological philosophy not as a neutral analysis, but expressly as "raising his hand against God."[36]

---

33. T. Sheehan, "Heidegger's 'Introduction to the Phenomenology of Religion' (1920/21)," *Personalist* 60 (1979): 312-24, here 320.
34. M. Heidegger, *Phänomenologie des religiösen Lebens*, GA 60 (Frankfurt am Main: Vittorio Klostermann, 1995). Cf. D. Kaegi, "Die Religion in den Grenzen der bloßen Existenz. Heideggers religionsphilosophische Vorlesungen von 1920/21," *Internationale Zeitschrift für Philosophie* 1 (1996): 133-46; M. Zaccagnini, *Christentum der Endlichkeit. Heideggers Vorlesungen "Einleitung in die Phänomenologie der Religion"* (Münster: LIT, 2003). M. Höfner, *Sinn, Symbol, Religion. Theorie des Zeichens und Phänomenologie der Religion bei Ernst Cassirer und Martin Heidegger* (Tübingen: Mohr Siebeck, 2008), esp. Section D.
35. Ibid., 308. Cf. Heidegger, *Phänomenologie des religiösen Lebens*, 234-37.
36. M. Heidegger, "Phänomenologische Interpretationen zu Aristoteles (Anzeige der hermeneutischen Situation) (sog. 'Natorp-Bericht,' 1922)," ed. H.-U. Lessing, in *Dilthey-Jahrbuch*

Second, in a critical turn away from the historicism of the history-of-religions approach (Troeltsch) and from Marburg irrationalism (Otto), he explored the topic of religion by means of a hermeneutic of religion within the framework of a hermeneutic of facticity whose outlines he developed in his critical engagement with Paul,[37] Augustine,[38] and Luther.[39] However, inasmuch as he attempted "to analyze early-Christian life experience as the paradigm for factual life in general," he maneuvered himself into the aporia of overlooking the specifically *religious* content of the Christian way of life.

> The correct insight, that the contents of experience can only be appropriately understood within the pragmatic context of their enactment, became . . . entwined, in Heidegger's analyses, with the problematic strategy of bringing the temporal enactment of early-Christian life experience to the fore, at the cost of its specific content. The tension between emphasizing the originative structural elements of life, on the one hand, and characterizing the enactment as the origin, on the other . . . was . . . resolved in Heidegger's phenomenology of religion to the benefit of the enactment. By contrast, the specific contents of Christian life, as they come to expression in the Pauline epistles, were either so obscured by Heidegger, or so greatly formalized, that they could be integrated into the characterization of the experience of temporality.[40]

Thus, in analyzing the concrete enactments of life, he turned away from the very things that made them concrete enactments of life. This aporia leads, in *Sein und Zeit*, not only to a constant oscillation between what Heidegger calls "ontic" and "ontological" but also to the methodological difficulty of distinguishing elements of ontic

---

für Philosophie und Geschichte der Geisteswissenschaften 6 (Göttingen: Vandenhoek & Ruprecht, 1989), 235–74; here 246n2.

37. Cf. G. Ruff, *Am Ursprung der Zeit. Studie zu Martin Heideggers phänomenologischen Zugang zur christlichen Religion in den ersten Freiburger Vorlesungen* (Berlin: Duncker & Humblot, 1997); E. E. Popkes, "Phänomenologie frühchristlichen Lebens. Exegetische Anmerkungen zu Heideggers Auslegung paulinischer Briefe," *Kerygma und Dogma* 52 (2006): 263–86.

38. Fr.-W. von Herrmann, "Gottsuche und Selbstauslegung. Das X. Buch der Confessiones des Heiligen Augustinus im Horizont von Heideggers hermeneutischer Phänomenologie des faktischen Lebens," *Studia Phaenomenologica* 1 (2001): 201–19.

39. Cf. O. Pöggeler, "Heideggers Luther-Lektüre im Freiburger Theologenkonvikt," in *Heidegger und die Anfänge seines Denkens (Heidegger-Jahrbuch 1)*, ed. A. Denker (Freiburg: K. Alber, 2004), 185–96; J. J. McGrath, "The Facticity of Being God-Forsaken: The Young Heidegger and Luther's Theology of the Cross," *American Catholic Philosophical Quarterly* 29 (2005): 273–90.

40. Höfner, *Sinn*, 317.

enactment from elements of ontological structure while at the same time seeking to construe and understand the one as the concretization of the other. The aporia appears also in Heidegger's efforts to effectually disguise the concrete ancestry of his analysis of *Dasein*.[41] The characteristics of the enactment of a particular ontic form of existence were thus presented as the ontological structural characteristics of the general enactment of the existence of *Dasein* in the world. The failure of the project was thus unavoidable.

4. The Aporia of a Phenomenological Theology

The phenomenological approach raises fundamental methodological questions when it comes to revelation, faith, and theology. Marion rightly asks, "Which horizon could allow a revelation?"[42] It appears that the question must be answered negatively, so long as the horizon defines the phenomenon. Thus, for the possibility of a phenomenological understanding of revelation, it is essential that it is not the horizon that determines the phenomenon, but the phenomenon that determines the horizon. Marion captures this thought in his concept of the "saturated phenomenon" and uses it also to address the problem of revelation.[43] Revelation is, understood in strictly phenomenological terms, "une apparition purement de soi et à partir de soi, qui ne soumet sa possibilité à aucune détermination préalable."[44] Or, as he puts it elsewhere, "Faith does not compensate, either here or anywhere else, for a defect of visibility. . . . [I]t alone renders the gaze apt to see the excess of the pre-eminent saturated

---

41. One can construe this situation pragmatically: *Sein und Zeit* was the writing Heidegger used to apply for a professorship in philosophy; thus, it was better to obscure the theological ancestry of its thoughts and argumentation. One can also understand this as the expression of a methodological error: the opinion that the circumstances of discovering an insight have no relevance worth considering when it comes to the function, significance, and validity of the insight. Heidegger's entire work speaks against this, however. Or, one can trace the situation back to an unexpressed and unconsidered theological attitude of Heidegger's—that in a theological description of phenomena, what will become clear is what is also true for the enactment of life in general.
42. J.-L. Marion, "Aspekte der Religionsphänomenologie: Grund, Horizont und Offenbarung," in *Religionsphilosophie heute*, ed. A. Halder et al. (Düsseldorf: Patmos, 1988), 100.
43. Cf. J.-L. Marion, *Étant donné. Essai d'une phénoménologie de la donation* (Paris: PUF, 1997).
44. J.-L. Marion, *Le visible et le révélé* (Paris: Cerf, 2005), 73–74.

phenomenon, the Revelation."[45] Thus, the whole weight is placed on the self-giving and self-disclosure of the revelation *as revelation*, and not on the phenomenal horizon of its perception. But even this leads us to no conclusion other than to say that revelation, so understood, *is not a phenomenon*, because it does not appear as a phenomenon. To describe it as an "absolute phenomenon" that transcends every horizon is not the description of a phenomenon but rather an indication of a boundary problem, articulated in a boundary term.

Boundary terms, however, are not defining terms; instead, they are critical indicators of the boundaries of meaningful use of our defining terms. They express nothing about something or concerning something, but rather mark the boundaries of our abilities to perceive or understand, the boundaries of meaningful use for our defining categories. To designate God as *causa sui* does not mean that God (has) caused Godself, but rather that applying the category of *causa* to God is misleading. And to designate revelation as an "absolute phenomenon" does not mean that it is a phenomenon beyond all possible perceptual horizons, but rather that applying the term *phenomenon* to revelation is misleading.

In a similarly fundamental way, linking the phenomenon one seeks to understand to participation and the perspective of the participant poses methodological difficulties. If the phenomenological analysis of such enacted phenomena necessarily requires participation in the phenomenon one seeks to analyze, must not the philosopher—in the case of faith—participate fully in the life of faith in order to analyze it?[46] Heidegger sought to resolve this problem in a well-known way that had significant consequences for the theology of Bultmann, who adopted this approach: Philosophy indicates only the formal structures of such enacted phenomena or phenomena of existence. In contrast to

---

45. J.-L. Marion, "They Recognized Him; and He Became Invisible to Them," *Modern Theology* 18 (2002): 145–52, 150.
46. This would erase the distinction between philosophy and theology. That one can, from the theological side, intend this programmatically is evidenced by E. Herms, "Theologie als Phänomenologie des christlichen Glaubens. Über den Sinn und die Tragweite dieses Verständnisses von Theologie," in *Phänomenologie. Über den Gegenstandsbezug der Dogmatik*, Marburger Jahrbuch Theologie 6, ed. W. Härle and R. Preul (Marburg: N. G. Elwert, 1994), 69–99. Heidegger had understood this as the self-assigned task of philosophy.

theology, philosophy is not "direction" but only "correction" for faith's manner of existence.[47] "The formal indication . . . of the ontological term does not have the function of binding, but the opposite, of releasing and pointing toward the specific, i.e., the faith-appropriate, original disclosure of the theological term."[48]

However, this does not resolve the actual problem. The fundamental question is not how philosophy and theology are to distinguish themselves from one another in their varying relationships to such enacted phenomena, but rather *if it makes any sense to speak of phenomena here at all.* The phenomenological cry, "To the things themselves!" has as its point, over against the modern "scientification" of life, to lead us back to the life-relationships themselves on which the scientific theories are built, to turn back to the phenomena, and through the staging (or the free variation) of things themselves to turn the attention anew to those aspects that the scientific method with its theoretical constructions tends to systematically obscure. The point of phenomenology thus was and is critical of theories and sciences; it is "interested above all in keeping open to the otherness, and thus in the descriptive query if things actually appear as the theories say they do."[49]

In the case of faith, this raises a number of problems. Revelation, the act of God, does not allow itself to be staged. For that, one would have to be able to specify a horizon in which this would be possible for the intentionality of the ego. But every horizon that thus "*a priori* sets the scene for coming phenomena, also sets the boundaries for what is possible, and hence necessarily excludes (or forbids) revelation."[50] This does not make revelation (the self-disclosure of God in the mode of its human appropriation) impossible, but it does make a phenomenology of revelation impossible. If the horizon of revelation is the concrete

---

47. Cf. G. Imdahl, *Das Leben verstehen. Heideggers formal anzeigende Hermeneutik in den frühen Freiburger Vorlesungen* (Würzburg: Königshausen & Neumann, 1997).
48. Heidegger, *Phänomenologie und Theologie*, 31.
49. M. Moxter, "Gegenwart, die sich nicht dehnt. Eine kritische Erinnerung an Bultmanns Zeitverständnis," in *Religion und Gestaltung der Zeit*, ed. D. Georgi, H.-G. Heimbrock, and M. Moxter (Kampen: Kok Pharos, 1994), 108-22, here 117.
50. Marion, "Aspekte der Religionsphänomenologie," 101.

process of appropriation in each specific (individual or communal) enactment of existence, then a "phenomenon" can only be something that is available and accessible to the participants who share in the enactment. But how can others have access to phenomena that are available only through participation, so that phenomenology can achieve its end of saving the phenomena from the distortions of theory and science? The things of faith are not amenable to the phenomenological method of free variation, and thus do not permit phenomenology's critical correction of theology. The things of faith can be discussed only in the mode of participatory enactment and thus in the form of concrete, historical faith-existence, which understands itself as the creation of divine self-disclosure. The formation of theological theories is thus always linked back to the varieties of faithful existence and to the self-understanding of the faithful, without being able to find therein a criterion for critiquing theological-theoretical abbreviations. Only the historical variety of the life of faith and the religious experiences of human beings can be described phenomenologically. Yet a "phenomenological" theology so understood would be nothing other than what Heidegger explicitly rejected as inadequate, a conception of theology as the study of Christianity as a historical event or—more generally—as a "science of man and his religious states and experiences."[51]

It is obvious: phenomena that are available as phenomena only through participatory enactment cannot be employed, by way of phenomenological methodology, for the correction of theological shortcomings. They lack either phenomenological accessibility (as with revelation), or they lack resistance to inadequate theoretical constructions (as with faith's historical manner of existence) because there is no recourse for describing such things independently. To be sure, the self-understanding of the faithful can become a topic for

---

51. Heidegger, *Phenomenology and Theology*, 15. That the attempt to base phenomenology of religion in a phenomenology of experience also leads to aporia is made clear by B. Waldenfels, "Phänomenologie der Erfahrung und das Dilemma einer Religionsphänomenologie," in *Religion als Phänomen. Sozialwissenschaftliche, theologische und philosophische Erkundungen in der Lebenswelt*, ed. W.-E. Failing (Berlin: de Gruyter, 2001), 63–84.

discussion because of the way in which it distinguishes itself from theological reconstructions, but insofar as the faithful self-understanding is itself in need of correction and critique, it must have recourse to something other than itself: to the *action of God*. This, however, is no phenomenon amenable to phenomenological description. Phenomenologically, one has recourse only to such enactments of existence that understand themselves, or may be understood by others, as appropriations of God's act of revelation, but not to such an act itself (whatever that might mean): "act of God" designates not a phenomenal reality, but rather a particular way to see and understand what is phenomenally given (phenomena) as well as those for whom they are phenomena. Those who speak of "the acts of God" see phenomena differently, but they do not see different phenomena.

5. God's Nonphenomenality

That those who speak of "the acts of God" do not see different phenomena is a matter of supreme significance. Expressions such as "God's action" or "God's revelation" thus cannot mean some phenomenon because God is not a phenomenon—however one understands the term *phenomenon*.[52] God can be addressed phenomenologically not as a phenomenon but, at most, as something unthematically concurrent with phenomena.[53] This was clear not only to Heidegger and Bultmann but also to Husserl and Tillich.[54]

It was with good reason that Husserl declined to identify God as a

---

52. This is also true for Marion's attempt to escalate the issue, by means of the concept of "saturated phenomenon," to the extreme point of fulfilled meaning, where horizontal variation is neither needed nor possible. Cf. Marion, *Étant donné*. This is simply the formulation of a boundary term, which is then used as a descriptive term for certain phenomena, instead of used critically to mark the boundary of meaningful use of the term *phenomenon* in regard to certain issues.
53. This is the fundamental problem of all attempts to develop a "phenomenological theology," whether they are concerned with interpreting the phenomenality of phenomena in general (cosmo-theological or fundamental-theological attempts) or in interpreting specific religious phenomena (phenomenology-of-religions attempts, based on religious experience). Cf. the differing approaches in S. W. Laycock and J. G. Hart, eds., *Essays in Phenomenological Theology* (Albany: State University of New York Press, 1986); W. Härle and R. Preul, eds., *Marburger Jahrbuch Theologie VI: Phänomenologie. Über den Gegenstandsbezug der Dogmatik* (Marburg: N. G. Elwert, 1994); and T. Söding and K. Held, eds., *Phänomenologie und Theologie* (Freiburg: Herder, 2009).
54. I limit myself to contemporary positions that attempted to find answers to similar questions.

phenomenon and instead spoke of God, in a Platonic sense, as "the idea of the most perfect being; as the idea of the most perfect life," as "super-reality," or as "super-existing."[55] For his phenomenological philosophy—strictly conceived in scientific fashion—"the highest conclusion is the question about the 'Principle' of the teleology disclosed concretely in its universal structures. Accordingly, the highest 'constitutional problem' is the question of the being of the 'super-being,' that is, of that principle that makes possible the existence of a coherent totality of transcendental intersubjectivity with the world constituted by it. Therefore, one can also describe this as the Platonic idea of the good."[56] A God that is so understood is not present as a phenomenon to any consciousness, but neither is such a God in a transcendental sense that universal consciousness that encompasses everything that can possibly be a phenomenon to any consciousness and thus also encompasses every consciousness itself as a phenomenon. God is neither a phenomenon of consciousness among others nor the universal consciousness for which all other phenomena exist.

Claudia Welz has rightly stressed this point in her critique of Steven W. Laycock. Laycock had understood Husserl's brief reference to "divine omniscience" in such a way that "Husserl's God is, as it were, a single, universal intentional act, spanning Absolute Subject and Absolute Object."[57] This universal "divine intentional act" becomes a phenomenon or "appearance" for us by being mediated through "the universal intersubjective community of finite minds."[58] Now, Husserl

---

55. E. Husserl, *Vorlesungen über Ethik und Wertlehre, 1908–1914*, ed. U. Melle (The Hague: Kluwer, 1988), 225–26. Cf. S. Strasser, "Das Gottesproblem in der Spätphilosophie Edmund Husserls," *Philosophisches Jahrbuch* 67 (1958–1959): 130–42; Strasser, "History, Teleology, and God in the Philosophy of Husserl," *Analecty Husserliana* 9 (1979): 317–33; L. Dupré, "Husserl's Thought on God and Faith," *Philosophy and Phenomenological Research* 29 (1968–1969): 201–15; and J. G. Hart, "A Précis of an Husserlian Philosophical Theology," in Laycock and Hart, *Essays in Phenomenological Theology*, 89–168. E. Husserl, *Briefwechsel, Band VII: Wissenschaftlerkorrespondenz* (Dordrecht: Springer, 1992), 21.
56. E. Husserl, *Briefwechsel Band VI: Philosophenbriefe* (Dordrecht: Springer, 1992), 461.
57. E. Husserl, *Zur Phänomenologie der Intersubjektivität, Erster Teil: 1905–1920*, Husserliana, vol. 13 (The Hague: Nijhoff, 1973), 8. Cf. C. Welz, *Love's Transcendence*, esp. 30–64. My discussion follows the analysis of Welz.
58. S. W. Laycock, "The Intersubjective Dimension of Husserl's Theology," in Laycock and Hart, *Essays in Phenomenological Theology*, 169–86, here 169–70. See also D. Zahavi, *Husserl und die transzendentale*

does, indeed, speak of God, the "ideal representative of absolute knowledge," as "omniscient consciousness," to whom one could "attribute the 'capability,'" of "looking into other consciousnesses ... because God would not have *one* field of vision, for example, but rather so many as there may be absolute consciousnesses."[59] That means that God "sees things from one side (with *my* consciousness) and 'simultaneously' from the other side (with the consciousness of the *other*)."[60] This is "conceivable only under the condition that God's being encompasses all other absolute being within itself."[61] And Husserl rightly asks, "Is this even conceivable?"[62] At the very least, it is clear that the "divine omniscient consciousness" under consideration can in no way be understood in the sense of a supersubjectivity correlated with all-encompassing unity, as a text on the Monadology from the beginning of the 1930s makes clear.[63]

> The all-inclusive universe of monads (*Monadenall*), a monadic unity of all things, is in the process of an augmentation and intensification *in infinitum*, and this process is necessarily the perennial development from sleeping monads to patent monads, the development to a world that is constantly constituting itself in monads, whereby these world-constituting monads, as patent monads, are not all the monads there are; still the entire universe is always involved in the foundations. And this world-constituting is the constituting of an ever-higher humanity and super-humanity, in which the universe becomes conscious of its own true being and takes on the form of something that freely constitutes itself as reason or perfection.
>
> God is not the all-inclusive universe of monads itself, but the entelechy that lies within it; God is the idea of a never-ending goal of development, of a "humanity" out of absolute reason, necessarily ruling the monadic being and ruling it of its own free will. This, being intersubjective, is of

---

Intersubjektivität (Dordrecht: Springer, 1996); and P. Hess, "Der Mensch muss sterben—das transzendentale Ich ist unvergänglich. Edmund Husserls Argumente für die Unsterblichkeit des transzendentalen Ichs" (PhD diss., University of Duisburg-Essen, 2009).

59. E. Husserl, *Ideen zu einer reinen Phänomenologie und phänomenologischen Philosophie—Erstes Buch: Allgemeine Einführung in die reine Phänomenologie* (1913), Husserliana, vol. 3/1 (The Hague: Springer, 1976), 350; Husserl, *Zur Phänomenologie der Intersubjektivität*, 9.
60. Ibid.
61. Ibid.
62. Ibid.
63. Cf. E. Husserl, *Zur Phänomenologie der Intersubjektivität, 3. Teil*, Husserliana, vol. 15 (The Hague: Springer, 1973), 608–10.

necessity an unfurling process, without which, despite the events of decay that necessarily accompany it, the universal being simply could not be, etc."[64]

God, thus, is considered to be the equivalent of neither a comprehensive total perspective nor of the totality of all individual perspectives, but rather of the entelechal tendency of the all-inclusive universe of monads to actualize all that is true and good and thus to take part in the "process of self-realization of the divinity."[65] The individual monads participate in this process, but the process is identical neither with any one of them nor with all of them.[66] A corollary of this notion of participation is that God is understood not as a phenomenon but rather as the condition of the possibility of phenomena that, as such, is not a phenomenon itself. God is neither a monad nor the universe of monads, "but rather the entelechy to be found within it"—that is to say, that which guides the universe of monads toward the perfection of that which is true and good. This idea cannot be turned around to form the thesis that, in the course of their existence, monads become the locus in which God appears indirectly as a phenomenon. That which makes phenomenal existence possible does not thereby itself become a phenomenon any more than God's revealing action, through the processes of appropriating revelation, appears as a phenomenon. If one argues that God's revealing action is, according to the self-understanding of the faithful, something that is unthematically concurrent with these phenomenal processes, then this revealing action can indeed be addressed theologically in the interpretation of such a faithful understanding, but it still cannot be addressed *as a phenomenon*. It remains an interpretation based on the

64. Ibid.
65. Ibid.
66. Contra Leibniz, these, according to Husserl, have windows: "Leibniz says monads have no windows. I, however, believe that every soul-monad has innumerable windows. Every understanding perception of another body is such a window, and every time when I say, 'Please, dear friend,' and he answers in an understanding way, out of our open windows an ego-act of my ego passes over into the friend's ego, and vice-versa. The reciprocal motivation between us has a true unity—yes a true unity is produced. Love truly reaches from soul to soul, and, in command, the will of the one truly and directly impacts the will of the other, or the one willing-subject impacts the other." *Zur Phänomenologie der Intersubjektivität, 1. Teil*, Husserliana, vol. 13 (The Hague: Springer, 1973), 473.

self-interpretation of faith, even when it is theologically interpreted in the sense of an interpretation of the fundamental self-interpretation of God.

Tillich also was clear beyond doubt that God's revelatory actions could not be understood as phenomena. He described revelation as the "breakthrough of the unconditional into the world of the conditional," which, as the unconditional, never "allows itself to be made into something conditional . . . to one field alongside others, to religion alongside culture," to one phenomenon among other phenomena.[67] Revelation is "unconditional transcendence showing itself as unconditional transcendence." As such, it can only ever be *one* thing (not different or several); it can only ever take place as an *event*, as the "unconditional and hidden making itself manifest in Being" (but not as a communication about it) and thus can only be revealed *unconditionally* (and not as "partial or obscure proclamation").[68] This "breakthrough of unconditional meaning through the meaning form" occurs as "being grasped by one who grasps unconditionally" and, thus, as what Tillich called "faith."[69]

> Faith is always revelational faith, because faith is acquiring unconditional content by means of thoroughly conditioned forms. Autonomous non-faith knows no revelation, but only the forms. . . . Heteronomous faith does not see the breakthrough character of revelation. It ascribes the absoluteness of revelation to the means of revelation itself, and thus destroys the autonomous form. The conflict between the heteronomous construal of revelation and the autonomous denial of revelation can be resolved only through insight into the *paradoxical-symbolic character of revelation.*[70]

It is precisely this character that precludes the possibility that revelation can be understood as a phenomenon. It is never "given" as

---

67. P. Tillich, "Religionsphilosophie" (1925), in *Main Works =Hauptwerke*, vol. 4: *Writings in the Philosophy of Religion = Religionsphilosophische Schriften*, ed. J. Clayton (Berlin: de Gruyter, 1987), 118–70, here 118. That religion is not one cultural sphere alongside others, not one "symbolic form" alongside others, is also to be read as a critique of E. Cassirer's philosophy of symbolic forms. Regarding the relationship to Heidegger, see Höfner's work, *Sinn*.
68. P. Tillich, "Offenbarung: Religionsphilosophisch" (1930), in *Main Works = Hauptwerke*, vol. 4, 237–42, here 239.
69. Tillich, "Religionsphilosophie," 160; Tillich, "Offenbarung," 239.
70. Tillich, "Religionspilosophie," 160.

such, but can only be experienced as conditioned forms being broken through, and even then only if the breakthrough is undergone and understood as the breaking through of unconditioned content of meaning. This, however, is always the case only in and for faith, because neither autonomous nonfaith nor heteronomous faith has any perception of revelation, since each abstractly addresses either the form or the content and, thus, does not truly perceive revelation. Only for faith does the unconditioned "show itself" in the conditioned, but what it shows to faith is not a phenomenon. It is rather the breaking through and the calling into question of the phenomenality of phenomena, which for others, for third parties, is not perceivable as such. These others always see only people who confess that they have faith, but they never see the faith they confess nor the being-grasped by the unconditioned within the conditioned that these understand as faith.

It follows, therefore, that God's action is not phenomenologically describable. It is not a phenomenon, and, as the unthematic corollary of phenomena, it comes into view only to the eyes of faith. Others can describe the way of life of faithfully acting people but cannot describe the action of God, which, according to their self-understanding, makes such a way of life possible, sustains it, and directs it. If theology takes God's action as its topic, it requires a different method than phenomenology; if it presents itself as phenomenology, it cannot take God's action as its topic.

11

Resonance Analysis of Revelation

The differences in understanding theology adumbrated in the foregoing were developed with exemplary, and complementary, one-sidedness by Bultmann and by Barth. The two were in agreement that Protestant theology would become superfluous as a distinct intellectual endeavor if conceived as a history-of-religions theory about Christianity and not as a resonance analysis of revelation. However, while the one developed this resonance analysis as a theology of faith, the other conceived it as a theology of revelation.

1. Bultmann's Theology of Faith

Bultmann sought to ground his theology in the responsive structure of faith, which confessed itself to be based on God's revelation. God's revelatory action is not phenomenally accessible; only faith in it—or, more precisely, the historical manifestations of the shift from unfaith to faith, which believers attribute to God alone—is accessible.

This approach led to two significant problems. First, talking about the responsive structure of faith suggests the common theological misunderstanding that faith is a human answer to a divine address.

But this is misleading. God's "address" never occurs except as mediated through signs; in the case of the gospel, it occurs in, with, and under human proclamation of the gospel. Furthermore, the fact and content of faith are to be understood as no less the work of God than the fact and content of the address to which faith responds. Hence, two pairs of relationships must always be distinguished theologically: on the one hand, the relationship of *human address* (proclamation) and *human response* (understanding the proclamation and acknowledging what is proclaimed), and, on the other hand, the relationship of *divine self-disclosure* (revelation; Word of God) and *the divinely given gift of participation in the self-disclosing divine life* (faith). Thus, just as one must construe a relationship between the *Word of God* (*verbum aeternum*) and human proclamation (*verbum externum; viva vox evangelii*), so one must construe a relationship between understanding the proclamation (*verbum externum*) and participating in the life of God (*verbum internum*). The structure of the situation of faith is not a relationship between God and human beings. It is, rather, the presence of God with human beings whom God includes in the divine life, both anaphorically (in retrospect) and cataphorically (in prospect).[1]

Second, if one begins theologically with the givenness of faith in its historical manifestations, one is confronted with the methodological challenge of reliably distinguishing manifestations of faith from other phenomena that are not manifestations of faith. But how is that possible? As Bultmann never tired of stressing, there are no neutral criteria for identifying salvific facts among historical facts, salvation

---

1. Anaphor and cataphor are rhetorical or linguistic terms that are used here in a figurative sense. Thus, a sentence (or phrase) *p* is anaphoric to a sentence (or phrase) *q* if *q* is the antecedent of *p* and the meaning of *p* is dependent upon *q*. For example: "Frida Kahlo lived with Diego Rivera" (*q*). "He treated her badly" (*p*). A corresponding dependence upon what has proceeded applies also to the Christian confession of faith in Jesus Christ: "In the resurrection of the Crucified One, God revealed Godself as merciful love" (*q*). "Christians have faith in Jesus Christ" (*p*). In the second example, just as in the first, it is impossible to understand the sentence (or phrase) *p* without going back to *q*. A similar thing is true of the cataphor. Thus, a sentence (or phrase) *p* is cataphoric to a sentence (or phrase) *q* when that which *p* says only becomes understandable through what is later said in *q*. An example: "She was exhausted" (*p*). "Therefore, Frida went to bed early" (*q*). Much the same is true of the Christian confession of hope: "Christians hope in God" (*p*). "Creative love has the last word" (*q*). On the linguistic issues of such backward- and forward-reaching relationships of meaning, cf. M. Consten, *Anaphorisch oder deiktisch?* (Tübingen: Max Niemeyer, 2004).

history within history, or some special group of faith-phenomena within the phenomena of life. There are people who are convinced to have faith, and there are others who vehemently deny faith. But how can one know if a person is manifesting faith or unfaith? The difference between faith and unfaith does not appear at the level of the phenomena (one group of phenomena versus another group of phenomena) but rather—to put it in the jargon of Marburg neo-Kantianism—only at the level of the *sequence* of the phenomena (one version of the totality of phenomena versus another version of the totality of phenomena). Faith does not add any new phenomena to the life of a person but rather sets all of life's phenomena in a new and different light. It opens a new sequence rather than simply adding new phenomena to the same old sequence.

The transition from unfaith to faith, therefore, is not gradual, smooth, or mediated. It is not more-or-less but strictly either-or, a "decision," as Bultmann, following the lead of Kierkegaard, says, between two alternative life sequences or fundamental life orientations. This decision has the character of something that has always already been decided and thus is not a choice among freely available options.[2] Every person lives existentially within this either-or, and there is no one who confronts it from some neutral position within which they could choose one or the other or neither of the two. Everyone, in fact, lives either in unfaith or in faith, even when those living in unfaith do not know it because the possibility of living in faith is unknown. No one lives in faith who did not come out of unfaith. And since no one, in and of themselves, can change from unfaith to faith, no one lives in faith without having God to thank for it. Faith knows itself to be based, anaphorically and cataphorically, in God's saving acts; this is manifested existentially in the either-or between living in faith and living in unfaith.

Bultmann sought to come to terms methodologically with this

---

2. Cf. C. Landmesser, "Der Mensch in der Entscheidung. Anthropologie als Aufgabe der Theologie in der Auseinandersetzung mit Rudolf Bultmann," in *Rudolf Bultmann (1884-1976)—Theologe der Gegenwart. Hermeneutik—Exegese—Theologie—Philosophie*, ed. Chr. Landmesser and A. Klein (Neukirchen-Vluyn: Neukirchener Verlag, 2010), 87–110.

existential either-or through a double step. First, he shifted the accent from the "saving facts," or salvation history (Heils*geschichte*), to the salvation-occurrence (Heils*geschehen*), or saving event. Second, he analyzed this indirectly, rather than directly, through the resonance-phenomena of faith in which it is implicitly present or presupposed. Thus, it is not the saving event (revelation and faith) that is a phenomenon, but only the way in which faith is manifested in human life and existence in history (life of faith). This would not exist if there were no faith, and it does exist only insofar as the saving acts of God, to which it owes its existence, are unthematically present with it.

The theological program indicated by this is well-known. Only a faith that manifests itself existentially and historically can be reflected upon: theology is an *ontic* discipline. However, such reflection fails its theological task and misses the point if that which is unthematically present with faith—God's saving acts—is not made explicitly the topic: This ontic discipline is *theology*. This indirect strategy for addressing the theological issues shaped all major elements of Bultmann's theology, even the existential analysis of biblical texts. The ontic givenness of faith manifests itself not in special salvific facts but in a new orientation of the life on God that results from an encounter with the kerygma. This new orientation does not come to expression in specific individual phenomena of life but in the shift from a life in unfaith to a life of faith. Theology must consider this kerygmatically conditioned shift if it is to understand both faith itself and the saving acts of God in terms of the historical phenomena of the life of faith. There is no faith without understanding, but understanding alone is not faith; rather, understanding functions as the attempt to make what occurs in faith understandable for oneself and for others. One does not have faith on one's own, and one also does not understand faith on one's own. Both the faith and the understanding of faith are attributed by the faithful to God: the faith to God's Word, in which God as God becomes present and understandable, and the understanding of faith to God's Spirit, through which the presence of God is both perceived (or understood) and accepted as true (or acknowledged).

2. Barth's Theology of Revelation

Barth proceeds differently. He does not set out from faith as an existential reality and a historical given because faith does not allow itself to be grasped unambiguously as a phenomenon. Instead, he understands faith on the basis of the self-revelation of God in Christ, which he in turn develops in a biblical and christological manner. By reference to Jesus Christ through the witness of Scripture, which presents Jesus in many ways as the Christ—as God's being with us humans (Son of God) and as our being with God (Son of Man)—Barth derives a criterion for distinguishing faith from its manifestations in the history of Christianity. However, he had to construct this criterion itself dogmatically because God's self-revelation is not disclosed in historical phenomena as such but can only be made an explicit topic on the basis of the biblical texts. To be sure, it is not Christology but rather the orientation on Jesus Christ that is the criterion of proper theology, as Barth stressed. But it is only by means of the witness of Scripture that the Jesus Christ in whom Christians have faith and on whom Christology reflects can be clearly identified as the common starting point both for a Christian orientation in life and for christological reflection. It is there, in the testimony of Scripture, that he comes to speech as Immanuel, as the historical occurrence of the self-revelation of God, in which the eternal God discloses Godself in time with eschatological finality as God for us humans. This witness to Christ offers (phenomenologically speaking) the "preconception" of that which theology must dogmatically reconstruct if it is to critically bring the Christ so witnessed to bear as the normative prius of all ecclesiastical proclamation and theological teaching.

The phenomenological procedure just sketched can be seen throughout the *Church Dogmatics*, most clearly in *CD* IV, 1. Chapter 13, "The Subject and the Issues of the Doctrine of Reconciliation," begins by describing in detail "The Work of God in Reconciliation" (§57), thus presenting the "inventory of phenomena" with which "The Doctrine of Reconciliation" (§58) has to do. This relationship between inventory of phenomena, on the one hand, and doctrine, on the other, appears not only in the overall structure but is repeated within the individual sections. The first section of §57 ("God with Us") begins with a "first general approach" to the matter to be discussed in the following, "sketched in the broadest strokes."[3] These things are described in more detail under seven points, which emphasize that (1) it has to do with the "description of one of the *acts of God*, or better, of *God* in this his *act*"; that (2) this act "as one among others [is] at the same time the goal of all divine acts"; that (3) the history between "God and the whole of creation" thus becomes, "at its heart and at its peak, salvation history"; that (4) God is thus designated "the one who loves in freedom" and the human being is designated as the one whose honor consists in "being destined by God for salvation"; that this (5) makes clear that the human being stands "somewhere completely different from where, in God's intention, he should stand," that the human is, in fact, a sinner; that (6), in light of this, "God has made himself the executor of his saving will" and thus "has become human, in order . . . to take on, in divine sovereignty, our situation"; and that (7) from this free and undeserved "God with us" a "we with God" also comes truly into view: "This 'we with God' that is included within the 'God with us' is the Christian *faith*, the Christian *love*, the Christian *hope*."[4] Therefore, theological reflection on faith, hope, and love must understand these phenomena of the Christian life in every detail in terms of the fundamental event of "God with us" of which they are corollaries and by which they are determined and defined. Because theology cannot do this without having this fundamental event clearly and unmistakably in mind, its methodology is directed toward these seven aspects of the fundamental event by which "among us humans a communication of this 'God with us'" has come to be and which "bears the name, Jesus Christ."[5] This is "*the epistemological principle*" for

---

3. Karl Barth, *Church Dogmatics*, ed. G. W. Bromiley and T. F. Torrance (Edinburgh: T&T Clark, 2004), vol. IV, 1, 2–3; hereafter *CD* IV.
4. (1) *CD* IV, 1, 4; (2) *CD* IV, 1, 6; (3) *CD* IV, 1, 7; (4) *CD* IV, 1, 8–9; (5) *CD* IV, 1, 9; (6) *CD* IV, 1, 11; (7) *CD* IV, 1, 14–15.
5. *CD* IV, 1, 16–17.

everything that is to be said theologically about God and humankind, and thus is the fundamental phenomenon by which all theology must be measured.[6] This fundamental phenomenon is something totally unique, a concrete occurrence, not some "special form of the common, which as such would be interchangeable."[7] One cannot find it just anywhere, but only precisely there where it came to appearance and showed itself as it is. This concrete event, which bears the name "Jesus Christ," thus becomes objectively accessible and describable in a methodologically reliable way only through the "report and testimony" of the Christian message in the New and Old Testaments.[8] Only insofar as it echoes and spells out this testimony does theology stay with its task.

The methodological circle of this "phenomenological" argumentation is immediately apparent: dogmatics constitutes the phenomenon (the "matter") by which all of dogmatics is to take its bearing, and even when this presents itself as a *reconstruction* of that to which the Scriptures testify, it nonetheless remains a dogmatic construction. As Bultmann's theology remains within the horizon of self-understanding, Barth's remains within the horizon of scriptural understanding.

Bultmann attempted to develop his understanding of God theologically strictly on the basis of human self-understanding, by taking the human self-understanding that is always present within faith as the key to a proper understanding of God. Accordingly, his theological development of the understanding of God remained bound to the horizon of human self-understanding in faith. Concerning God's action, he was able to say only that, on the basis of human self-understanding, in faith's distinction between sin and grace it was necessarily implied, but only unthematically.

For Barth, however, it was exactly the opposite: everything was about how God understands Godself and us. He attempted to develop the human understanding of God and self strictly on the basis of the

---

6. *CD* IV, 1, 17.
7. *CD* IV, 1, 21.
8. *CD* IV, 1, 17.

divine self-understanding; this he found in the dogmatic recapitulation of the witness of Scripture as the self-interpretation of God, both as God is within Godself (Trinity) and as God makes Godself known for us in the revelation-event with its concrete christological and pneumatological dimensions. In the community of the Father, Son, and Spirit, so ran his thesis, God always understood Godself as freely overflowing love to those who were different, and God interpreted this self-understanding for us humans in history through the revelation-event of the cross and resurrection of Jesus. Therefore, it is not human self-understanding but divine self-interpretation that is the key to understanding God—that is, as God must be understood by us if God is truly to be understood as God. But insight into this revelatory event depends totally on the witness of Scripture. Therefore, just as Bultmann developed his theology around his existential analysis of human existence within the horizon of human self-understanding in faith, Barth developed his theology around his exegesis of Scripture within the horizon of a dogmatic reconstruction of the self-revelation of God in Jesus Christ.

3. Systematic Indeterminacy and Dogmatic Construction

Bultmann and Barth thus face corresponding problems when it comes to theologically clarifying just what is meant by the metaphor of "God's action."

Bultmann sought to discuss this theological reference point by starting from faithful existence. In other words, he attempted to think outward from the diastatic-diachronic time-structure of faith, which, anaphorically, confesses itself to be grounded in God's action and, cataphorically, hopes for a final clarification of that which "God's action" means for the truth of human life. Between such retrospective and prospective indeterminacy, however, what is actually meant by this metaphor seems to evaporate into arbitrary contingency. As a result, the otherness of this point of reference in relation to its respective thematizations can be maintained only negatively; the fundamental phenomenological intent cannot be developed *positively*.

On the other hand, if one follows Barth, starting positively from the self-disclosing revelatory act of God and developing its divine otherness as its content, one opens oneself up to the accusation of dogmatic construction. In this case, it seems that the phenomenological intent can only be protected by presenting the description meant to provide a phenomenological correction as a construction itself. God is a phenomenon only where God manifests Godself as such: in Jesus Christ. *That* God does so there is, however, not phenomenally evident. Rather, it becomes evident only because and insofar as God by God's action as Spirit allows it to become evident to humans. That Christ is the phenomenal God only becomes evident within the horizon of that which is presented in Pneumatology. Without the Spirit, there is no recognition that Jesus Christ is God's act of revelation as a historical phenomenon. And without this recognition, there is no possibility of identifying God's presence within faith or faith within history.

By way of the phenomenology of faith, the acts of God, therefore, never come into view; what comes into view is only the human testimony of faith, which credits the existence of faith, anaphorically, to that which it calls "God's action" and which, cataphorically, hopes that the meaning of this metaphor will become clear in the future of the world. By way of the theology of revelation, in contrast, "God's action" is dogmatically constituted on the basis of the testimony of Scripture, thereby abandoning the path of phenomenological description. Either way, it appears that a phenomenological theology proves a contradiction in terms. Neither recourse to faith nor to the self-revelation of God provides an adequate phenomenal starting point.

4. An Event-Hermeneutic of the Anaphoric-Cataphoric Structure of Faith

Faith and the self-revelation of God can ground a phenomenology only if theology becomes radical and sees itself as an *event-hermeneutic of the anaphoric-cataphoric structure of faith*, developed as an exploratory (investigatory) and imaginative (visionary) hermeneutics of the self-presentation of God in human life. What would this mean?

As Bultmann has shown, a theology that seeks to ground itself in objective saving facts or in a particular history of salvation is forced into epistemological and theological impasses: it is not able to identify its starting point in any generally accepted way—that is, within the horizon of human history—but can present it only in mythological fashion. Therefore, instead of focusing on *salvation history*, he sought to focus on the life-illuminating *salvation-event* of the Christian kerygma.[9]

The hermeneutical theology of Bultmann's students Ebeling and Fuchs went a step further. They identified this salvation-event more precisely as a *language-event* or *word-event*, respectively, in which humans are interpreted in such a way, through God's self-presentation, that they understand God, themselves, and their world anew in light of the Christian proclamation.[10] Humans are thus the locus, but not the primary actors, of such interpretation. In agreement with the later Heidegger, the hermeneutical focus shifts from existence and history to language, stressing that we always live in a world that is disclosed and interpreted in language.[11] The point of Christian communication of faith, then, consists neither in confirming this interpretation nor in adding another to it. Rather it is, put negatively, to *dislocate* humans within their worlds of meaning (to make their prior orientation radically problematic: Christian disorientation) and, put positively, to orient them anew in another way (Christian reorientation). Such disorientation and reorientation make it possible for them, in light of the presence of God, to gain a radically new view of this world and of their life in this world.[12]

---

9. Cf. R. Bultmann, "Heilsgeschehen und Geschichte. Zu Oscar Cullmann, 'Christus und die Zeit'" *ThLZ* 73 (1948): 659–66, here 665.
10. Cf. J. M. Robinson, "Die Hermeneutik seit Karl Barth," in *Die Neue Hermeneutik*, ed. J. M. Robinson and J. B. Cobb (Zürich: Zwingli, 1965), 13–108, here 83–84.
11. Cf. G. Noller, ed., *Heidegger und die Theologie. Beginn und Fortgang der Diskussion* (München: Kaiser, 1967); A. Jäger, *Gott. Nochmals Martin Heidegger* (Tübingen: Mohr Siebeck, 1978), 1–133.
12. In this respect, Christian language processes are *processes of disturbance* and *differentiation* in regard to our familiar ways of dealing with life and the world. Christians are not called to confirm the existing and the given, to justify it, or to legitimize it. Instead, they are called to critically consider what within it is viable for the future and thus to be promoted, and also what has no such viability and is thus to be overcome or brought to an end.

This new way of viewing life is not an additional or new life-phenomenon. To be sure, the Christian way of life that is so reoriented does take on phenomenal forms by which "Christian life" can be empirically distinguished from other ways of living. But this way of life does not exist except within the variety of its interpretations, and none of them is, per se, what is spoken of within it as an "act of God." Whoever seeks to find what is meant by that term as a phenomenon among phenomena will find only interpretations among interpretations; they will find nothing that offers itself to interpretation as an act of God.[13] Wherever people testify to God's action as that which has changed them from a self-centered life to a life oriented around God, they locate this change of orientation retrospectively-anaphorically and prospectively-cataphorically in a context that they metaphorically call "God's action."

With the abductive metaphor of "God's action" (which, looking backward, can be made concrete as *revelation, creation*, and so on, and which, looking forward, can be specified as *redemption, consummation*, and so forth), they make reference to something that in the appearance of phenomena does *not* appear. Instead, it accompanies and defines the appearance as origin, background, and goal, even though it is only there by withdrawing itself: the absent presence of God.

That this is so does not appear in the phenomena as such but rather shows itself first to the eyes of faith. Phenomenally, God is *not present* but God is also not simply *not there*. God is present *with* the phenomena as phenomenally absent—as that which is unthematically present with the phenomena but which cannot be disclosed as such by the phenomena themselves. Only with the eyes of faith and faith's

---

13. The criticisms of H. Braun or F. Buri regarding Bultmann's speaking objectively of the acts of God are applicable here. Cf. H. Braun, "Die Problematik einer Theologie des Neuen Testaments," in *Gesammelte Studien zum Neuen Testament und seiner Umwelt* (Tübingen: Mohr Siebeck, 1967), 325–41; F. Buri, "Entmythologisierung oder Entkerygmatisierung der Theologie," in *Kerygma und Dogma* II (1952), 85–101. Their therapeutic proposals, however—to understand the word *God* as a way of saying *agape*, a particular type of human solidarity (Braun), or to radicalize demythologizing into de-kerygma-tizing—throw out the baby with the bathwater. There is no need to choose between these alternatives: either mythical speech about God or an ethic of human solidarity and respect for life. There are other possibilities, especially that of taking seriously the metaphorical character of talking about "acts of God" and making this the hermeneutical guidepost for theological thinking.

interpretation can it be made explicit and become explicitly thematized. At the level of phenomena, it appears both in retrospect and in prospect as a *gap*. This gap cannot be thematized as a phenomenon because it is no phenomenon but instead marks the *standpoint* and the *horizon* from which or within which phenomena come into view, to the eyes of faith, in a different and new way—namely, as *God's good, albeit corrupted, creation*. It is the *blind spot* of faith, which is not a phenomenon among phenomena; it is rather the basis from which and upon which phenomena (can) appear at all as creation or as manifestations of faith.[14] Phenomena may be so thematized only on the basis of faith, which, looking back on its genesis and looking forward to its goal, metaphorically understands as the "action of God" that which is not phenomenally graspable but to which it owes its existence and upon whose effective power it hopes. Then, using a variety of terms of theological reflection and orientation, it brings this to speech and defines it more precisely as the Word of God, revelation, creation, redemption, and the like.

The methodological starting point for such theological explication is, for Barth, the witness of Scripture that must be discussed with reference to God's self-revelation as its "whence" and to God as the "whither" of faith. For Bultmann, however, it is the phenomenal complex of faith, which uses the metaphor of "God's action" to testify both to that to which it owes its existence and to that upon which it hopes. For both, this implies four things. First, from the theoretical view of scholarly description, the point of reference for both the anaphoric and the cataphoric—looking backward and looking ahead—can be defined only *negatively*, as that to which the phenomena given at the outset *themselves refer*; it cannot, however, in and of itself, be grasped as a phenomenon. Scientifically, one can neither assert

---

14. If faith and the manifestations of faith are viewed from another standpoint, that is, as Luhmann puts it, if its observations are themselves observed, then it comes into view as the way of faith and the life of faith of certain persons or groups—that is, as the *faith of Christians*. As a historical and empirical phenomenon, however, it appears always as a mixture of Christian and non-Christian elements, and thus is, at best, a more or less clear process of the transformation of concrete human life into a Christian life. This process is always open to deepening and improvement, but it is never an unambiguous manifestation of faith in the life of humans.

that that this reference point for faith exists nor even contend that it could exist.[15] Furthermore, even to undertake such a negative phenomenology requires that one adopt the perspective of a participant as the starting point. If that is not done, the result is not a negative phenomenology of faith but rather its negation: either in retrospect or prospect, one does not negatively describe a gap; one describes nothing. Third, from the participants' perspective, the metaphorical designations of both the anaphoric and cataphoric reference may vary with the concrete facts on the basis of which they are conceived and developed: one does not need to use the metaphor "God's action" to speak of that which is spoken of with that term. Fourth, whatever metaphors are chosen by the participants to bear witness to that which Scripture or faith assumes as its indispensable basis or longs for as its hoped-for goal, one cannot discuss this without also discussing *all* phenomena from this point of view in light of that which in the self-disclosure of the phenomena is *not* disclosed but nonetheless irrefutably accompanies and determines its self-disclosure, even though it is only there by means of its withholding itself.

From this phenomenal gap in both the past and the future, which constitutes the anaphoric whence and the cataphoric whither of faith and which is brought to speech metaphorically as "God's action," a new light shines upon everything. What is addressed thereby is not some special, new phenomenon among or alongside others, but rather *a new view of all phenomena*—not because one desires it, although one could also not do so, but rather because one cannot do otherwise than understand oneself and everything else, both retrospectively and prospectively, in a radically new and different way through becoming aware of this gap.

---

15. R. Bultmann, "Ist voraussetzungslose Exegese möglich?," *Theologische Zeitschrift* 13 (1957): 409–17, here 411–12: "While, for example, the Old Testament historical writings tell of God breaking into history, historical scholarship cannot ascertain an act of God. But it can take faith in God and in God's action seriously. As historical scholarship it cannot simply maintain that such faith is an illusion and that there are no acts of God in history. But as a scholarly discipline it cannot itself hold them to be true and deal with them."

12

Radical Theology

Radical theology develops and reflects on the anaphoric-cataphoric dynamic of faith, looking back to its whither and looking forward to its whence. It describes no new phenomena (experience), but instead describes all phenomena anew (experience with experience). It thus develops a *new point of view* (standpoint and horizon) from which all phenomena are to be newly seen and understood.

From other standpoints, this new point of view may appear to be merely a *different* viewpoint, one other variant within a series of (cultural or religious) phenomena. This is not wrong. In fact, that it can be seen in this way is essential. This makes it possible for this standpoint to actually refer to *the experiences of this life.* (The "experience with all experience" itself belongs to this world and not to some other world.) It also makes it possible, and necessary, for people, within the horizon of their reflections on the experiences of this life, to refer back to themselves as phenomena of this life. (In one's perspective on everything, one can and must also address and reflect on oneself as a cultural or religious phenomenon.)

This does not mean, however, that the standpoint or point of view of faith can be understood fully or adequately by seeing it as merely one standpoint or point of view among others. It is always possible to formulate points of view in which faith and its view of life can be compared to a series of other phenomena. But to do so is to reduce faith and its view of life to the question of a common denominator within a certain construct, rather than to apprehend it phenomenologically in its irreducible uniqueness.

Only where such apprehension occurs will the radical otherness of its point of view become clear, regardless of its manifold similarities to others. From this point of view, the world is differentiated into a former (undifferentiated) sequence and a new (differentiated) sequence: within the former sequence—not out of it!—a new sequence arises that does not continue the former but sheds a new and differentiating light on everything. It develops a *twofold view* of human life in this world by asking of everything, in the light of *the eschatological distinction between old and new*, whether it, in the light of God's presence, has a future or not. Thus, the fullness of what is phenomenally accessible is observed from the point of view of *becoming*: in fact, with a twofold accent on *the becoming of the new* and *the passing of the old*, on *a world that is coming to be* and *a world that is passing away*. With this dynamic doubling of its view of the world and of life, radical theology sets itself apart not only from every monistically conceived philosophy but also from all scholarly disciplines that work empirically and historically. It becomes a scholarly undertaking sui generis.

1. Heidegger's Limit of Understanding

Heidegger had sensed this, but not truly understood it. After a long back and forth about whether he would publish his lecture "Phenomenology and Theology" together with Bultmann's lecture on revelation, Heidegger finally declined his friend's request on December 18, 1928. "The way I posed the question in the lecture, in regard to theology as a scholarly discipline, is not only too narrow, but unsustainable. The positivism of theology, which I do believe to have captured, is somewhat different from that of the sciences. Theology stands apart from the sciences in an entirely different way than philosophy does. But more about that some other time."[1] Heidegger never developed his thought beyond this negative insight. He had identified theology's difference from philosophy as consisting in theology's nature as a positive discipline. But philosophy's difference from theology was not yet made clear. Heidegger recognized the problem—"if neither philosophy nor a science," what then is theology?—but he had no solution.[2] "Personally, I am indeed convinced that theology is *not* a science, but I am not yet in a position *truly to show* that, and certainly not in a way that would *positively* capture the great function of theology within intellectual history."[3] He could not find a way because he thought as a philosopher and not as a theologian. Theology is, in fact, not one of the positive sciences because its focus is not on a subtopic (such as religion), but on the whole. However, it views the whole not as philosophy does, but "in a totally different way." How it does so, Heidegger was not able to say. Theology, in its twofold distinction from the sciences and from philosophy, remained a puzzle for him.

Even later, this never changed. The difference between philosophy and theology was clear to him, but wherein it was based and how it was to be explored was not. This can still be seen in the notes from a seminar session on March 4, 1961, which Heidegger, together with G. Ebeling, led on Luther's disputation *De homine* and Luther's disputation on John 1:14.[4] "Prof. Heidegger emphasized," in reference to the antithetical "Lutheran view of the relationship of *ratio* and *fides*," that "for him it came down to the contradistinction from faith."

> "It was already doubtful" that one "with the help of syllogisms could transfer valid findings from one branch of thought to another . . . between separate disciplines in the natural sciences. Much less could truth within

---

1. M. Heidegger and R. Bultmann, *Rudolf Bultmann, Martin Heidegger, Briefwechsel 1925-1975*, ed. Andreas Großmann and Christoph Landmesser, intro. Eberhard Jüngel (Frankfurt am Main: V. Klostermann; Tübingen: Mohr Siebeck, 2009), 87.
2. M. Heidegger and E. Blochmann, *Briefwechsel 1918-1969* (Marbach am Neckar: Deutsche Schillergesellschaft, 1989), letter to Elisabeth Blochmann from August 8, 1928.
3. Ibid.
4. Heidegger and Bultmann, *Briefwechsel*, 287-305. The following citations are found on 297-99.

philosophy be asserted as true for theology, since the difference between the two was infinitely greater than that between individual scientific disciplines. The matter of theology stands not only *contra*, but also *extra, intra, supra, infra, citra, ultra omnem veritatem dialecticam.* Luther . . . over and over expressly emphasized . . . that the subject matter of theology could not be confined by the judgments and constrictions of human reason. In the field of theology, only the dialectic between the Word of God and faith was valid."

Faith and reason, theology and philosophy, therefore had to be considered each in reference to its own field. "The matter of theology, however, is not in the realm of *ratio*." As a result, one must refer to the role of language, and "Prof. Heidegger emphasized" that the "formal function of language . . . should by no means [be] underestimated." "A word in the field of theology receives its relevance only through its theological interpretation even though theological and philosophical speech shares a common vocabulary. Thus the conflict between theology and philosophy must be carried out in large part as a conflict about language in its formal function." Even though, text-critically, one cannot always tell which thoughts are to be ascribed to Heidegger and which to Ebeling or to other participants in the seminar (and even though some phrasing is strongly reminiscent of Ebeling's thinking and is more likely to be ascribed to him than to Heidegger), it remains clear that Heidegger in this conversation still stressed the *difference* between philosophy and theology. It is also clear that he did not see language as offering the horizon for resolving the nature of their relationship; instead, language was a warning sign that brought their differences into view.

It is precisely this twofold distinction of theology, both from the sciences and from philosophy, that reveals just how radical theology is: it is neither one science among the sciences, nor is it a rival of philosophy. Both are bound to the realities to which they belong. Theology, however, is about the possible. It is neither an ontic nor an ontological discipline, but rather—if anything—a *discipline of the possible*. In contrast to the sciences and philosophy, theology devises no defining concepts by means of which reality can be grasped in description, but rather develops—to express it from their perspectives—*limiting* concepts, which critically restrict the claims of science and philosophy to say all that can be said, from the standpoint of reality, about the world and about human life in the world. Or—to state it in terms of its own perspective—it offers terms of theological orientation, which help in critically examining how human life in faith is newly oriented in a radical way. The world is more than that what appears to be the case; life is more than whatever we make of it; and both are more than what comes to speech within science and philosophy.

This is what theology addresses by understanding everything in terms of the silent power of the possible, which from the viewpoint of faith is revealed as the horizon of human life *coram deo*. It speaks of no other world than this one, but speaks of this world differently inasmuch as it observes this world *from another point of view* and *within a different horizon* (from the point of view of the priority of possibility above reality through its orientation around God as the reality of the possible). It thus sees all things in a radically different way. Theology explicates and reflects on faith not as a particular phenomenon in the world, but as a *new way of seeing the world*, in which it becomes clear that the world is more than what is or what can be through the continuation of what is. Reality depends on and profits from the possibilities that are offered to it, not those already inherent within it. Only thus is there a history of reality, which is not only the execution over time of the possible variations within a pattern of being (as a long tradition of Christian theology thought in the wake of Aristotle), nor the emergence of new realities on the basis of the possibilities of earlier realities (as contemporary process-metaphysics contends), but rather a primordial becoming of that which is genuinely new (*creatio ex nihilo*).[5]

The theological problem of the panentheistic metaphysics of

---

5. Cf. P. Clayton and P. Davies, eds., *The Re-emergence of Emergence: The Emergenist Hypothesis from Science to Religion* (Oxford: Oxford University Press, 2006); P. Clayton, *Mind and Emergence: From Quantum to Consciousness* (Oxford: Oxford University Press, 2004). *Mind and Emergence* was translated to the German by G. Schenki Robinson as *Emergenz und Bewusstsein. Evolutionärer Prozess und die Grenzen des Naturalismus* (Göttingen: Vandehoek & Ruprecht, 2008).

emergence is a fundamental methodological failure: it attempts to think of the world within God (and not of the world as God, of God as the world, of God without the world, or of the world without God). However, it thus objectifies God and the world without giving adequate consideration to the hermeneutical presuppositions and theological consequences of its methods or to the frames of reference and mental horizons of its efforts. Neither "world" nor "God" is the name of an object that can be theoretically delineated and scientifically researched. Instead, we live in the world, insofar as we live in a worldly way, and we live *coram deo*, insofar as we live within the divine power of the possible, which does not owe its existence to us, but we to it. Just as the sciences, strictly speaking, are concerned not with the world but in the world (in worldly ways) with their specific problems, so God is no phenomenon of the world, but rather the viewpoint and the horizon from which and within which our life and our world is disclosed as creation. The world is not a phenomenon, but the horizon for the perception of phenomena. And God's creative work is the framework for understanding all worldly phenomena as creation; it is not one of the phenomena thus perceived and understood.

In the attempts of emergence metaphysics, the theologically justified effort to think of God and the world in their relation to one another is carried out with an aporetic methodology: it tries to think through this relationship beginning from the world and within its horizon and not from God and within God's horizon, all the while without clarifying exactly what "world" or "God" signifies, or why any recourse to God is required in order to understand the processes of the world. God and world are linked to one another in an objectifying manner and then sketched into the unified emergence framework of a continuum reaching from the physical through the mental to the transcendental, without ever achieving clarity about the horizon of meaning of this attempt. Thus, the world is understood in an everyday scientific perspective in accord with the theories of the natural sciences and, *viewed in this way*, is embedded within a more comprehensive God-structure that is also *viewed in this way*. Instead of understanding the world (as both nature and culture) anew, within the horizon of its relationship to God, in terms of creation theology, God is made into the metaphysical framework for the physically-psychically-mentally-transcendentally understood world. Thus, either the topic of God is metaphysically "naturalized" —that is, developed within the horizon of a scientific theory of the world as its framework—or the world is understood scientifically while God is understood theologically, in which case a methodological breach has been committed by discussing world and God within differing horizons and thus without direct connection to one another. It is no coincidence that panenetheistic approaches regularly oscillate between monistic metaphysical conceptions, which think of God in "worldly" terms, and methodologically inconsistent dualistic conceptions, which think in "worldly" ways of the world and in "godly" ways of God. In both cases, God and the world are not thought of together, homogeneously, as Creator and creation. The first does not truly think of a creation, but rather of an emergent world-process. The second does not truly think of a relationship between God and world, but only of a purely external correlation of unrelated entities.

Radical theology is different, thinking of the possible not within the framework of an emergence-continuum from the real, but rather focusing on the transformation of the real through the divine power of the possible, on the becoming of what is genuinely new. It aims at the whole, as does philosophy, but it does so *from a different standpoint* and *with a different point of view*: sub ratione dei, as they used to say.

2. Sub Ratione Dei

This *ratio* of the presence of God is no phenomenon. It is rather the point of view from which phenomena, in faith, appear as signs of God's present absence, pointing toward that which is unthematically present in the phenomenality of phenomena. It is something without which phenomena would not exist, but which itself never appears as a phenomenon. God is not "there" as a phenomenon, but rather as the reality of that which is possible, thus conferring added value to that

219

which we experience as phenomena. The totality of actual and possible phenomena may now be experienced not merely *as the world* (in a worldly way), but at the same time also differently, namely *as creation* (in the way of faith), so that *the world* is now seen and understood *as God's creation*.

Phenomena as such do not manifest themselves *as* creation, and thus do not appear so for each and every person. As the beauty of the world becomes manifest to human eyes, it reveals its created nature only where phenomena are seen and experienced *by* creatures *as* creation—that is, as signs of the absent presence of the creator. Without understanding oneself as a creature, one cannot see and understand the world as creation. One does not discover one's own createdness by studying nature or by studying oneself, but only by being made aware of it through a communication with others that leads to one's own course of life being interrupted in a radical way (dislocation) and set on a new course (reorientation).[6]

It is this life-changing shift of standpoint and view that theology addresses when it speaks of God's action, revelation, word of God, creation, faith, unfaith, and so on. These are not the names of phenomenal events (religious events or experiences as opposed to profane); they are rather *categories of theological thinking and reflection* for describing and unfolding the new (not self-evident) reorientation of Christian life in faith and its different (not self-evident) view of everything. *Revelation* is thus the theological category for explicating that to which faith anaphorically relates as its foundation, when it is confessed as faith in Jesus Christ. Nonfaith, accordingly, is the theological category used by faith to indicate not its genesis but its past, that is to say, the place from which it came, although it did not arise from that place. *Creation* is also such a category of theological orientation and not a description of phenomena that can be

---

6. The fundamental Christian rituals of Baptism and the Lord's Supper are also ritualized communal acts of remembering this all-encompassing dislocation and reorientation of life, without which there is no faith and thus no Christian life. One does not procure these for oneself but rather experiences them as something in which one passively, together with others, is included by God's effectual presence.

ascertained either scientifically or philosophically. The only possible subject for scientific research is that which can be grasped in terms of differences in empirical or historical experience, that is to say, which, within the horizon of the empirical or the historical, is sometimes and under certain conditions the case, but not always and not under all conditions. Likewise, in a world so disclosed, all that can be explored philosophically as the possibility-horizon of reality is that which, in principle, could be experienced as a concrete phenomenon in terms of such differences in the realm of the experienceable. The predicate "is created" ("Creation"), however, cannot realistically be applied only to some phenomena, but not others: the distinction between *created* and *uncreated* is not a phenomenal difference in experience. Rather, if anything at all can be rightly identified as created by God, than *all* that is real and possible must also be so identified. Creation is not a term of definition or classification, but rather a term of orientation. It not only expresses something about that of which it is predicated, but also about those who predicate it: that they understand *themselves* as creatures among creatures. All who understand themselves in this manner necessarily adopt a particular outlook toward that which they designate as creation. Among other things, this outlook implies that nothing worldly will be treated as God or as divine, and also that nothing divine will be treated as worldly. Whoever speaks of creation says that everything real and possible is due to God, to whom it owes its existence. And whoever says that, but does not show God the respect due to God, is guilty not simply of an error of thought but of existential self-contradiction.

3. The Ontological Plasticity of Phenomena

In order for such a *relecture* or rereading of the phenomena of the world and of one's own life to be possible, these phenomena must *possess ontological plasticity*. That is to say, when considering what they are, they are *susceptible to multiple determinations and interpretations* and can truthfully be *understood in different ways*. The common model of fact and interpretation, of objective reality and subjective meaning, is particularly unhelpful for grasping the problem that here arises. This is so, first of all, because facts are not ontological givens, but always semiotic results of interpretation (they are *facta*, the result of some doing). Furthermore, that which, in the act of interpretation, is distinguished as the *interpretandum* from the *interpretans* is not ontologically rigid, but instead *plastic*, and thus may be understood in differing ways, all of which can be "right," "true," or "accurate" in different respects, or to differing degrees. Christians do not experience the phenomena of their life and world simply as *phenomena* (experience), but, simultaneously or in retrospect, they also understand them in another way, as *signs of the presence of God* (experience with the experience).[7] They are so understood because they become signs for humankind of God's presence *through Godself* as faith specifies. They are thus an experience with the experience that is not arbitrary, but, in the concrete case, unavoidable, and true to the character of the world as God's creation.[8] The world is not creation because it is experienced so; rather, it is so experienced because it is creation. No one is compelled to experience the world in this way, but one cannot experience it in this way without also understanding oneself as a creature. Once you understand yourself so (and thus the world as well), then everything that before had been undergone, seen, and experienced in one way appears in another light, although the new experience does not simply erase or replace the old experience but reinterprets it. The phenomena of the world are ontologically plastic and may be defined truthfully in more than one way. This can be seen both in the dynamics of scientific knowledge, which always seeks

---

7. To be sure, they are not understood *as* signs of the presence of God, but as *signs* for it. Just as, in the practices of our life, we do not deal with something *as* a table, tree, or person, but deal with tables, trees, and people, so in faith we do not live in the world *as* creation but rather *in creation*. Only in reflecting on this circumstance, and thus within the horizon of theological, philosophical, or scientific distancing from this practice of life, can and does one compare this with other ways of living; only against the background of such a comparison can one then also, in a reflective, self-referential way, speak of experiencing the world *as* creation.
8. In this sense, Jesus (a particular historical phenomenon, generally recognizable) is confessed by Christians as the Christ (the definitive sign of God's merciful presence among humans). Unlike the historical recognition of Jesus through one's own comprehension, this confession is attributed by Christians to the working of God's spirit, which imparts a metaphorical surplus to that which is historically recognizable, thus making possible a deeper insight into reality.

to surpass itself and remains tied to no one hypothetical explanation of the reality of the world, and in the non-self-evident, radically disorienting, and freshly reorienting insight that one is a creature and that the world at large is God's creation.

No one must understand oneself and one's world in this way, but everyone can do so. The possibility of such multiple interpretations is inherent within the dynamic symbolic structure of phenomena themselves. In short, phenomena are always symbolic events, in which "something is disclosed through something as something for someone." Within the unity of what occurs, such symbolic events are both informed by reality and interpretive of reality, inasmuch as *"something through something appears for someone as something,"* and *"by someone for someone something is interpreted as something."*[9] Every phenomenon is a concrete symbolic event in which the selection of four horizons of possibility and three dimensions of reality are so knotted together that the string of preceding phenomena, without which this symbolic event would not be possible, must always be extended by a further symbolic event, which in turn makes other symbolic events possible, without which it would not be (or have been) possible.[10] Every phenomenon has others at its back, and every phenomenon leads on to others.

Accordingly, phenomena are characterized by four constitutive structural elements: Whatever appears is always something *with and among others* (with-structure); it appears *as something* (as-structure); it appears as something *for someone* (for-structure); and it appears as something for someone *through something* (through-structure).[11] Thus, no phenomenon appears alone, and no phenomenon can be understood in only one correct way. Instead, phenomena, on the basis of their with-, as-, for-, and through-structures, are complexly intertwined. Therefore, neither the sequence of what precedes nor the

---

9. Cf. I. U. Dalferth, *Die Wirklichkeit des Möglichen. Hermeneutische Religionsphilosophie* (Tübingen: Mohr Siebeck, 2003), 128.
10. Ibid., 19–22.
11. Cf I. U. Dalferth, "Weder möglich noch unmöglich. Zur Phänomenologie des Unmöglichen," *Archivio di Filosofia / Archives of Philosophy* 78 (2010): 49–66.

horizons of what may follow is defined, or can be defined, in only one way. Every phenomenon possesses an essential ontological plasticity precisely because it is a symbolic event among other symbolic events within time.

4. Horizons of Possibility and Dimensions of Reality

Every phenomenal symbolic event is distinguished by four fundamental semiotic dimensions: the relationship between sign and sign (the syntactic dimension), the relationship between sign and signified (the semantic dimension), the relationship between sign and sign-interpreter (the pragmatic dimension), and the relationship between sign and sign-bearer (the material or medial dimension). As a result, each such event is thus also linked to *four horizons of possibility* and *three dimensions of reality*.

The four horizons of possibility for sign-events are the reference to the *sum of possible signs* (the totality of possible signifiers), the *sum of what can be signified* ("the signifiable"), the *sum of all possible sign-interpreters* (the totality of possible communities of interpretation), and the *sum of what can be experienced* ("the experienceable"). In the syntactic sign-dimension, every sign-event refers to the *sum of possible signs (or sign-codes)*, and thus actualizes only one possibility from the totality of the possible sign- and communication-repertoire. In the semantic dimension, it refers to *the sum of what can be signified*, and thus actualizes—insofar as it follows the laws of logic—a possible world. In the practical dimension, it refers to the *sum of all possible interpreters*, but actualizes only one among all possible communities of signs, communication, and interpretation. Finally, in the material or medial dimension, it refers to the sum of all that can be experienced, but makes use of something as a bearer of signs (a medium) that can be appreciated, at least in principle, by a particular community of interpretation.

Every sign-event takes place as a specific combination of these four horizons of possibility. By means of certain signs (or sign-codes), a possible world is actualized for one or more sign-interpreters by using certain resources of the real world. Sign-events continuously transform possibilities into facts or actual states of affairs that are then available as concrete projections of meaning because they can be negated in terms of the difference between truth and falsehood. That is to say, through the negation of certain possibilities in the formation of structures of meaning, in reality a distancing from reality is concretely created, thus opening room for freedom. This is so because in the real world possible worlds of meaning come into existence through sign-events. These worlds of meaning not only semiotically transcend the real world without leaving it behind but also represent it in less complex and thus more comprehensible ways. It is the difference between reality and a complexity-reducing concept or projection of reality that makes a responsible use of freedom even possible.

The *three dimensions of reality* to which all sign-events constitutively remain bound, in spite of all transcending or modification of that which is given as given, are sign-interpreters (society), sign-codes (culture), and sign-media (nature); these are always presupposed. We consider sign-media to be everything that can be perceived directly or indirectly by our senses. They always are *natural phenomena* that represent the order of *nature* that is given and that we do not constitute ourselves.[12] As beings who construct signs, who influence behavior with signs, and who produce and communicate knowledge through signs, we remain bound to nature because we are dependent on material sign-bearers that we can use and receive.

Sign-codes, the repertoire of signs and rules for the use of signs, that we make use of individually or communally are always *cultural phenomena* because we are social beings. They represent the historical ordering of culture, which although always coming to us as something given are also always (co)constituted by us and thus, in principle, changeable and shapable. Cultural patterns are (historical) products of our communal activity and thus expressions of our freedom, which sets the rules for itself. Natural patterns, in contrast, are the predetermined

---

12. Nature is thus defined by our bodily senses; to the degree that these are technically altered, what we mean by "nature" will also be defined differently.

general conditions of all our actions and thus are an expression of (empirical) necessities, which can be summarized in laws. Insofar as our cognitive acts make use of signs, and thus of the existence of sign-media and sign- codes, they are always concretely negotiating between the law-bound order of nature, which is set in place *before* all our action, and the rule-bound order of culture, which is set in place *by* our action. The resulting tension between our *being bound to the natural order* and *our freedom in regard to the cultural order* (to which we are also bound, although in a different way) is a fundamental structural characteristic of human life and of human freedom; it is manifest in every act of life. On the one hand, there is nothing that we can believe, know, recognize, intentionally do, or communicate without sign-media, which owe only their function, not their existence, to us. On the other hand, we cannot do any of this without sign-codes, which owe both their function and existence to us.

5. The Ordinary Way of Seeing: Real and Ideal

The three semiotically differentiated dimensions of reality inherent in sign-events use the keywords *Nature, Culture,* and *Society* to specify the three fundamental fields of human knowledge and cognition. Through the use of signs, cultural worlds of meaning are constituted within the natural world—cultural worlds without which the complex communal life of human societies could not exist. For example, Christians (interpreters) use the English word *God* (medium) as a sign for God (the signified). What they do when they do that can be observed scientifically, that is, empirically and historically described and (as far as possible) explained in terms of the three dimensions of reality: *nature* (sign-medium), *culture* (symbolic world), and *society* (sign-interpreters).[13]

Everything that scientifically can and does come into view in this

---

13. Considered semiotically, not only the natural sciences but also the cultural and social sciences (the human sciences) are sciences of reality, which should neither be played off against one another nor be reduced to some methodological common denominator. They investigate the world in different ways, starting from dimensions of reality that are mutually dependent on one another.

way is commonly distinguished (following the guiding distinction between *real* and *ideal* that has become dominant within modernity) as the realm of the *real* (Christian usage of the term *God*) as opposed to the realm, constituted by the usage of signs, of the *ideal* (the God signified by the term *God*). This is the ordinary way of looking at things currently, one that largely defines our everyday life and the world in which we live, even with our increasingly digitalized practices of communication. This is the methodological and theoretical basis of all our scientific ways of approaching the world of nature, culture, and society as those scientific approaches have developed since the seventeenth century. In the scientific-theoretical (self-)interpretation of these approaches that is currently dominant, this appears in the form of naturalism, in one variety or another: either it is a point of dogma that only the world of the empirically and historically accessible real exists (ontological or metaphysical naturalism),[14] or there is skepticism (methodological naturalism)[15] that sees no good reason to accept any world other than that of a reality that can be researched scientifically.[16] Both approaches can appear in various forms.[17] Despite all their differences in detail, these philosophical conceptions of naturalism are characterized by a shared conviction that no real and ideal "worlds" exist, that there is no dual "reality" of the real and the ideal. Instead, only the scientifically (empirically or historically) comprehensible real world exists. Since everything ideal

---

14. Cf. D. Papineau, "Naturalism," in *The Stanford Encyclopedia of Philosophy*, March 2010, http://plato.stanford.edu/entries/naturalism/index.html/. "The driving motivation for ontological naturalism is the need to explain how different kinds of things can make a causal difference to the spatiotemporal world."
15. R. Feldman, "Methodological Naturalism in Epistemology," in *The Blackwell Guide to Epistemology*, ed. J. Greco and E. Sosa (Malden, MA: Blackwell, 1999), 170–86; Feldman, "Naturalized Epistemology," in *The Stanford Encyclopedia of Philosophy*, Fall 2006, http://plato.stanford.edu/archives/fall2006/entries/epistemology-naturalized/; J. Kim, "The American Origins of Philosophical Naturalism," *Journal of Philosophical Research*, APA Centennial Volume (2003), 83–98.
16. On the related debate about religion and God, see A. Plantinga, "Methodological Naturalism?," in *Facets of Faith and Science*, ed. J. van der Meer (Lanham, MD: University Press of America, 1996), 91–130; P. Draper, "God, Science, and Naturalism," in *The Oxford Handbook of Philosophy of Religion*, ed. W. Wainwright (Oxford: Oxford University Press, 2005), 272–303; and D. Dennett, *Breaking the Spell: Religion as a Natural Phenomenon* (Viking: Penguin Books, 2006).
17. See Papineau, "Naturalism"; and Feldman, "Naturalized Epistemology."

is merely a product of meaning in the real world, it can be reduced to nothing more.

According to this common conception, phenomena can exist only in the realm of the real, because everything ideal is not a phenomenon, but constituted, by means of phenomenal sign-events, as the ideal correlate of such sign-events. All worlds of meaning can thus be considered as cultural phenomena and understood as the correlates of sign-processes within the horizon of the real. In order to scientifically investigate the sign-events of Christian life in this manner, no faith is required, but rather its opposite: a practical or methodological nonfaith. One need not accept what Christians say and do in order to study those things empirically. It is sufficient to consider these phenomena in an empirical and historical manner. So long as one does that, it is irrelevant whether one has faith or not: the use of the scientific method remains unaffected by this difference of standpoint. The methods of empirical and historical scholarship are not in the least affected, nor are their intended results, if one practices them as a Christian or as a non-Christian, as a person of faith or of unfaith. They provide scientific answers to scientific questions, thus helping by verifiable means to find scientific solutions to scientific problems—no more, but also no less.

Not only in fact, but also in principle, nothing of what Christians call "God," "act of God," "creation," and the like is considered by such methods. With empirical and historical methods, one can consider only the cultural phenomena of Christianity, but the whole realm of Christian ideality is not itself a field of investigation for the sciences of reality. There is no empirical science of creation or historical study of God, no real science of God or of God's action. God plays no role in the scholarly description and explanation of the world in the historical and empirical disciplines, and, moreover, there is no place for the whole system of theological terms of orientation (creation, revelation, act of God, providence, redemption, and so forth). Such terms have no business there because they do not say anything that cannot just as easily be said without them. They are not prescientific or pseudoscientific terms of description and explanation, but rather terms of orientation for the life of faith or for the theology that critically reflects upon this life. The two things are not to be mixed together. As Bultmann rightly stressed:

> While, for example, the Old Testament historical writings speak of the active intervention of God in history, historical scholarship cannot verify an act of God, but can only take note of faith in God and God's actions. As historical scholarship, of course, it cannot simply maintain that such faith is an illusion and that there are no acts of God in history. But it cannot itself, as a scholarly discipline, observe such acts and reckon with them; it can only allow everyone the freedom to decide for themselves if they will see an act of God in an historical event that itself can be understood as having purely historical causes.[18]

6. Radical Conversion: Old and New

All of this is different in the perspective of radical theology. Such a theology employs all scientific methods and can bring them to bear on all phenomena that are studied by the sciences, including these scientific disciplines and radical theology itself. But it does so from another perspective and within another horizon: the perspective and the horizon of *faith*.

Even the distinction between *faith* and *unfaith* belongs, in the thought of radical theology, to the terms of theological orientation; the two do not represent a pair of descriptive terms by means of which anthropological, moral, or religious phenomena can be described. The expressions "faith" and "unfaith" do function in such a way in everyday usage—as descriptive terms by which empirical phenomena can be classified and assigned to different sets. But they are not so used theologically, at least not by Protestant theology within the horizon of the theology of the Reformation. This differing usage of "to have faith" or "to not have faith" (everyday usage: terms of description) and "faith" or "unfaith" (theological usage: terms of orientation) provides

---

18. R. Bultmann, "Ist voraussetzungslose Exegese möglich?," *ThLZ* 13 (1957): 409–17, here 411–12. That it is not arbitrary or purely subjective caprice to see such an act of God in an historical event, must, of course, be developed more fully in what follows.

repeated occasion for confusion and mistakes. Doubtless there are empirical humans who believe something (*p*) and others who do not believe that (*-p*); within the horizon of the ordinary way of viewing things, guided by the orienting distinction between real and ideal in this doxastic variety, they may rightly be described as believing or unbelieving people. But that misses the theological point when *p* has to do with religious beliefs. Theologically, within the horizon of faith, guided by the orienting distinction between faith and unfaith, *all* people come under consideration, both religious believers (in the ordinary way of seeing) and those who are not religious believers. By no means does theology intend to say that the former live *in faith* while the latter live *in unfaith*. In specific cases, it can be exactly the opposite: that the religious believers live *in unfaith* while those who are not religious believers live *in faith*. The decisive factor is not what humans do (have faith or not have faith), but is instead how what they do is to be judged in light of God's relationship to them and their relationship to God, which is the focus of the orienting distinction between faith and unfaith. All people, whatever they do or allow, live, when judged in reference to God, either in faith or in unfaith; no person lives without living in either one or the other relationship to God. Theologically, therefore, *faith* and *unfaith* function together as the fundamental distinction of a Christian orientation to life. They do not describe differing types of life-phenomena; instead, *sub ratio dei*, they express a different comprehensive perspective on all phenomena of life. People believe many things (or they do not believe), but they do so—speaking theologically—either in faith or in unfaith, and whatever they do or do not do (believe or not believe) is not to be confused with the place and the horizon at which or within which they do it (faith or unfaith).

The standpoint of faith is not a standpoint within the ordinary way of viewing things, but instead presupposes a fundamental shift of standpoint or radical conversion, a shift (as can be said from the new standpoint and only from the new standpoint) from unfaith to faith, from the *old life* to the *new*. This shift in standpoint to that of faith is *radical* for several reasons: It opens a new way of looking at everything. It occurs as a shift from one total or comprehensive system of orientation (old life) to another that is likewise all-encompassing (new life). It is neither something that can be compelled, nor something that one can achieve on one's own.

This shift of perspective is radical, first of all, because it is not simply a change of position within the horizon of the normal way of viewing things. Instead, it leads to seeing not only some things, but everything, including the standpoint of faith itself from which one sees all things new, in a new and different way. The perspective of faith opens not simply a different view, but a *new* view upon the *whole* world. In this new view, the shift of perspective from before to after is to be differentiated from the evaluative distinction between old and new. It is not simply the before that is the old and the now that is the new. Instead, old and new are to be distinguished *within* what has gone before, *within* the present, and *within* the future. Whatever in the past pointed forward to the life of faith must be distinguished from that which now is seen to be the old that has been surpassed and brought to an end. Whatever in the present which as new has a future must be distinguished from that which as the overcome reality of the old still has its effects but is condemned to be destroyed and to disappear because it has no future. The continuity of life's course in before and after is so thoroughly displaced by the distinction between old and new that everything—the before, the now, and the after—is seen in a newly differentiated way: a person's life is thus defined, understood, and lived as a life of faith.

Second, the perspective of faith cannot be attained directly, but only by means of a transition away from an ordinary perspective. Within the story of a life, the perspective of faith always has a before that can be remembered in the now. No one is born as a person of faith; every person of faith has become so in the course of his or her life, changing from a person who lived however he or she lived into a person who can, should, and wants to live in the presence of God. The ordinary ways of looking at things that precede faith can be described—not per se, but only from the perspective of faith—as perspectives of practical nonfaith or of active unfaith (in the form of denial of faith, superstition, or impugning of faith). No course of life, within the ordinary perspective of life, stands out as a nonfaithful or an unfaithful way of life. It may be judged to be morally good or evil, but this moral judgment within the ordinary perspective provides, as such, no starting point for the distinction between the old life and the new life within the perspective of faith. Conversely, every course of life within the common perspective can also appear in the new perspective, albeit not under the moral judgment of good or bad, but under the previously inaccessible distinction between sin (sinner) and grace (justified sinner). Since that which is morally good can, thankfully, also be performed by sinners and that which is morally evil can, regrettably, also be performed by justified sinners, the moral distinction offers no reliable basis for understanding the radical difference between faith and nonfaith. Instead, the moral must undergo a critical metajudgment from the perspective of faith. Morality and faith are not natural relatives but instead stand in a complicated relationship with one another.

Just as the prior standpoint, the customary way of seeing, is a total perspective applying to everything, the new standpoint of faith is also a total perspective on everything. Thus, both standpoints are also capable of considering the other, although in markedly different ways. From the perspective of the ordinary way of seeing, guided by the orienting distinction between real and ideal, faith appears to be only another perspective within the same horizon. However, from the perspective of faith, the ordinary way of seeing appears as a fundamentally different total perspective. Likewise, from the perspective of the common way of seeing, the change to faith appears to be a relative change—a change from a nonreligious life to a religious life or from one type of religious life to a another type of religious life—rather than an absolute or radical change to an entirely new life. Conversely, from the perspective of faith, there are two comprehensive frameworks of orientation that must be distinguished from one another and referred to one another, so that it becomes not only possible but also necessary to locate and describe the life of every single person and of humankind as a whole in terms of the difference between these two mutually exclusive perspectives on everything. While, within the horizon of the customary perspective, faith appears to be only *another* (in this case, religious) variant of human life, from the standpoint of faith itself it is revealed to be a *new* view of the *whole* world. This new view differs from the *old* view of the *whole* world—from the standpoint of unfaith—in kind, not simply in degree. It thus recognizes a *twofold view of everything*: only within the horizon of faith can faith and unfaith be distinguished; only within the horizon of the new can new and old be distinguished. Not only can they be distinguished, but they must be.

Third, one cannot bring about this change of perspective on one's own, either as a person of faith or as one of nonfaith. The person of nonfaith cannot do so because the perspective of faith, within the ordinary way of looking at things, is not a radically different perspective. If it is perceived at all, it is seen as only a different, namely religious, perspective within the same horizon, a perspective one can adopt or not adopt at will. Adopting or not adopting is something each person must freely choose, deciding for or against. Clearly, in such a case it would make sense to ask what the reasons are for this change (or lack of change) to a religious point of view, whether that be a change (or lack of change) from a nonreligious life to a religious life, or a change (or lack of change) from one religious standpoint to another. It is also clear that such reasons, when they exist at all, will seldom be convincing to others and never be convincing to all others. Most are only more or less illuminating, and that which may be sufficient for one is seldom so for others.

People of faith, however, see themselves and everything else from this new perspective, and do not require arguments to be moved to a change of perspective. They experience this change not as a choice but as something they undergo, and thus they have to deal with a decision that has already happened, not with one they have yet to make. They also seek reasons and arguments. But their search does not have the function of reaching a decision through the weighing of pros and cons, but rather the function of understanding the decision made, understanding the experienced change, and also making that change and themselves understandable to others. However, the reasons and arguments that are decisive for people of faith themselves are not necessarily convincing for people without faith because they are not formulated from the perspective of the ordinary way of looking at things, but from the perspective of faith. People of faith understand their change to the standpoint of faith as God's gracious gift, enriching their lives in ways they never deserved and never imagined. Accordingly, they describe this change as a redirecting of human life, thanks only to God, toward the self-disclosing, creative presence of God. They describe it as being made aware of the truth of a possibility that frees life, in contrafactual (dislocating), correcting (bettering), or culminating (perfecting) ways, to perceive all that is real and all that is possible as God's good creation. The world with all its realities and possibilities proves to be more than it is or can be on its own when it also becomes for us what God's presence makes it to be: God's good creation.

7. Radically New: Faith and Unfaith

Lived faith is the way of practicing the truth of this possibility that cannot be inferred, but only offered, to us. The view of faith differentiates itself from the view of nonfaith in this way: by means of a radical conversion, that which natural perspectives on reality dismiss as "merely" ideal (as opposed to what is real) comes to be understood as an indicator of a standpoint recognizing the genuine reality of all that is real and possible. The God to whom Christians refer with the sign *God* is no mere ideal projected on a grand scale, but rather the *Creator*, and everything seen in natural perspectives on reality as nature, culture, and society, as well as the horizons of possibility within these dimensions of reality, is to be distinguished from this Creator as the divine *creation*. Accordingly, it is not the distinction between real and ideal that that is the fundamental, orienting distinction of this new orientation on life, but rather the distinction between *Creator* and *creation*, between the creative *reality of the possible* (God) and the *world with its realities and possibilities* (creation).[19] To be guided by this distinction means to live in faith. Failure to do so, in practice, is *nonfaith*, while failure to do so, in active denial of faith, is *unfaith*.

Radical theology takes its orientation from the fundamental difference between Creator and creation, seen in faith as the self-disclosed distinction of the Creator from the creation. As such, radical theology is *theocentric theology*. Insofar as this distinction is not clear per se but becomes manifest only through an event wherein Creator and creation become distinct (through the Creator's self-distinction from the creation), radical theology is essentially a theocentric *event-theology* (in respect to God) or a theocentric *occurrence-theology* (in respect to humankind). Because of this, it derives its understanding of God and of everything else from the uncontrollable event of a radical transformation from the old life to the new. In the orienting horizon of faith, this is understood as the change, due to God alone, from unfaith or nonfaith to faith. No one must change from the perspective of nonfaith or unfaith to that of faith. However, such change is possible for everyone (*de dicto*), even though no one can make this change in and of themselves (*de re*).

This radical change of perspective to faith, and the *new way of looking at all things* that results from it, is the topic that radical theology explores. (The change of perspective is radical because it is discontinuous and unconstrained; wherever it does occur, it occurs freely on its own.) Radical theology no longer speaks of God only as

---

19. This is not simply modifying or renaming the distinction between real and ideal as that of creation and creator. That would miss the actual point and help promote the misunderstanding that the perspective of faith is nothing but a religious redescription of that which has already been described scientifically as it "really" is. On the contrary: creation, distinguished from the creator, encompasses both the real and the ideal. The creator, meanwhile, remains distinguished from them both: the creator is neither an empirical or historical phenomenon within the horizon of the realities of nature, culture, or society nor a cultural phenomenon of meaning within the horizon of the ideal. What Christians mean by *God* can never be wrapped up in what they say with this sign. The creator is in no way a part or aspect of creation, but rather the one who through the divine relationship to it makes it what it is: God's creation.

the *meaning-product of religious speech about God*. That is to say, it speaks not only *sub ratione mundi* of a historical-cultural understanding of God, and thus of what certain people at certain times meant by the sign *God*. Instead, it discusses God as the *ground of the changed perspective* that leads to understanding *oneself* as *God's creature* and to seeing the world of nature, culture, and society along with all of its attendant possibilities *sub ratione dei*, in light of *the presence of God*—to perceiving and understanding this world *as the creation of the Creator*.

8. Radically Different: Creator and Creation

This has two important consequences. First, whoever uses "God" to mean the Creator, to whom one owes this change of perspective to that of faith, must at the same time understand God as the one without whom nothing that is could be and without whom nothing that might be would be possible. God must be understood as the absolute precedent and origin of all that is real and possible, as the indispensable creative reality of the possible. God is thus not to be thought of only by means of limit terms (as something of which nothing greater can be thought) nor by means of a theology of negation (as something that is greater than everything that can possibly be thought). Both discuss God within the horizon of a way of thinking that is not determined by the change of perspective to faith and the accompanying reorientation in regard to unfaith—an unfaith that is never transparent to itself as such, but can be perceived only from the view of faith, and that thus encompasses all past and present efforts of human thinking to understand the world, humanity, and God. The worthiness and greatness of this way of thinking—but also its tragedy and its impasses—can be seen clearly, in its full consequences, only in light of the change in perspective to the new place of relationship to God brought about by God alone. In short, this way of thinking can be seen clearly only within the new orienting horizon of faith.

This adds nothing, materially. No new phenomena are added to the manifold variety of human experience and thought in the world. But all of these things are now seen—within this new viewpoint, guided by the distinction between faith and unfaith—as creation. As creation, they all will be evaluated differently. In principle, nothing in the world is thus distinguished, theologically, from anything else. Orienting distinctions, such as those between sacred and profane or between religious and secular, lose their theological valence. In light of the fundamental distinction between Creator and creation, they are all together on the side of that which is made, in contrast to the reality of the Creator. As creation, everything comes from God. The decisive difference is not any distinction within creation, but the distinction between everything created and the Creator who distinguishes between creation and Creator by marking the divine creativity from the created world. God thereby creates the possibility of relating to all things different from God in differentiated ways (as Creator, Redeemer, and Perfecter) without ever becoming identical to them or failing to be distinguishable from them. God's creative being thus reveals itself, within the orienting horizon of faith, as the fundamental and indispensable *positive reality* to which everything else, in its differentiated determinateness, owes its existence: without it, they would not be. This creative reality, for its part, is only understandable as such because, and insofar as, it makes itself concretely understandable within the horizon of creation. To understand it as such is the same thing as changing to the perspective of faith.

Accordingly, God's creative being is not imaginable or understandable apart from this change in perspective that is due to God alone. *God is the one who, through the divine Word and through the Spirit, makes God understandable as God.* God does this by becoming, in the gospel of Jesus Christ, so present as God with humankind that a fundamentally new horizon of understanding is opened up, one in which people learn to see God, themselves, their lives, and their world anew—in short, to understand all things anew, and to live anew.[20] This is evident at all levels of Christian life:

In the life of faith, this fundamental change of orienting horizon,

---

20. The phrase "gospel of Jesus Christ" is to be understood as *gen. auctoris* in reference to the person of Jesus Christ and as *gen. obj.* in reference to the gospel that Christians proclaim about him.

which comes about through God making Godself present among humankind, is experienced purely as something one undergoes and as the undeserved gift of God. It is consummated as conversion, turning away from the old life lived at a distance from God and turning to new life in fellowship with God.

In the life of the Christian community, the symbolic act of Baptism presents this change of orientation as the radical end of the old and as the beginning of a radically new life: immersion in water symbolizes the death of the old and the rebirth of a new person. Receiving a new name in the name of the triune God marks this change as the entrance into a radically new community—not dependent on any earlier ties—with all those who orient their life by God's good presence, as it is understandably revealed and efficaciously conveyed in the gospel of Jesus Christ—as the efficacious presence of the one who is totally and ultimately good by creating good out of evil, justice out of injustice, life out of death.

Theologically, this radical change of orienting horizon is to be understood as the change to faith from unfaith, a change due only to God. Within a universal horizon, in reference to the eschatological change from the old creation to the new creation that occurs in the story of Jesus Christ, it appears as the orienting distinction between old and new. Within the individual life-horizon of each person, in reference to the soteriological change from the old life to the new arising from the efficacy of the gospel, it appears as the orienting distinction between being lost (*Unheil*) and being saved (*Heil*). Both distinctions represent the same event, the change to faith from unfaith, in relation to different defining horizons.

Based on this fundamental change and its various symbolic representations—in manifold, situation-specific concretions, such as Father, Son, Spirit, Creator, Reconciler, Redeemer, Perfecter, and so on—God's divine being becomes approachable and thinkable. The doctrine of the Trinity is a systematic compacting of these concretions into a core formula that applies not only to God but to the entire frame of reference offered by faith. In the Trinitarian compaction of these concretions of the understandings of God's divine being, critically linked to one another, criteria emerge that allow for everything that is understood as "God," "human," "world," "life," and so forth to undergo a differentiated new description and a critical evaluation within the orienting horizon of faith.

Out of this arises something more: whoever understands the world as creation not only makes clear that they see themselves as creatures, they also, of necessity, express *more* about themselves and the world than what appears in a purely phenomenal way. The contingent facticity of the world of phenomena only becomes a sign of its created nature when this facticity is perceived by those who understand themselves as creatures, as the locus of the input of possibilities *through God and from God*. Only then will the world in its worldliness be understood as the creation of the Creator.

Thus, in theological thinking, the point of the distinction between real and ideal is reversed. That which, in the natural perspectives on reality, is seen as ideal is understood theologically as a hint of what is truly real—namely, the Creator. In contrast, both the scientific real and the cultural ideal are seen as products of this creative reality—that is, as creation. The everyday orienting distinction between real and ideal is revealed, in light of the theological orienting distinction between creation and Creator, to be bound within the horizon of creation. Creation is distinct from the Creator, who relates to creation while distinguishing Godself from creation. Only that which is possible and not impossible can become real. What is real can only come to be when the possible is distinguished from the impossible. In theological perspective, however, possible and impossible are whatever God makes possible or impossible. The modal fundamental distinction between the possible and the impossible is constituted through the real fundamental distinction of the Creator from the creation.[21] The world

---

21. Modal terms (possible, impossible, necessary, unnecessary, contingent, noncontingent) are always designations by or for something or someone. They do not stand as absolutes, but are always related to something or someone. In modernity, these are propositions (alethic modalities) or beliefs (epistemic modalities). In the Aristotelian tradition, this something was the world (this, and only this, is possible, which really was, is or will be). In Christian thought, it is God who allows the world to really exist as creation by distinguishing Godself from it, thus making

with its distinction between real and ideal only becomes real because God makes the possible possible, the impossible impossible, and reality real. God does so by distinguishing Godself as Creator from the creation, thus allowing the world as the divine creation within the horizon of God's distinction between the possible and the impossible to become real.

The key distinction between *real* and *ideal* is replaced by the key distinction between *Creator* and *creation*, both within lived faith and in faith's theological reflection. This replacement, along with the redefinition of the first distinction in light of the second (the distinction between *real* and *unreal* is assigned to *creation*, which is to be distinguished from the *Creator*), presupposes that one *can* undergo such a radical change of orientation and perspective, that it is possible *to be so dislocated* (to abandon the old place of orientation) and *to orient oneself anew* (to see everything else differently from this new place). In order to demonstrate this possibility, one is not required to carry out such a change of perspective, even though the possibility would be demonstrated by carrying out the change. Just as the natural perspective on reality is developed from a position of *factual* or *methodological* unfaith, so the theological perspective is developed from a position of *factual* or *methodological* faith. One does not need to have faith in order to follow the thinking of theology. One must, however, at least as a thought experiment, follow along with faith's radical change of orientation in order to see what the thinking of theology consists of.[22]

---

the possible possible, making the impossible impossible, and making the real real. For a more detailed presentation and analysis of these issues, see I. U. Dalferth, "Possibile Absolutum: The Theological Discovery of the Ontological Priority of the Possible," in *Rethinking the Medieval Legacy for Contemporary Theology*, ed. A. K. Min (Notre Dame, IN: University of Notre Dame Press, 2014), 91–129.

22. For this reason, theology should not be understood as a science among the sciences, but instead as a radical *scienza nuova*, a critical-reflective interpretive practice that uses all the procedures and results of the sciences in order to describe and analyze all realms of life (everyday, cultural, scientific, societal, political, economic, religious, and so forth) in light of the fundamentally new orientation of faith. By means of this critical reflection, it thus seeks to clarify what it means to reorient life from the ground up within the horizon of faith and to live in a new way. Cf. I. U. Dalferth, *Evangelische Theologie als Interpretationspraxis. Eine systematische Orientierung* (Leipzig: EVA, 2004).

9. The Radical Presence of Radical Otherness

The change of perspective from nonfaith to faith is a sign-event that does *not simply continue one sequence* or *open a new sequence within another*, but rather opens a fundamentally new horizon for the understanding of both. The meaning of this sign-event is thus found precisely in its enactment. This means that the content-sense (what), the relational-sense (who), and the enactment-sense (how) coincide in such a way for the persons affected that, by using the sign *God* (which here indicates the sum of all other signs in *usus fidei*), God through God becomes understandable as God in such a way that those affected have no other choice but to understand God as their Creator, themselves as God's creatures, and their world as God's creation.

The event of the change of standpoint from nonfaith to faith thus has this structure: "*God through God becomes understandable for someone as God,*" that is, as Creator, as the Giver of all that is good, as merciful Father, and so forth. Regarding God, this means that God is experienced simultaneously as radically present and radically other, as the one who (as is indicated by the sign *God* with its distinction between sign and signified) reveals Godself freely and beyond grasp as the present absence (the presence of God's hiddenness) and the absent presence (hiddenness of God's presence) within all use of signs. God's presence is no phenomenon, but rather—to the eyes of faith—something that is implicitly copresent within the phenomenality of phenomena: an indicator of the absent presence of God. To speak of this absent presence does not express God's noneffectiveness or nonpresence, but rather the opposite—the absolutely unconditional, presence-constituting creativity of God, which calls what is not into being and holds whatever is (although it could just as easily not be) in existence. God is not "there" as a phenomenon, but rather as the one who lends to the occurrence of phenomena at the locus of human beings the surplus value of being creation and, therefore, the locus of God's absent presence. Only for humans are there phenomena, and only for people of faith are phenomena God's creation. As creation, phenomena are where God is present.

Accordingly, God's presence is not *experienced* as such, but as that which is there *with* the phenomena, without itself being a phenomenon. More precisely—and this is what makes it a *radical* presence of a *radical* otherness—it is that which is there with very concrete phenomena in such a way that they are understood as signs of God's presence, without God ever becoming a mere sign Godself. God is always different from the sign *God*. (This is a grammatical comment about how the sign *God* is used in a Christian manner). One can use signs, but not God; only because God is distinct from all signs, as the signified and not merely as sign, can *God* be used as a sign.

Therefore, phenomena can only become signs for God when (a) the distinction between sign and signified is absorbed *in the experiencing*, so that the *presence* of the phenomenon is experienced as the *presence* of God and when (b) the *phenomenon* and *God* can and must be distinguished *in thought* in such a way that it is understood as a worldly sign of God. This is because that whose presence is directly experienced (the phenomenon) becomes only a sign for that whose presence is also experienced with the phenomenon (God), all without the phenomenon itself becoming what it signifies nor the signified becoming a phenomenon. God is present *with* this phenomenon, but not *as* this phenomenon; this phenomenon is a *sign* for God but not identical with God. Therefore, God's radical presence is the presence of God's radical otherness. Only where a phenomenon is so experienced that it is understood as a sign of the present absence of God does there exist what one calls, in a questionably abbreviated manner, an "experience of God." If the *presence* of the phenomenon is not experienced as the *presence* of God, then only a worldly phenomenon, not God, is experienced. If *God* is not, in thought, distinguished from the phenomenon in question, it is not understood as a sign for God, and God, accordingly, is not understood at all.

When phenomena are experienced (seen, heard, tasted, felt) as *signs of God's presence*, they then offer *more* to understand than they indicate in and of themselves. This other way of seeing, experiencing, and understanding presupposes a radical change of perspective, apart from which there is no "experience of God." This change of perspective is radical in a twofold sense: one sees *more* in phenomena when one sees them as signs of God's presence, and that happens only when one also sees *oneself* differently, namely as the locus of the absent presence of God. But *that* one sees things and oneself in this manner cannot be achieved on one's own. Rather, according to people of faith, it is thanks only to God that phenomena become God's signs, that humans become the locus of God's presence, and that God makes Godself present in an understandable way. Only where God makes God understandable for someone as God does the change of perspective come about; only then can phenomena be understood as signs for God; only then can God can be understood by means of these signs.

Therefore, only that which *through God becomes* a sign of God's hidden presence ("self-revelation of God": Jesus Christ) and also *through God is understood* as a sign of God's hidden presence ("understanding the self-revelation of God as self-revelation": faith in Jesus Christ) is a *reliable* sign of God's presence. The former is seen by Christian faith as the heart of the event expressed in the confession of Jesus as the Christ: Jesus is made by God to be a reliable sign of God's hidden presence among and for us humans. Theologically, this is reflected on and developed in Christology and in the corollary doctrines of God (the Trinity) and of humankind (anthropology). The latter is what constitutes faith in Jesus as the Christ: that Jesus Christ is a reliable sign for God's hidden presence is understood in faith and confessed as truth made certain by God. Theologically, this is considered and developed in Pneumatology and in the corollary doctrines of faith (justification) and of the community of faith (ecclesiology). Taken all together, this underscores the fact that no phenomenon as such is a sign of God's hidden presence. Rather, phenomena become such signs only through Godself. This is true both in regard to their as-structure (sign *of God*) as well as their for-structure (sign of God *for us*). They become signs *for God's presence* only because

God reveals Godself for us in them; they become *signs* for God's presence only when in faith, thanks to God's self-revelation, they become so understood.

10. Radical Contingency and the Trinity

This point has both theological and hermeneutical implications. Hermeneutically, it means that the specific terms used for considering and understanding God always reflect the nature of the situation in which this change of orientation came about. Therefore, there is not simply one "right" definition of God. Instead, there are a number of appropriate understandings of God that intertwine in multitudinous ways and are always being refined. Strictly speaking, one can only speak of an understanding *of God*—and not just of a more or less appropriate *understanding* of God—when there is an event of understanding God, an event in which the content-sense (what), the relational-sense (who), and the enactment-sense (how) coincide in such a way that "God is revealed through God as God for someone." If one replaces "for someone" in this formulation with "people of faith," one arrives at Bultmann's position; replace it with "in Jesus Christ for all" and one arrives at Barth's position. Both have to do with an event, and the meaning of the enactment of the event is this: there can be theological recourse to salvation history (*Heilsgeschichte*) only by recourse to a *saving event (Heilsgeschehen) that communicates and makes itself understandable as such.*

If that is radically thought through, then "God" means nothing other than the event in which *God*, by means of certain phenomena of our experience of the world or of self, *through God* (who makes these phenomena the locus of God's understandable, self-disclosing presence) becomes understandable for someone *as God*. This defines the presence of this event as a saving presence, reveals the ontological plasticity of this phenomenal event, specifies that the understanding of God arising within it is dynamic and contingent upon the fact that it is God who makes Godself understandable for others as God, and thus differentiates the understanding of the one addressed into a before and after, which can be theologically formulated and explored using the guiding distinction between old and new.

Inasmuch as this event is necessarily *for someone*, it has to do with someone who is thereby set apart. This someone need not be an individual; it can also be a number of people who through this experience are set apart from other individuals and groups and constituted as a new social group. What is decisive, either for an individual or for a group, is that a difference is established: those affected understand themselves and everything else no longer just as they did before, but in a new and different way, a discontinuous way. In the place of I ("there"), otherness breaks out, which makes it necessary to speak of "the old I and the new I," of "I, but not I." Theologically, this is to be considered under the twin figures of creation and sin. "Creation" is that which distinguishes the *old* and *new I* from the one who here through God discloses God as God (the distinction between Creator and creature). Sin is that which distinguishes the *new I* from the *old I* (the difference between sinner and creature). Here and now, the *I/we* that existed 'then' becomes both strange and understandable in a new way; this is so because, and to the degree that, God becomes understandable in a certain way as God.

This event can be so understood and explained only because and to the degree that it itself has a concrete sign-structure. It is a sign-event, more precisely a concrete sign-event, in the threefold respect that it makes use of *specific signs* for something *specifically signified* within a *specific signification-event*. In the Christian tradition, the first is symbolized as the "Word of God" ("word of the cross"), the second as "God" ("Father, Son, and Holy Spirit"), the third as the historically concrete event of "word and faith." This event is radically contingent because, once again in a threefold way, it refers very specifically to a certain history. It thus raises three fundamental questions. First, in reference to Jesus, why this one and no other? Second, in reference to the designation of Jesus as Word of God, why so and not otherwise? And, third, in reference to the event that always occurs anew, that people come to have faith in this Jesus as God's word for them, why these people and not—yet—others? There is no satisfactory answer to any of these questions without referring to God. However, just referring to God offers no clarification of this threefold contingency. Instead, it holds the questions open in principle.

The fact that God has revealed Godself as God, according to Christian understanding, within this radical contingency has led Christian theology to think of God in a *Trinitarian* manner. Trinitarian theology safeguards the radical contingency of God in thinking about God. Trinitarian theology is thus not merely an answer to the three questions named above. Instead, it is the enduring memory that theology may not and cannot demand clarity regarding the contingent occurrence that precedes it and forms its basis. Even when it has said and clarified all that it can understand, theology recognizes open questions that it is not able to answer. They are simply part and parcel of the contingency of the event that it seeks to explore.

The chain of thought that leads to the Trinity is hermeneutically obvious and theologically consequential: if God is understood only insofar as *God makes God understandable for us as God*, then God must be thought of as the one who is in a position to make God understandable as God, or, to put it more precisely, who is the very one who freely makes God understandable to others as God by means of others than God: God is the one who freely discloses God as *God for all* to others through others. The theological tradition has sought to make this understandable by explicating the Johannine prologue with reference to its distinction between *God* and the *Word of God*: God is the one who from eternity makes Godself communicable for others in the divine Word. This Word of God comes to speech for us both in Jesus Christ as *deus loquentis persona* and in becoming present through the *verbum externum* of the gospel to those who hear and understand the testimony of the gospel in such a way that they are moved by the Spirit to reorient their lives from nonfaith to faith. This occurs because the *verbum externum*, through God the Spirit, becomes so understandable as God's Word that they begin to understand, both positively (as creatures) and negatively (as sinners), what it means to be God's creatures: the undeserving addressees of God's unconditional love, care, attention, and affection.

The doctrine of the Trinity, theologically developed with a view to understanding God, is thus not a speculative theory about God. It is rather the event-hermeneutical sum total of the life-changing reorientation of people, who, through the working of God's Word and Spirit, come of their own free will and insight to shift from nonfaith to faith. This is not because they thereby attain a goal they had always sought on their own to attain, but rather because, in the light of the gospel, they can do no other without living contrary to their own deepest insight.

11. Radical Witness

The *radical presence* (self-occurring), *radical otherness* (everything altered, in the sense of seeing all things new, from another perspective and within another horizon than before), and *radical contingency* (from *there* [Jesus], *this* [God's saving work] for *these* [particular people]) can be considered theologically only because and insofar as they phenomenally come to speech in a particular way in *the witness of faith*. This witness is itself a contingent historical phenomenon, characterized by all the particularities of historical phenomena. This is true from its first appearance, through the biblical testimonies, up to the always-differing ways in which it is borne witness to in history, both verbally and through the practice of life. Theologically, it can be grasped only as witness, but no witness that can be grasped theologically is identical to the event to which it bears witness. In the witness of faith, memories of past witness and the actualization of new witness are superimposed upon one another so that one can and must read every witness not only in terms of what it retrospectively and anaphorically presupposes and continues, but also in terms of that which it prospectively, creatively, or imaginatively initiates, releases, or makes possible. That which is radically present, other, and contingent can only be understood and considered because and insofar as it is *borne witness to*. And it can only be understood and considered *as* radically present, other, and contingent because and insofar as it *in a radical sense is always witnessed afresh*, that is, that it consists in nothing other than the preceding witness being continued in new witness.

There is no premature exit from this long chain of witnesses. What inimitably comes to speech cannot be made accessible by abridging it to be nothing more than a special case of the common. Instead, one must repeatedly say it anew, neither neutralizing it by fixing it in particular terms nor seeking to come to grips with its radicality in reasoning by turning its conceptual representation into a dynamic progression from concept to concept. Rather, as a recurring memory it can only be kept alive by being continuously spoken anew and borne witness to. *Continuing witness* is the means of its transmission, and this requires two things to be made clear: as *witness* it brings *something other than itself* to speech, and as *radical* witness it makes clear that what it brings to speech can be understood only insofar as it makes itself present by becoming—sometimes, unpredictably, in a way that is not methodologically controllable, but nonetheless truly and repeatedly—understood anew.

12. Distancing and Disorientation

It will not be understood, however, with distanced coolness or by disinterested contemplation. It will be understood only "passionately" or not at all, as Kierkegaard rightly stressed. Thus, it always appears in the same way: not through simply taking intellectual notice of it from one's given perspective and standpoint, but rather through a radical change of life, a change both of position and orientation. The cheap accusation that this is blind decisionism fundamentally misunderstands the phenomenon: the event of such a change of orientation does not take place through one's own choice, or as an arbitrary decision, or in pure immediacy; it takes place through the *occurrence of a concrete sign-event* in one's life. The medium of the sign, the language, the word—and thus the contingency of the concrete historical details of a life that can be related in narrative and discussed in argumentation—do not fall away but instead are radically revalued.

For in this sign-event the signified so coincides with its sign that the presence of the sign *God* ("word of God") becomes the presence of God for the recipient (hearer or reader). God comes as Word in human words to human beings, and they do not remain who they were.

In fact, this removal of the distinction between sign (word) and signified (Word) at the place of sign-usage leads, at the place of the sign-using human, to distinctions that were not possible before. This event thus appears in the life of a person as the occurrence of an existential *dislocation and disorientation* through which a distanced position to the usual and customary becomes possible, a distance without which there is no reflective orientation to life. *Dislocating* here means "to be changed from something to something through something or someone." That is, it has to do with a change of place in the widest sense of a *change of orientation*: another perspective opens up another horizon of orientation. If such a change takes place through oneself, as a *self-alteration*, then this event can then be described actively, as *something one does*. If, on the other hand, it takes place through other things, through others or an other, then it has to do with an *alteration from outside*, and the event is described passively as *something that occurs to* one or that one *undergoes*.

Whoever is dislocated no longer has the prior perspective (before) but another (after). Before, one did *not* live in faith; *now* one lives in faith. This change can be described in two ways. First, one can present it as an alteration from *being so* to *being different*. Then it has to do with a becoming different, inasmuch as one is now *something* that one was not before: one immigrates to the United States, joins a church, becomes a Christian. One who before was not a U.S. citizen, not a church member, not a Christian, now is. Second, one can also describe this change as a transition from *nonbeing* (nonfaith) to *being* (faith). It has to do with a *becoming* or *becoming new*, inasmuch as one now *is* while before one was *not*: one is born, one lives in faith, one becomes Christian. As distinct from the first case, being Christian, so understood, is not a special way to live as a human (that is, a special form of human existence). It is instead the unexpected experience of living as a new human being (and thus a new human existence). Even those who become Christian in the first sense must still become so in the second sense, as Kierkegaard never tired of stressing. His critical distinction between *Christendom* and *Christianity*, which Heidegger took up in his lecture "Phenomenology and Theology," refers precisely to this distinction between *becoming different* (the alteration of situation within a life) and *becoming* or *becoming new* (the beginning of a [new] life). When it comes to pass that one not only lives *differently* but truly *lives* at all, that is no alteration of situation. It is a new *becoming*, which one cannot ascribe to oneself but only to another. Indeed, in the strictest sense, when it has to do with a becoming from nonbeing into being, only God, as the Creator of this creation, is to be thanked.

Radical theology employs both ways of seeing the matter as it seeks to understand the origins of faith. It understands the change from nonfaith to faith not only as a becoming different but as a becoming new. To put it more sharply: it understands *this* becoming different *as* a becoming new. *Understanding* thus occurs *backward. Seen from faith*, what came before is described as *nonfaith. Living it*, however, occurs *forward*. A person of nonfaith becomes a person of faith. Only afterward can it be seen at all that earlier one did not simply not have faith but instead *had lived in unfaith*. From the perspective of the one who has newly become a person of faith, this is a change from nonbeing to being. One is now *what* one earlier was not (becoming different), but one understands this as *becoming new*: one *is* now, while earlier one *was not*. Therefore, people of faith cannot understand themselves as people of faith without thanking the Creator rather than themselves or only other people: they *are*, even though they did not have to be and also might not have been.

Inasmuch as this change from people of nonfaith to people of faith is understood as a *becoming new*, the thinking of radical theology has a fundamentally metaphorical and paradoxical structure. It describes the becoming different—from the perspective of the one who has become new—*as* becoming new (faith). It thus understands *backward*, from faith, what was lived *forward* as the change from unfaith to faith.

Inasmuch as it holds fast to both, thus speaking two languages and linking two discourses in a particular order, it preserves the reciprocal otherness of the two ways of seeing. At the same time, it makes clear that only from faith can nonfaith be spoken of us as unfaith, while from the other point of view, faith appears only to be one variation of the (religious) life of human beings. Unfaith can be thought of only from faith, and unfaith can thus never become a topic of thought for someone who will not or cannot think in this way.

13. Reorientation

From this dislocation and disorientation regarding what came before arises the task of a *constant reorientation*. The event of dislocation, the change of place and orientation, divides the life of a person into a *before* and an *after*. However, the before is not simply the old, nor the after the new. From a scientific perspective (even that of religious studies), this change of orientation appears to be only a becoming different, a change to a particular way of living religiously. It thus appears, empirically and historically, to be a particular cultural phenomenon. *Old*, here, is what is past and previous, biographically and historically, while new is the present and current.

From the perspective of radical theology, however, this becoming different in Christian faith is understood as a *becoming new* through God. This necessitates that the before not be equated with the old and that the after not be equated with the new. Instead, both the before *and* the after must be critically evaluated from the point of view of their relationship to the presence of God. Regarding the before, one must distinguish between that which passes away and has come to an end (the old) and that which points ahead to the future (as a token of the new). Regarding the after, one must always distinguish between that which has a future and can be built up (new life) and that which comes to its end and is torn down (old life). This distinction must also be made constantly when considering the present because much that is current and supersedes the past is not really new, but old through and through. The necessary powers of judgment and distinction must be developed;

else one cannot escape the mistake of confusing the current with the new and the earlier with the old. It is not that simple. The old is to be found in the current, just as the new is to be found in the earlier. Distinguishing the times is not to be equated with distinguishing between old and new. Instead, past, present, and future must always be critically judged in the light of the old and the new. So long as life goes on, the need for this critical judgment continues. The existential change of orientation that comes about through becoming aware of the presence of God requires always that both the before and the after—the past, present, and future of a life—be evaluated, judged, and understood in a differentiated way in the light of God's presence.

Bultmann described this existential change of orientation in a traditional manner: *people come to faith*. Barth set a different accent: *faith comes to people*. Hermeneutical theologians such as Ebeling or Fuchs expressed it with terms like *word-event* and *speech-event*, redescribing God's working of change in human life as a sign-event that makes itself understandable. However one speaks of this radical change of orientation that puts everything in a new light, the decisive thing is that theological reflection distinguishes, with full clarity, the fact *that* this change occurs from all attempts to understand *what* there occurs. That God gains attention in the life of humans, and that humans thereby begin to orient themselves anew with a view toward God, is not a necessity and is not to be understood theologically as a necessity. But if God were to gain no such attention, and if there were no such radical change of orientation in human life, then there would be nothing to understand theologically.

14. God's Creative Presence as the Topic of Theology

This life-changing experience of God's presence—not the historical, social, or religious reality of Christianity, of the church, or of the life of Christians in and of themselves—makes theology possible and makes theological reflection necessary. There are many religions, but no theology is needed to understand them. Christianity is a historical and social phenomenon that can also be studied without theology.

Christians and churches can be studied profitably from a number of points of view. Theologically, however, all of that is interesting only for the sake of the task that Christians as churches and as individuals have in the world: to call attention to God by means of what they say (or do not say) and do (or do not do). To witness to God's presence, to the fact that God freely makes Godself present for the sake of God's creation, is the point of their existence in the world.

This explicit witness distinguishes Christians, in a theologically relevant way, from other people. It is precisely this witness that makes it clear that they are merely what others also could be: a living witness to the possibility of understanding oneself and everything else in the light of the presence of God, a living indication of the benefit that means for a life, but also of the difficulties that such a life must reckon with.

That people do, in fact, come to understand and to live their lives in such a way remains the elusive prerequisite of Christian witness. Christians can neither effectuate this nor precipitate it; they can only anaphorically bear witness to it. The condition that makes this radical change of life and orientation possible is the elusive event of which the Christian witness speaks, that makes it real, to which Christian faith owes its existence, and about which radical theology reflects: the in-breaking of the new within human lives. This in-breaking can occur in a surprising and conspicuous way or as a gradually growing change that is hardly appreciable and that is clearly apparent only in retrospect. In one way or the other, the life of people becomes transparent to the presence of God for them. This leads them, in the light of God's presence, not only to understand the past, present, and future of their lives in a radically new way, but also to live their lives in an entirely new way—as a life of faith, in thankfulness to God and in astonishment over their own unfaith.

Bibliography

Albrecht, Christian. *Historische Kulturwissenschaft neuzeitlicher Christentumspraxis. Klassische Protestantismustheorien in ihrer Bedeutung für das Selbstverständnis der Praktischen Theologie.* Tübingen: Mohr Siebeck, 2000.

Altizer, Thomas J. J. *The Contemporary Jesus.* Albany: State University of New York Press, 1997.

———. *The Gospel of Christian Atheism.* Philadelphia: Westminster, 1966.

Altizer, Thomas J. J., and W. Hamilton, eds. *Radical Theology and the Death of God.* Harmondsworth: Penguin, 1968.

Angehrn, Emil. *Interpretation und Dekonstruktion. Untersuchungen zur Hermeneutik.* Wielerswist: Königshausen & Neumann, 2003.

Bader, Günter. "Erfahrung mit der Erfahrung." In *Wirkungen hermeneutischer Theologie, FS Gerhard Ebeling,* edited by Hans F. Geisser and Walter Mostert, 137–53. Tübingen: Mohr Siebeck, 1983.

Badiou, Alain. *L'être et l'événement.* Paris: Seuil, 1988.

Barker, Jason. *Alain Badiou: A Critical Introduction.* London: Pluto, 2002.

Barth, Karl. *Church Dogmatics.* Vol. 4, 1–3.2. Edited by G. W. Bromiley and T. F. Torrance. Edinburgh: T&T Clark, 1961, 1967, 1988.

———. *Rudolf Bultmann. Ein Versuch, ihn zu verstehen.* Zurich: Evangelischer, 1964.

Barth, Ulrich. *Gott als Projekt der Vernunft.* Tübingen: Mohr Siebeck, 2005.

———. *Religion in der Moderne.* Tübingen: Mohr Siebeck, 2003.

———. "Theoriedimensionen des Religionsbegriffs. Die Binnenrelevanz der sogenannten Außenperspektive." In *Religion in der Moderne,* 29–87.

____. "Was ist Religion? Sinndeutung zwischen Erfahrung und Letztbegründung." In *Religion in der Moderne*, 3–27.

____. "Zur Barth-Deutung Eberhard Jüngels." *Theologische Zeitschrift* 40 (1984): 296–320, 394–415.

Bayer, Oswald. "Hermeneutische Theologie." In *Glauben und Verstehen. Perspektiven hermeneutischer Theologie*, edited by Ulrich H. J. Körtner, 39–55. Neukirchen-Vluyn: Neukirchener Verlag, 2000.

Bertram, Georg W. *Hermeneutik und Dekonstruktion: Konturen einer Auseinandersetzung in der Gegenwartsphilosophie*. Munich: Fink, 2002.

Beuscher, Bernd. "WinWord. Die Sprachlichkeit des Evangeliums und das Nadelöhr der Medien. Eine semiotische Orientierungsskizze." In *Hermeneutik und Ästhetik. Die Theologie des Wortes im multimedialen Zeitalter*, edited by Ulrich H. J. Körtner, 98–133. Neukirchen-Vluyn: Neukirchener Verlag, 2001.

Bogdal, Klaus-Michael. "Problematisierungen der Hermeneutik im Zeichen des Poststrukturalismus." In *Grundzüge der Literaturwissenschaft*, edited by Heinz L. Arnold and Heinrich Detering, 137–56. Munich: dtv, 1996.

Bormann, Claus V. "Hermeneutik: I. Philosophisch-theologisch." *TRE* 15 (1986): 108–37.

Braun, Herbert. "Die Problematik einer Theologie des Neuen Testaments." In *Gesammelte Studien zum Neuen Testament und seiner Umwelt*, 325–41. Tübingen: Mohr Siebeck, 1967.

Brkic, Pero. *Martin Heidegger und die Theologie. Ein Thema in dreifacher Fragestellung*. Mainz: Matthias-Grünewald-Verlag, 1994.

Bultmann, Rudolph. "Der Begriff der Offenbarung im Neuen Testament." In *Glauben und Verstehen III*, 1–34.

____. *Glauben und Verstehen I*. Tübingen: Mohr Siebeck, 1980.

____. *Glauben und Verstehen II*. Tübingen: Mohr Siebeck, 1952.

____. *Glauben und Verstehen III*. Tübingen: Mohr Siebeck, 1960.

____. "Heilsgeschehen und Geschichte. Zu Oscar Cullmann, *Christus und die Zeit*." *Theologische Literaturzeitung* 73 (1948): 659–66.

____. "Ist voraussetzungslose Exegese möglich?" *Theologische Zeitschrift* 13 (1957): 409–17.

____. "Das Problem der Hermeneutik." In *Glauben und Verstehen II*, 211–35.

———. "Das Problem der 'natürlichen Theologie.'" In *Glauben und Verstehen I*, 294–312.

———. "Das Problem einer theologischen Exegese des neuen Testamentes." *Zwischen den Zeiten* 3 (1925): 334–57.

———. *Theologische Enzyklopädie*. Edited by Eberhard Jüngel and Klaus W. Müller. Tübingen: Mohr Siebeck, 1984.

———. "Welchen Sinn hat es, von Gott zu reden?" In *Glauben und Verstehen I*, 26–37.

Bultmann, Rudolph, and Martin Heidegger. *Rudolf Bultmann, Martin Heidegger, Briefwechsel 1925-1975*. Edited by Andreas Großmann and Christoph Landmesser, with an introduction by Eberhard Jüngel. Frankfurt am Main: V. Klostermann; Tübingen: Mohr Siebeck, 2009.

Buren, Paul van. *The Secular Meaning of the Gospel: Based on an Analysis of Its Language*. New York: Macmillan, 1963.

Buri, Fritz. "Entmythologisierung oder Entkerygmatisierung der Theologie." *Kerygma und Dogma* II (1952), 85–101.

Capelle, Philippe. *Philosophie et Théologie dans la pensée de Martin Heidegger*. Paris: Cerf, 2001.

Caputo, John. *Demythologizing Heidegger*. Bloomington: Indiana University Press, 1993.

———. *Heidegger and Aquinas: An Essay on Overcoming Metaphysics*. New York: Fordham University Press, 1982.

———. "Heidegger and Theology." In *The Cambridge Companion to Heidegger*, edited by Charles Guignon, 270–88. Cambridge: Cambridge University Press, 1993.

———. *More Radical Hermeneutics: On Not Knowing Who We Are*. Bloomington: Indiana University Press, 2000.

———. *The Mystical Element in Heidegger's Thought*. Rev. ed. New York: Fordham University Press, 1986.

———. *On Religion*. London: Routledge, 2001.

———. *Philosophy and Theology*. Nashville: Abingdon, 2006.

———. *The Prayers and Tears of Jacques Derrida: Religion without Religion*. Bloomington: Indiana University Press, 1997.

———. "The Question of Being and Transcendental Phenomenology: Heidegger's Relationship to Husserl." *Research in Phenomenology* 7 (1977): 84–105.

———. *Radical Hermeneutics: Repetition, Deconstruction, and the Hermeneutic Project*. Bloomington: Indiana University Press, 1987.

———. "Radical Theology from Hegel to Zizek." Syllabus, Fall 2009. http://religion.syr.edu/courses/fall2009_pdfs/rel667.pdf.

———. *The Weakness of God: A Theology of the Event*. Bloomington: Indiana University Press, 2006.

———. *What Would Jesus Deconstruct? The Good News of Postmodernism for the Church*. Ada, MI: Baker Academic, 2007.

Caputo, John, and Gianni Vattimo. *After the Death of God*. Edited by Jeffrey W. Robbins. New York: Columbia University Press, 2007.

Caspar, Bernhard. "Die Gründung einer philosophischen Theologie im Ereignis." *Dialegesthai: Rivista telematica di filosofia* 5 (2003), http://mondodomani.org/dialegesthai.

———. "Transzendentale Phänomenalität und ereignetes Ereignis. Der Sprung in ein hermeneutisches Denken im Leben und Werk Franz Rosenzweigs." In *Vom Rätsel des Begriffs. FS F.W. von Herrmann*, edited by Paola-Ludovika Coriando, 359–63. Berlin: Duncker & Humblot, 1999.

Cassirer, Ernst. *An Essay on Man*. New Haven: Yale University Press, 1944.

———. *Philosophy of Symbolic Forms* (1923–1929). New Haven: Yale University Press, 1965.

Clayton, Philip. *Mind and Emergence. From Quantum to Consciousness*. Oxford: Oxford University Press, 2004.

Clayton, Philip, and P. Davies, eds. *The Re-emergence of Emergence: The Emergenist Hypothesis from Science to Religion*. Oxford: Oxford University Press, 2006.

Cobb, John B., ed. *The Theology of Altizer: Critique and Response*. Philadelphia: Westminster, 1970.

Consten, Mandfred. *Anaphorisch oder deiktisch?* Tübingen: Max Niemeyer, 2004.

Couzen-Hoy, David. *The Critical Circle: Literature, History and Philosophical Hermeneutics*. Berkeley: University of California Press, 1978.

Cupitt, Don. *Radical Theology: Selected Essays*. Santa Rosa, CA: Polebridge, 2006.

Dalferth, Ingolf U. "Alles umsonst. Zur Kunst des Schenkens und den Grenzen der Gabe." In *Von der Ursprünglichkeit der Gabe. Jean-Luc Marios*

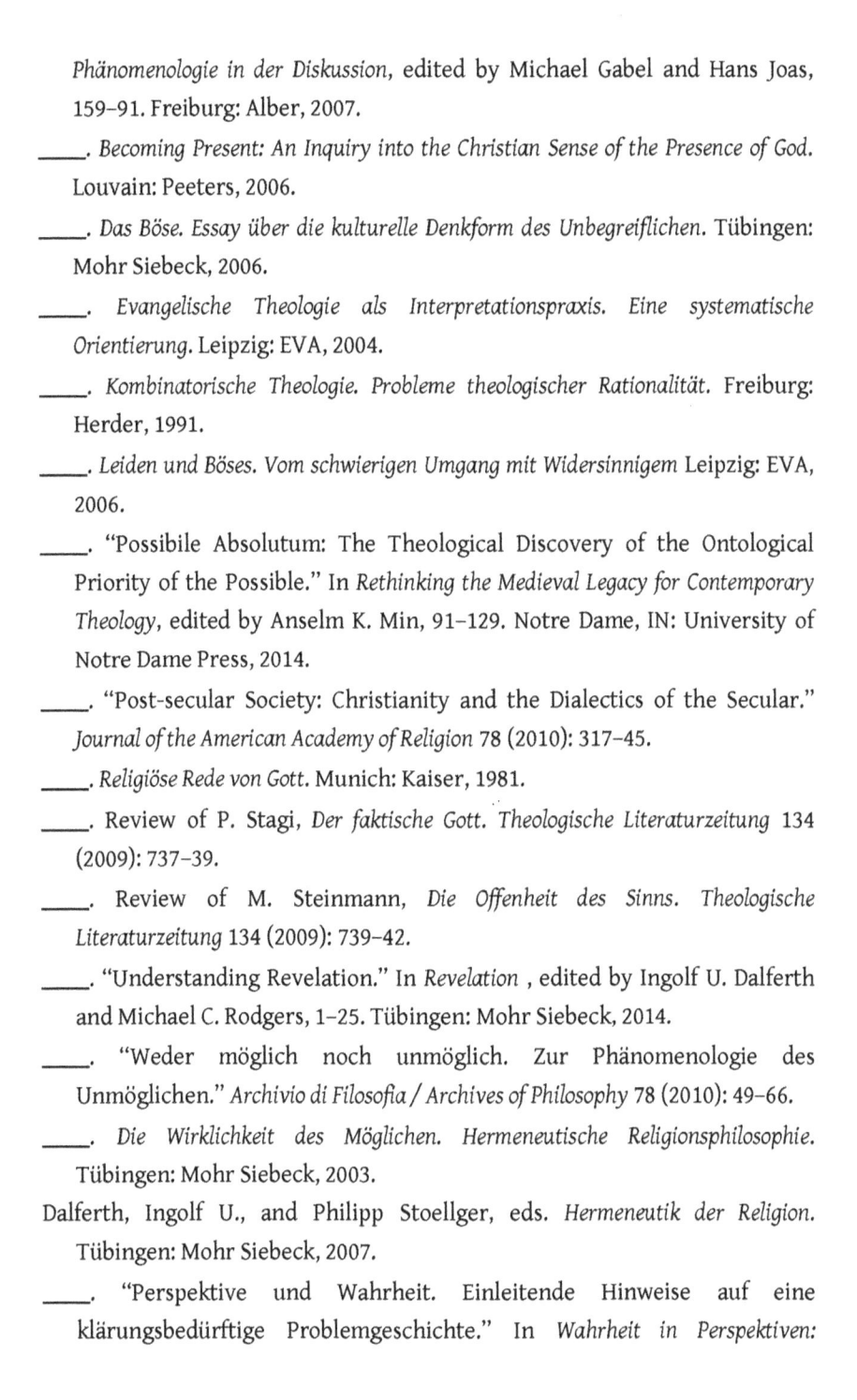

Phänomenologie in der Diskussion, edited by Michael Gabel and Hans Joas, 159–91. Freiburg: Alber, 2007.

———. *Becoming Present: An Inquiry into the Christian Sense of the Presence of God.* Louvain: Peeters, 2006.

———. *Das Böse. Essay über die kulturelle Denkform des Unbegreiflichen.* Tübingen: Mohr Siebeck, 2006.

———. *Evangelische Theologie als Interpretationspraxis. Eine systematische Orientierung.* Leipzig: EVA, 2004.

———. *Kombinatorische Theologie. Probleme theologischer Rationalität.* Freiburg: Herder, 1991.

———. *Leiden und Böses. Vom schwierigen Umgang mit Widersinnigem* Leipzig: EVA, 2006.

———. "Possibile Absolutum: The Theological Discovery of the Ontological Priority of the Possible." In *Rethinking the Medieval Legacy for Contemporary Theology*, edited by Anselm K. Min, 91–129. Notre Dame, IN: University of Notre Dame Press, 2014.

———. "Post-secular Society: Christianity and the Dialectics of the Secular." *Journal of the American Academy of Religion* 78 (2010): 317–45.

———. *Religiöse Rede von Gott.* Munich: Kaiser, 1981.

———. Review of P. Stagi, *Der faktische Gott. Theologische Literaturzeitung* 134 (2009): 737–39.

———. Review of M. Steinmann, *Die Offenheit des Sinns. Theologische Literaturzeitung* 134 (2009): 739–42.

———. "Understanding Revelation." In *Revelation*, edited by Ingolf U. Dalferth and Michael C. Rodgers, 1–25. Tübingen: Mohr Siebeck, 2014.

———. "Weder möglich noch unmöglich. Zur Phänomenologie des Unmöglichen." *Archivio di Filosofia / Archives of Philosophy* 78 (2010): 49–66.

———. *Die Wirklichkeit des Möglichen. Hermeneutische Religionsphilosophie.* Tübingen: Mohr Siebeck, 2003.

Dalferth, Ingolf U., and Philipp Stoellger, eds. *Hermeneutik der Religion.* Tübingen: Mohr Siebeck, 2007.

———. "Perspektive und Wahrheit. Einleitende Hinweise auf eine klärungsbedürftige Problemgeschichte." In *Wahrheit in Perspektiven:*

Probleme einer offenen Konstellation, edited by Ingolf U. Dalferth and Philipp Stoellger, 1–28. Tübingen: Mohr Siebeck, 2004.

———. "Wahrheit, Glaube und Theologie. Zur theologischen Rezeption zeitgenössischer wahrheitstheoretischer Diskussionen." *Theologische Rundschau* 66 (2001): 36–102.

Damasio, Antonio. *The Self Comes to Mind: Constructing the Conscious Mind*. New York: Random House, 2010.

Danneberg, Lutz, and Hans-Harald Müller. "Wissenschaftstheorie, Hermeneutik, Literaturwissenschaft. Anmerkungen zu einem unterbliebenen und Beiträge zu einem künftigen Dialog über die Methodologie des Verstehens." *Deutsche Vierteljahrsschrift für Literaturwissenschaft und Geistesgeschichte* 58 (1984): 177–237.

Danz, Christian. *Gott und die menschliche Freiheit. Studien zum Gottesbegriff in der Neuzeit*. Neukirchen-Vluyn: Neukirchener Verlag, 2005.

———. *Wirken Gottes. Zur Geschichte eines theologischen Grundbegriffs*. Neukirchen-Vluyn: Neukirchener Verlag, 2007.

Derrida, Jacques. *Dissemination*. Vienna: Passagen Verlag, 1995.

———. *Eine gewissen unmögliche Möglichkeit, vom Ereignis zu sprechen*. Trans. S. Lüdemann. Berlin: Merve, 2003.

Dennett, Daniel. *Breaking the Spell: Religion as a Natural Phenomenon*. New York: Penguin Books, 2006.

Devitt, Michael, and Kim Sterelney. *Language and Reality: An Introduction to the Philosophy of Language*. Oxford: Blackwell, 1987.

Diem, Hermann. *Theologie als kirchliche Wissenschaft*. Vol 2, *Dogmatik*. Munich: Kaiser, 1960.

———. "Zur Problematik theologischer Wahrheitsfindung." *Theologische Literaturzeitung* 95 (1970): 161–72.

Draper, Paul. "God, Science, and Naturalism." In *The Oxford Handbook of Philosophy of Religion*, edited by William Wainwright, 272–303. Oxford: Oxford University Press, 2005.

Dupré, Louis. "Husserl's Thought on God and Faith." *Philosophy and Phenomenological Research* 29 (1968–1969): 201–15.

Ebeling, Gerhard. "Die Bedeutung der historisch-kritischen Methode für die protestantische Theologie und Kirche." In *Wort und Glaube*, 1–49.

_____. *Dogmatik des christlichen Glaubens I*. Tübingen: Mohr Siebeck, 1987.

_____. *Dogmatik des christlichen Glaubens III*. Tübingen: Mohr Siebeck, 1979.

_____. *Einführung in theologische Sprachlehre*. Tübingen. Mohr Siebeck, 1971.

_____. "Elementare Besinnung auf verantwortliches Reden von Gott." In *Wort und Glaube*, 349–71.

_____. "Erwägungen zur Lehre vom Gesetz." In *Wort und Glaube*, 255–93.

_____. "Existenz zwischen Gott und Gott." In *Wort und Glaube II*, 257–86.

_____. "Die Frage nach dem historischen Jesus und das Problem der Christologie." In *Wort und Glaube*, 300–318.

_____. "Glaube und Unglaube im Streit um die Wirklichkeit." In *Wort und Glaube*, 393–406.

_____. "Hermeneutische Theologie?" In *Wort und Glaube II*, 99–120.

_____. "Karl Barths Ringen mit Luther." In *Lutherstudien III*, 428–573. Tübingen: Mohr Siebeck, 1985.

_____. "Die Klage über das Erfahrungsdefizit der Theologie." In *Wort und Glaube III*, 3–28.

_____. *Luther. Einführung in sein Denken*. Tübingen: Mohr Siebeck, 1964.

_____. "Das Problem des Bösen als Prüfstein der Anthropologie." In *Wort und Glaube III*, 205–24.

_____. *Theologie und Verkündigung. Ein Gespräch mit Rudolf Bultmann*. Tübingen: Mohr Siebeck, 1962.

_____. "Theologie zwischen reformatorischem Sündenverständnis und heutiger Einstellung zum Bösen." In *Wort und Glaube III*, 173–204.

_____. "Theologische Erwägungen über das Gewissen." In *Wort und Glaube*, 429–46.

_____. "Das Verständnis von Heil in säkularisierter Zeit." In *Wort und Glaube III*, 349–61.

_____. "Weltliches Reden von Gott." In *Wort und Glaube*, 372–80.

_____. *Das Wesen des christlichen Glaubens*. Tübingen: Mohr Siebeck, 1959.

_____. "Wort Gottes und Hermeneutik." In *Wort und Glaube*, 319–48.

_____. *Wort und Glaube*. Tübingen: Mohr Siebeck, 1967.

_____. *Wort und Glaube II*. Tübingen: Mohr Siebeck, 1969.

_____. *Wort und Glaube III*. Tübingen: Mohr Siebeck, 1975.

———. "Zum Verständnis von R. Bultmanns Aufsatz: 'Welchen Sinn hat es, von Gott zu reden?'" In *Wort und Glaube II*, 343–71.

Eco, Umberto. *Lector in fabula*. Munich: dtv, 1998.

———. *The Limits of Interpretation*. Bloomington: Indiana University Press, 1990.

———. *The Role of the Reader: Explorations in the Semiotics of Texts*. Bloomington: Indiana University Press, 1979.

Feldman, Richard. "Methodological Naturalism in Epistemology." In *The Blackwell Guide to Epistemology*, edited by John Greco and Ernest Sosa, 170–86. Malden, MA: Blackwell, 1999.

———. "Naturalized Epistemology." In *The Stanford Encyclopedia of Philosophy*, Fall 2006. http://plato.stanford.edu/archives/fall2006/entries/epistemology-naturalized/.

Felski, Rita. "After Suspicion." In *Profession*, 2009, 28–35.

Figal, Günter. *Gegenständlichkeit. Das Hermeneutische und die Philosophie*. Tübingen: Mohr Siebeck, 2007.

Fischer, Hermann. "Natürliche Theologie im Wandel." *Zeitschrift für Theologie und Kirche* 80 (1983): 85–102.

Fitzgerald, Timothy. *The Ideology of Religious Studies*. Oxford: Oxford University Press, 2000.

Franz, Helmut. "Das Wesen des Textes." *Zeitschrift für Theologie und Kirche* 59 (1962): 182–225.

Fuchs, Ernst. "Alte und neue Hermeneutik." In *Glaube und Erfahrung*, 193–230.

———. "Antwort auf die amerikanischen Beiträge." In *Die neue Hermeneutik*, edited by James M. Robinson and John B. Cobb, 299–311. Zurich: Zwingli, 1965.

———. "Das Christusverständnis bei Paulus und im Johannesevangelium." In *Jesus Christus. Das Christusverständnis im Wandel der Zeiten*, Marburger Theologische Studien 1, edited by Hans Grass and Werner G. Kümmel, 11–20. Marburg: N. G. Elwert, 1963.

———. *Glaube und Erfahrung. Zum christologischen Problem im Neuen Testament*. Tübingen: Mohr Siebeck, 1965.

———. *Hermeneutik*. Tübingen: Mohr Siebeck, 1970.

———. "Das hermeneutische Problem." In *Zeit und Geschichte: Dankesgabe an*

Rudolf Bultmann zum 80. Geburtstag, edited by Ernst Dingler, 357–66. Tübingen: Mohr Siebeck, 1967.

———. *Jesus. Wort und Tat*. Tübingen: Mohr Siebeck, 1971.

———. "Kanon und Kerygma." In *Wagnis des Glaubens. Aufsätze und Vorträge*, edited by Eberhard Grötzinger, 21–41. Neukirchen: Neukirchener Verlag, 1979.

———. *Marburger Hermeneutik*. Tübingen: Mohr Siebeck, 1968.

———. "Das Neue Testament und das hermeneutische Problem." In *Glaube und Erfahrung*, 136–73.

———. "Neues Testament und Wort Gottes." *Theologische Literaturzeitung* 97 (1972): 1–16.

———. "Das Problem der theologischen Hermeneutik." In *Gesammelte Aufsätze I: Zum hermeneutischen Problem in der Theologie*, 116–37.

———. "Das Sprachereignis in der Verkündigung Jesu, in der Theologie des Paulus und im Ostergeschehen." In *Zum hermeneutischen Problem in der Theologie*, 281–305.

———. "Was ist ein Sprachereignis? Ein Brief." In *Zur Frage nach dem historischen Jesus*, 424–30. Tübingen: Mohr Siebeck, 1960.

———. "Was ist existentiale Interpretation?" In *Zum hermeneutischen Problem in der Theologie*, 107–15.

———. "Das Wort Gottes." In *Zum hermeneutischen Problem in der Theologie*, 323–33.

———. *Gesammelte Aufsätze I: Zum hermeneutischen Problem in der Theologie. Die existentiale Interpretation*. Tübingen: Mohr Siebeck, 1959.

Gadamer, Hans-Georg. *Truth and Method*. Second, revised edition. Translation revised by J. Weinsheimer and D. G. Marshall. London/New York: Sheed and Ward and the Continuum Publishing Group, 2004.

———. "Vorwort zur 2. Auflage [von Wahrheit und Methode]." In *Gesammelte Werke 2, Hermeneutik II*, 437–448. Tübingen: Mohr Siebeck, 1986.

Gethmann-Seifert, Annemarie. *Das Verhältnis von Philosophie und Theologie im Denken Martin Heideggers*. Freiburg: K. Alber, 1974.

Gill, Jerry H. *Ian Ramsey: To Speak Responsibly of God*. London: Allen and Unwin, 1976.

Göckeritz. Hermann G., ed. *Friedrich Gogartens Briefwechsel mit Karl Barth, Eduard*

Thurneysen und Emil Brunner. With an introduction by H. G. Göckeritz. Tübingen: Mohr Siebeck, 2009.

Gräb, Wilhelm. "Massenmedien—Religion—Hermeneutik." In Dalferth and Stoellger, *Hermeneutik der Religion*, 215–29.

Gräb, Wilhelm, and Birgit Weyel, eds. *Handbuch Praktische Theologie*. Gütersloh: Gütersloher Verlagshaus, 2007.

Gremmels, Christian, and W. Herrmann. "Hermeneutik und Gesellschaftstheorie (Theologie, Hermeneutik und Gesellschaft)." In *Hermeneutik als Kriterium für Wissenschaftlichkeit? Der Standort der Hermeneutik im gegenwärtigen Wissenschaftskanon*, edited by Uwe Gerber, 48–65. Loccum: Ev. Akademie Loccum, 1972.

Grondin, Jean. *Einführung in die philosophische Hermeneutik*. Darmstadt: Wissenschaftliche Buchgesellschaft, 2001.

Großmann, Andreas. "Zwischen Phänomenologie und Theologie: Heideggers 'Marburger Religionsgespräch' mit Rudolf Bultmann." *Zeitschrift für Theologie und Kirche* 95 (1998): 37–62.

Güttgemanns, Erhardt. "'Gottesgerechtigkeit' und strukturale Semantik. Linguistische Analyse zu dikaiosuðnh qeouÜ." In *Studia linguistica neotestamentica*, 59–98. Munich: Kaiser, 1971.

Habermas, Jürgen. "Der Universalitätsanspruch der Hermeneutik." In *Hermeneutik und Ideologiekritik*. Frankfurt am Main: Suhrkamp, 1971.

Härle, Wilfried, and Eilert Herms. "Deutschsprachige protestantische Dogmatik nach 1945." *Verkündigung und Forschung* 27 (1982): 2–100; *Verkündigung und Forschung* 28 (1983): 1–87.

Härle, Wilfried, and Reiner Preul, eds. *Marburger Jahrbuch Theologie VI: Phänomenologie. Über den Gegenstandsbezug der Dogmatik*. Marburg: N. G. Elwert, 1994.

Hallward, Peter. *Badiou: A Subject to Truth*. Minneapolis: University of Minnesota Press, 2003.

———. *Out of This World: Deleuze and the Philosophy of Creation*. London: Verso, 2006.

Hart, James G. "A Précis of an Husserlian Philosophical Theology." In *Essays in Phenomenological Theology*, edited by Steven W. Laycock and James G. Hart, 89–168. Albany: State University of New York Press, 1986.

Hegemann, Helene. *Axolotl Roadkill*. Berlin: Ullstein, 2010.

Heidegger, Martin. *Beiträge zur Philosophie; Besinnung; Über den Anfang* (1941). Frankfurt am Main: V. Klostermann, 2005.

———. *Beiträge zur Philosophie (Vom Ereignis) (1936-1938)*. GA 65. Frankfurt am Main: V. Klostermann, 1994.

———. *Besinnung (1938/39)*. GA 66. Frankfurt am Main: V. Klostermann, 1997.

———. *Brief über den "Humanismus"* (1946). In *Wegmarken*, 313–64. GA 9. Frankfurt am Main: V. Klostermann, 1996.

———. "Einblick in die Notwendigkeit der Kehre" (1964). In *Vom Rätsel des Begriffs* (FS F.-W. v. Herrmann), edited by Paola- Ludovika Coriando, 1–3. Berlin: Duncker & Humblot, 1999.

———. *Die Geschichte des Seyns*. GA 69. Frankfurt am Main: V. Klostermann, 1998.

———. *Ontologie: Hermeneutik der Faktizität*. GA 63. Frankfurt am Main: Suhrkamp, 1995.

———. *Phänomenologie des religiösen Lebens*. GA 60. Frankfurt am Main: Vittorio Klostermann, 1995.

———. *Phänomenologie und Theologie*. Frankfurt am Main: Klostermann, 1970. Translated into English by James G. Hart and John C. Maraldo as *Phenomenology and Theology*, in *The Piety of Thinking: Essays by Martin Heidegger*, 5–21 (Bloomington: Indiana University Press, 1976).

———. "Phänomenologische Interpretationen zu Aristoteles (Anzeige der hermeneutischen Situation) (sog. 'Natorp-Bericht,' 1922)," edited by Hans- Ulrich Lessing. In *Dilthey-Jahrbuch für Philosophie und Geschichte der Geisteswissenschaften* 6, 235–74. Göttingen: Vandenhoek & Ruprecht, 1989.

———. *Sein und Zeit*. Tübingen: Max Niemeyer, 1967. Translated into English by John Macquarrie and Edward Robinson as *Being and Time* (London: SCM, 1962), and by J. Stambaugh as *Being and Time* (New York: State University of New York Press, 1996).

———. *Seminar in Zähringen, Vier Seminare*. Edited by Curd Ochwaldt. Frankfurt am Main: V. Klostermann, 1977.

———. "Zeit und Sein" (1962). In *Zur Sache des Denkens*, 1–26. Tübingen: Niemeyer, 1988.

———. "Zum Martin Heidegger, 'Der Satz der Identität'" (1957), in *Identität und Differenz*, 9–30. Stuttgart: Klett-Cotta, 1999.

Heidegger, Martin, and Elisabeth Blochmann. *Briefwechsel 1918-1969.* Marbach am Neckar: Deutsche Schillergesellschaft, 1989.

Henrich, Dieter. *Fluchtlinien. Philosophische Essays.* Frankfurt am Main: Suhrkamp, 1982.

Henrix, Hans H. Review of *Das Wort wurde messianischer Mensch. Die Theologie Karl Barths und die Theologie des Johannesprologs*, by Jochen Denker. *Theologische Revue* 105 (2009): 223–27.

Herms, Eilert. "Die Einführung des allgemeinen Zeichenbegriffs. Theologische Aspekte der Begründung einer reinen Semiotik durch Ch. W. Morris." In *Theorie für die Praxis. Beiträge zur Theologie*, 164–88. Munich: Kaiser, 1982.

———. "Offenbarung" (1985). In *Offenbarung und Glaube. Zur Bildung des christlichen Lebens*, 168–220. Tübingen: Mohr Siebeck, 1992.

———. "Theologie als Phänomenologie des christlichen Glaubens. Über den Sinn und die Tragweite dieses Verständnisses von Theologie." In *Phänomenologie. Über den Gegenstandsbezug der Dogmatik*, Marburger Jahrbuch Theologie 6, edited by W. Härle and R. Preul, 69–99. Marburg: N. G. Elwert, 1994.

———. *Theologie—eine Erfahrungswissenschaft.* Munich: Kaiser, 1978.

Herrmann, Friedrich-Wilhelm von. "Gottsuche und Selbstauslegung. Das X. Buch der Confessiones des Heiligen Augustinus im Horizont von Heideggers hermeneutischer Phänomenologie des faktischen Lebens." *Studia Phaenomenologica* 1 (2001): 201–19.

———. *Wege ins Ereignis. Zu Heideggers "Beiträgen zur Philosophie."* Frankfurt am Main: V. Klostermann, 1994.

Hess, Peter. "Der Mensch muss sterben—das transzendentale Ich ist unvergänglich. Edmund Husserls Argumente für die Unsterblichkeit des transzendentalen Ichs." PhD dissertation, University of Duisburg-Essen, 2009. https://duepublico.uni-duisburg-essen.de/servlets/DerivateServlet/Derivate-23372/Gesamt_22_10_2009.pdf.

Hock, Klaus. *Einführung in die Religionswissenschaft.* Darmstadt: WBG, 2002.

Höfner, Martin. *Sinn, Symbol, Religion. Theorie des Zeichens und Phänomenologie der Religion bei Ernst Cassirer und Martin Heidegger.* Tübingen: Mohr Siebeck, 2008.

Hoffmann, Veronika. *Vermittelte Offenbarung. Ricoeurs Philosophie als Herausforderung der Theologie*. Mainz: Matthias-Grünewald-Verlag, 2007.

Houser, Nathan, and Christian J. W. Kloesel, eds. *The Essential Peirce, Selected Philosophical Writings, Volume 2 (1893-1913)*. Bloomington: Indiana University Press, 1998.

Husserl, Edmund. *Briefwechsel, Band VI: Philosophenbriefe*. Dordrecht: Springer, 1992.

———. *Briefwechsel, Band VII: Wissenschaftlerkorrespondenz*. Dordrecht: Springer, 1992.

———. *Ideen zu einer reinen Phänomenologie und phänomenologischen Philosophie—Erstes Buch: Allgemeine Einführung in die reine Phänomenologie (1913)*. Husserliana, vol. 3/1. The Hague: Springer, 1976.

———. *Logische Untersuchungen*. Tübingen: Max Niemeyer, 1986.

———. *Vorlesungen über Ethik und Wertlehre, 1908-1914*. Edited by Ullrich Melle. The Hague: Kluwer, 1988.

———. *Zur Phänomenologie der Intersubjektivität, 3. Teil*. Husserliana, vol. 15. The Hague: Springer, 1973.

———. *Zur Phänomenologie der Intersubjektivität, Erster Teil: 1905-1920*. Husserliana, vol. 13. The Hague: Springer 1973.

Imdahl, Georg. *Das Leben verstehen. Heideggers formal anzeigende Hermeneutik in den frühen Freiburger Vorlesungen*. Würzburg: Königshausen & Neumann, 1997.

Jäger, Alfred. *Gott. Nochmals Martin Heidegger*. Tübingen: Mohr Siebeck, 1978.

Janicaud, Dominique. *La phénoménologie éclatée*. Combas: L'Eclat, 1997.

———. *Le tournant théologique de la phenomenologie française*. Combas: L'Eclat, 1991.

Jenson, Robert W. *The Knowledge of Things Hoped For: The Sense of Theological Discourse*. New York: Oxford University Press, 1969.

Jung, Matthias. *Das Denken des Seins und der Glaube an Gott. Zum Verhältnis von Philosophie und Theologie bei Martin Heidegger*. Würzburg: Königshausen & Neumann, 1990.

Jüngel, Eberhard. *Barth-Studien*. Gütersloh: Gütersloher Verlagshaus, 1982.

———. "Das Dilemma der natürlichen Theologie und die Wahrheit ihres Problems. Überlegungen für ein Gespräch mit Wolfhart Pannenberg." In *Entsprechungen*, 158–77.

_____. *Entsprechungen: Gott-Wahrheit-Mensch. Theologische Erörterungen*. Munich: Kaiser, 1980.

_____. *Erfahrungen mit der Erfahrung. Unterwegs bemerkt*. Stuttgart: Radius, 2008.

_____. "Evangelium und Gesetz. Zugleich zum Verhältnis von Dogmatik und Ethik." In *Barth-Studien*, 180–209.

_____. "Das Gesetz zwischen Adam und Christus. Eine theologische Studie zu Röm 5,12–21." In *Unterwegs zur Sache*, 145–72.

_____. "Glauben und Verstehen. Zum Theologiebegriff Rudolf Bultmanns." In *Wertlose Wahrheit, Zur Identität und Relevanz des christlichen Glaubens. Theologische Erörterungen III*, 31–36. Munich: Kaiser, 1990.

_____. *Gott als Geheimnis der Welt. Zur Begründung der Theologie des Gekreuzigten im Streit zwischen Theismus und Atheismus*. Tübingen: Mohr Siebeck, 2001. Translated into English by Darell L. Guder as *God as the Mystery of the World: On the Foundation of the Theology of the Crucified One in the Dispute between Theism and Atheism* (Eugene, OR: Wipf & Stock, 2009).

_____. "Der Gott entsprechende Mensch." In *Entsprechungen*, 290–317.

_____. *Gottes Sein ist im Werden. Verantwortliche Rede vom Sein Gottes bei Karl Barth. Eine Paraphrase*. 4th ed. Tübingen: Mohr Siebeck, 1998. Translated into English by John Webster as *God's Being Is in Becoming: The Trinitarian Being of God in the Theology of Karl Barth* (Edinburgh: Bloomsbury T&T Clark, 2004).

_____. "Gott—um seiner selbst willen interessant. Plädoyer für eine natürlichere Theologie." In *Entsprechungen*, 193–97.

_____. "Ein paulinischer Chiasmus. Zum Verständnis der Vorstellung vom Gericht nach den Werken in Röm 2,2–11." In *Unterwegs zur Sache*, 173–78.

_____. *Paulus und Jesus*. Tübingen: Mohr Siebeck, 1967.

_____. "The Truth of Life: Observations on Truth as the Interruption of the Continuity of Life." In *Creation, Christ and Culture. Studies in Honour of T. F. Torrance*, edited by Richard W. Mackinney, 231–36. Edinburgh: T&T Clarke, 1976.

_____. *Unterwegs zur Sache. Theologische Bemerkungen*. Munich: Kaiser, 1972.

_____. "Die Welt als Möglichkeit und Wirklichkeit. Zum ontologischen Ansatz der Rechtfertigungslehre." In *Unterwegs zur Sache*, 206–33.

Kaegi, Dominic. "Die Religion in den Grenzen der bloßen Existenz. Heideggers religionsphilosophische Vorlesungen von 1920/21." *Internationale Zeitschrift für Philosophie* 1 (1996): 133–46.

Kenny, Anthony. *The Self.* Milwaukee, WI: Marquette University Press, 1988.

Kierkegaard, Søren. *Abschliessende Unwissenschaftliche Nachschrift. Gesammelte Werke*, vol. 16. Gütersloh: Gütersloher Verlagshaus, 1982.

———. *Philosophische Brocken. De omnibus dubitandum est,* translated by E. Hirsch. *Gesammelte Werke*, vol. 10. Düsseldorf: Eugen Diederichs Verlag, 1960.

———. *Die Tagebücher*, vol. 1. Düsseldorf: Eugen Diederichs Verlag, 1962.

Kim, Jaegwon. "The American Origins of Philosophical Naturalism." *Journal of Philosophical Research*, APA Centennial Volume (2003): 83–98.

Kleffmann, Tom. "Systematische Theologie—zwischen Philosophie und historischer Wissenschaft. Eine Auseinandersetzung mit Martin Heidegger." *Neue Zeitschrift für Systematische Theologie und Religionsphilosophie* 46 (2004): 207–25.

Knuth, Hans C. *Verstehen und Erfahrung. Hermeneutische Beiträge zur empirischen Theologie.* Hannover: Lutherhaus, 1986.

Körtner, Ulrich H. J. *Einführung in die theologische Hermeneutik.* Darmstadt: Wissenschaftliche Buchgesellschaft, 2006.

———. *Hermeneutische Theologie. Zugänge zur Interpretation des christlichen Glaubens und seiner Lebenspraxis.* Neukirchen-Vluyn: Neukirchener Verlag, 2008.

———. *Theologie des Wortes Gottes. Positionen—Probleme—Perspektiven.* Göttingen: Vandenhoeck & Ruprecht, 2001.

———. "Zur Einführung: Glauben und Verstehen. Perspektiven Hermeneutischer Theologie im Anschluß an Rudolf Bultmann." In *Glauben und Verstehen. Perspektiven hermeneutischer Theologie,* edited by Ulrich H. J. Körtner, 1–18. Neukirchen-Vluyn: Neukirchener Verlag, 2000.

Korsch, Dietrich. *Dialektische Theologie nach Karl Barth.* Tübingen: Mohr Siebeck, 1996.

———. *Religionsbegriff und Gottesglaube. Dialektische Theologie als Hermeneutik der Religion* (Tübingen: Mohr Siebeck, 2005).

Landmesser, Christoph. "Der Mensch in der Entscheidung. Anthropologie als Aufgabe der Theologie in der Auseinandersetzung mit Rudolf Bultmann." In *Rudolf Bultmann (1884-1976)—Theologe der Gegenwart. Hermeneutik—*

Exegese—Theologie—Philosophie, edited by Christoph Landmesser and Andreas Klein, 87–110. Neukirchen-Vluyn: Neukirchener Verlag, 2010.

Lauster, Jörg. *Religion als Lebensdeutung. Theologische Hermeneutik heute*. Darmstadt: Wissenschaftliche Buchgesellschaft, 2005.

Lawrence, Frederick G. "Hans-Georg Gadamer and the Hermeneutic Revolution." *Divyadaan: Journal of Philosophy and Education* 19, nos. 1–2 (2008): 31–54.

———. "The Hermeneutic Revolution and Bernard Lonergan: Gadamer and Lonergan on Augustine's Verbum Cordis—the Heart of Postmodern Hermeneutics." *Divyadaan: Journal of Philosophy and Education* 19, nos. 1–2 (2008): 55–86.

———. "Martin Heidegger and the Hermeneutic Revolution." *Divyadaan: Journal of Philosophy and Education* 19, nos. 1–2 (2008): 7–30.

———. "The Unknown 20th-Century Hermeneutic Revolution: Jerusalem and Athens in Lonergan's Integral Hermeneutics." *Divyadaan: Journal of Philosophy and Education* 19, nos. 1–2 (2008): 87–118.

Laycock, Steven W. "The Intersubjective Dimension of Husserl's Theology." In *Essays in Phenomenological Theology*, edited by Steven W. Laycock/James G. Hart, 169–86. Albany: State University of New York Press, 1986.

Laycock, Steven W., and James G. Hart, eds. *Essays in Phenomenological Theology*. Albany: State University of New York Press, 1986.

Leeuw, Gerardus van der. *Phänomenologie der Religion*. Tübingen: Mohr Siebeck, 1970.

Leiter, Brian. "The Hermeneutics of Suspicion: Recovering Marx, Nietzsche, and Freud." In *The Future for Philosophy*, edited by Brian Leiter, 74–105. Oxford: Oxford University Press, 2004.

Lonergan, Bernard. *Insight: A Study of Human Understanding*. Vol. 3 of *Collected Works*. Edited by Frederick E. Crowe and Robert M. Doran. Toronto: University of Toronto, 1992.

———. *Method in Theology*. London: Herder & Herder, 1973.

Lorenz, Rüdiger. *Die unvollendete Befreiung vom Nominalismus. Martin Luther und die Grenzen hermeneutischer Theologie bei Gerhard Ebeling*. Gütersloh: Gütersloher Verlagshaus, 1973.

Löwith, Karl. "Phänomenologische Ontologie und protestantische Theologie."

Zeitschrift für Theologie und Kirche NF 11 (1930): 365–99. Reprinted in *Heidegger und die Theologie. Beginn und Fortgang der Diskussion*, edited by Gerhard Noller (Munich: Kaiser, 1967), 95–124.

Mädler, Inken. *Transfigurationen. Materielle Kultur in praktisch-theologischer Perspektive*. Gütersloh: Gütersloher Verlagshaus, 2006.

Manovich, Lev. *Black Box—White Cube*. Berlin: Merve Verlag, 2005.

———. *The Language of New Media*. Cambridge, MA: MIT Press, 2001.

Marion, Jean-Luc. "Aspekte der Religionsphänomenologie: Grund, Horizont und Offenbarung." In *Religionsphilosophie heute*, edited by Alois Halder et al., 84–103. Düsseldorf: Patmos, 1988.

———. *Étant donné. Essai d'une phénoménologie de la donation*. Paris: PUF, 1997.

———. "They Recognized Him; and He became Invisible to Them." in *Modern Theology* 18 (2002): 145–52.

———. *Le visible et le révélé*. Paris: Cerf, 2005.

McGrath, Sean J. "The Facticity of Being God-Forsaken. The Young Heidegger and Luther's Theology of the Cross." *American Catholic Philosophical Quarterly* 29 (2005): 273–90.

Mersch, Dieter. *Was sich zeigt. Materialität, Präsenz, Ereignis*. Munich: Wilhelm Fink Verlag, 2002.

Montgomery, John W. *The "Is God Dead?" Controversy*. Grand Rapids, MI: Zondervan, 1966.

Moxter, Michael. "Gegenwart, die sich nicht dehnt. Eine kritische Erinnerung an Bultmanns Zeitverständnis." In *Religion und Gestaltung der Zeit*, edited by Dieter Georgi, Hans-Georg Heimbrock, and Michael Moxter, 108–22. Kampen: Kok Pharos, 1994.

———. "Die Phänomene der Phänomenologie." In *Religion als Phänomen. Sozialwissenschaftliche, theologische und philosophische Erkundungen in der Lebenswelt*, edited by Wolf-Eckart Failing, Hans-Georg Heimbrock, and T. A. Lotz, 85–95. Berlin: de Gruyter, 2001.

Müller-Schöll, Nikolaus, ed. *Ereignis. Eine fundamentale Kategorie der Zeiterfahrung. Anspruch und Aporien*. Bielefeld: Transcript, 2003.

Nancy, Jean-Luc. *La déclosion*. Déconstruction du christianism, 1. Paris: La Cebra, 2005.

Noller, Gerhard, ed. *Heidegger und die Theologie. Beginn und Fortgang der Diskussion.* Munich: Kaiser, 1967.

Osthövener, Claus-Dieter. "Weltvertrauen und Gottvertrauen. Theologische Bemerkungen zu dem humanen Phänomen des Vertrauens." In *Phänomenologie und Theologie*, edited by Thomas Söding and Klaus Held, 106-20. Freiburg: Herder, 2009.

Pannenberg, Wolfhart. "Hermeneutik und Universalgeschichte." In *Grundfragen systematischer Theologie*, 91-122. Göttingen: Vandenhoek & Ruprecht, 1979.

———. "Über historische und theologische Hermeneutik." In *Grundfragen systematischer Theologie*, 123-58. Göttingen: Vandenhoek & Ruprecht, 1979.

Papineau, David. "Naturalism." In *The Stanford Encyclopedia of Philosophy*, March 2010, http://plato.stanford.edu/entries/naturalism/index.html/.

Perry, John. The Self (1995) (https://faculty.washington.edu/smcohen/453/PerrySelf.pdf).

Petzold, Matthias. "Die Theologie des Wortes im Zeitalter der neuen Medien." In *Hermeneutik und Ästhetik. Die Theologie des Wortes im multimedialen Zeitalter*, edited by Ulrich H. J. Körtner, 57-97. Neukirchen-Vluyn: Neukirchener Verlag, 2001.

Phillips, Dewi Z. *The Concept of Prayer*. London: Routledge & K. Paul, 1965.

———. *Faith after Foundationalism*. London: Routledge, 1988.

———. *Faith and Philosophical Enquiry*. London: Routledge & K. Paul, 1970.

———. *Religion without Explanation*. Oxford: Blackwell, 1976.

Plantinga, A. "Methodological Naturalism?" In *Facets of Faith and Science*, edited by Jitse van der Meer, 91-130. Lanham, MD: University Press of America, 1996.

Pöggeler, Otto, ed. *Heidegger. Perspektiven zur Deutung seines Werkes.* Königsstein: Kiepenheuer & Witsch, 1984.

———. "Heideggers Luther-Lektüre im Freiburger Theologenkonvikt." In *Heidegger und die Anfänge seines Denkens (Heidegger-Jahrbuch 1)*, edited by Alfred Denker, 185-96. Freiburg: K. Alber, 2004.

———. *Philosophie und Hermeneutische Theologie. Heidegger, Bultmann und die Folgen.* Munich: W. Fink, 2009.

Popkes, Enno E. "Phänomenologie frühchristlichen Lebens. Exegetische

Anmerkungen zu Heideggers Auslegung paulinischer Briefe." *Kerygma und Dogma* 52 (2006): 263–86.

Puntel, Lorenz B. *Sein und Gott—ein systematischer Ansatz in Auseinandersetzung mit M. Heidegger, É. Lévinas und J.-L. Marion*. Tübingen: Mohr Siebeck, 2010.

Rahner, Karl. *Grundkurs des Glaubens. Einführung in den Begriff des Christentums*. Freiburg: Herder, 1977.

Ramsey, Ian. *Christian Discourse: Some Logical Explorations*. London: Oxford University Press, 1965.

———. *Christian Empiricism*. Edited by J. H. Gill. London: James Clarke, 1974.

———. *Miracles: An Exercise in Logical Map Work*. Oxford: Clarendon, 1952.

———. *Models and Mystery*. London: Oxford University Press, 1964.

———. *Models for Divine Activity*. London: SCM, 1973.

———. *Religious Language: An Empirical Placing of Theological Phrases*. London: Macmillan, 1957.

Ricoeur, Paul. *Die Interpretation: ein Versuch über Freud* (1965). Frankfurt am Main: Suhrkamp, 1974.

———. "Philosophische und theologische Hermeneutik." In *Metapher. Zur Hermeneutik religiöser Sprache*, mit einer Einführung von Pierre Gisel, edited by Paul Ricoeur and Eberhard Jüngel, 24–45. Munich: Kaiser, 1974.

Robinson, James M. "Die Hermeneutik seit Karl Barth." In *Die Neue Hermeneutik*, edited by James M. Robinson and John B. Cobb, 13–108. Zürich: Zwingli, 1965.

Rölli, Marc, ed. *Ereignis auf Französisch. Von Bergson bis Deleuze*. Munich: Wilhelm Fink, 2004.

Rosenzweig, Franz. *Der Stern der Erlösung*. GS 2. Frankfurt am Main: Suhrkamp, 1993.

Ruff, Gerhard. *Am Ursprung der Zeit. Studie zu Martin Heideggers phänomenologischen Zugang zur christlichen Religion in den ersten Freiburger Vorlesungen*. Berlin: Duncker & Humblot, 1997.

Salis, John. "Radical Phenomenology and Fundamental Ontology." *Research in Phenomenology* 6 (1976): 139–50.

Scheliha, Arnulf von. "*Dogmatik, ‚ihre Zeit in Gedanken gefasst'? Die dogmatische Aufgabe zwischen historischer Kritik und christologischer Gegenwartsdeutung.*" In *Systematische Theologie heute. Zur Selbstverständigung einer Disziplin*, edited by

Hermann Deuser, and Dietrich Korsch. Gütersloh: Gütersloher Verlagshaus 2004, 60–84.

Schenk, Wolfgang. "Hermeneutik III. Neues Testament." *TRE* 15 (1986): 144–50.

Schleiermacher, Friedrich D. E. *Hermeneutics and Criticism and Other Writings.* Translated and edited by A. Bowie. Cambridge: Cambridge University Press, 1998.

———. *Hermeneutik.* Edited by H. Kimmerle. Heidelberg: Carl Winter, 1959.

Schluchter, Wolfgang, and Friedrich Wilhelm Graf, eds. *Asketischer Protestantismus und der "Geist" des modernen Kapitalismus.* Tübingen: Mohr Siebeck, 2005.

Schneider, Irmela. "Konzepte von Autorschaft im Übergang von der 'Gutenberg-' zur 'Turing'-Galaxis." *Zeitenblicke* 5, no. 3 (2006), http://www.zeitenblicke.de/2006/3/Schneider/index_html.

Schultz, Werner. "Die Grundlagen der Hermeneutik Schleiermachers, ihre Auswirkungen und ihre Grenzen." *Zeitschrift für Theologie und Kirche* 50 (1953): 158–84.

Schwöbel, Christoph. "Offenbarung und Erfahrung—Glaube und Lebenserfahrung. Systematisch-theologische Überlegungen zu ihrer Verhältnisbestimmung." In *Marburger Jahrbuch Theologie III: Lebenserfahrung,* 68–122. Marburg: N. G. Elwert, 1990.

Sheehan, Thomas. "Heidegger's 'Introduction to the Phenomenology of Religion' (1920/21)." *Personalist* 60 (1979): 312–24.

Shields, David. *Reality Hunger: A Manifesto.* New York: Vintage, 2010.

Söding, Thomas, and Klaus Held, eds. *Phänomenologie und Theologie.* Freiburg: Herder, 2009.

Stagi, Pierfrnacesco. *Der faktische Gott.* Würzburg: Königshausen & Neumann, 2007.

Steinmann, Michael. "Der frühe Heidegger und sein Verhältnis zum Neukantianismus." In *Heidegger und die Anfänge seines Denkens (Heidegger-Jahrbuch 1),* edited by Alfred Denker, 259–93. Freiburg: K. Alber, 2004.

———. *Die Offenheit des Sinns. Untersuchungen zu Sprache und Logik bei Martin Heidegger.* Tübingen: Mohr Siebeck, 2008.

Stewart, David. "The Hermeneutics of Suspicion." *Journal of Literature and Theology* 3 (1989): 296–307.

Stoker, Hendrik G. *Das Gewissen. Erscheinungsformen und Theorien.* Bonn: F. Cohen, 1925.

Strasser, Stephan. "Das Gottesproblem in der Spätphilosophie Edmund Husserls." *Philosophisches Jahrbuch* 67 (1958-1959): 130-42.

———. "History, Teleology, and God in the Philosophy of Husserl." *Analecta Husserliana* 9 (1979): 317-33.

Strawson, Galen. "The Self." *Consciousness Studies* 4 (1997): 405-28.

———. *Selves: An Essay in Revisionary Metaphysics.* Oxford: Oxford University Press, 2009.

Taylor, Charles. *Hegel and Modern Society.* Cambridge: Cambridge University Press, 1979.

———. *A Secular Age.* Cambridge, MA: Harvard University Press, 2007.

———. "Self-Interpreting Animals." In *Human Agency and Language: Philosophical Papers 1*, 45-76. Cambridge: Cambridge University Press, 1985.

———. *Sources of the Self: The Making of Modern Identity.* Cambridge, MA: Harvard University Press, 1989.

Teevan, Donna. *Lonergan, Hermeneutics, and Theological Method.* Milwaukee, WI: Marquette University Press, 2005.

Tillich, Paul. *Main Works = Hauptwerke.* Vol. 4: *Writings in the Philosophy of Religion = Religionsphilosophische Schriften.* In the original English and German. Edited by J. Clayton. Berlin: de Gruyter, 1987.

———. "Offenbarung: Religionsphilosophisch" (1930). In *Main Works = Hauptwerke*, vol. 4, 237-42.

———. "Religionsphilosophie" (1925). In *Main Works = Hauptwerke*, vol. 4, 118-70.

———. "Die Überwindung des Religionsbegriffs in der Religionsphilosophie (1922)." In *Main Works = Hauptwerke*, vol. 4, 73-90.

Trawny, Peter. *Martin Heidegger.* Frankfurt am Main: Campus, 2003.

Trowitzsch, Michael. *Verstehen und Freiheit. Umrisse einer theologischen Kritik der hermeneutischen Urteilskraft.* Zürich: TVZ, 1981.

Vahanian, Gabriel. *The Death of God: The Culture of Our Post-Christian Era.* New York: George Braziller, 1961.

———. *Wait without Idols.* New York: George Braziller, 1964.

Vanhoozer, Kevin J., ed. *The Cambridge Companion to Postmodern Theology.* Cambridge: Cambridge University Press, 2003.

Vattimo, Gianni. *Jenseits vom Subjekt*. Edited by Peter Engelmann. Graz: Böhlau, 2005.

Vattimo, Gianni, and Richard Rorty. *Die Zukunft der Religion*. Edited by S. Zabala. Frankfurt am Main: Suhrkamp, 2006.

Vetter, Helmut. "Hermeneutische Phänomenologie und Dialektische Theologie. Heidegger und Bultmann." In *Glauben und Verstehen. Perspektiven hermeneutischer Theologie*, edited by Ulrich Körtner, 19–38. Neukirchen-Vluyn: Neukirchener Verlag, 2000.

Waardenburg, Jaques. *Religionen und Religion*. New ed. Berlin: de Gruyter, 1996.

Waldenfels, Bernhard. *Antwortregister*. Frankfurt am Main: Suhrkamp, 1994.

———. *Bruchlinien der Erfahrung. Phänomenologie, Psychoanalyse, Phänomenotechnik*. Frankfurt am Main: Suhrkamp, 2002.

———. *Grenzen der Normalisierung. Studien zur Phänomenologie des Fremden 2*. Frankfurt am Main: Suhrkamp, 1998.

———. "Die Macht der Ereignisse." In *Ereignis auf Französisch* , edited by M. Rölli, 447–58. Munich: Fink, 2004.

———. *Ordnung im Zwielicht*. Frankfurt am Main: Suhrkamp, 1987.

———. *Phänomenologie der Aufmerksamkeit*. Frankfurt am Main: Suhrkamp, 2004.

———. "Phänomenologie der Erfahrung und das Dilemma einer Religionsphänomenologie." In *Religion als Phänomen. Sozialwissenschaftliche, theologische und philosophische Erkundungen in der Lebenswelt*, edited by Wolf-Eckart Failing, 63–84. Berlin: de Gruyter, 2001.

———. *Schattenrisse der Moral*. Frankfurt am Main: Suhrkamp, 2006.

———. *Sinnschwellen. Studien zur Phänomenologie des Fremden 3*. Frankfurt am Main: Suhrkamp, 1999.

———. *Der Stachel des Fremden*. Frankfurt am Main: Suhrkamp, 1990.

Wansing, Rudolf. "Im Denken erfahren. Ereignis und Geschichte bei Heidegger." In *Ereignis auf Französisch. Von Bergson bis Deleuze*, edited by Marc Rölli, 81–102. Munich: Wilhelm Fink, 2004.

Webster, John B. *Eberhard Jüngel: An Introduction to His Theology*. Cambridge: Cambridge University Press, 1986.

Welz, Claudia. *Love's Transcendence and the Problem of Theodicy*. Tübingen: Mohr Siebeck, 2008.

Wenzel, Knut. *Glaube in Vermittlung. Theologische Hermeneutik nach Paul Ricoeur.* Freiburg: Herder, 2008.

White, Ern. "Between Suspicion and Hope: Paul Ricoeur's Vital Hermeneutic." *Journal of Literature and Theology* 5 (1991): 311–21.

Wiman, Christian. *My Bright Abyss: Meditation of a Modern Believer.* New York: Farrar, Straus & Giroux, 2013.

Zaccagnini, Marta. *Christentum der Endlichkeit. Heideggers Vorlesungen "Einleitung in die Phänomenologie der Religion."* Münster: LIT, 2003.

Zahavi, Dan. *Husserl und die transzendentale Intersubjektivität.* Dordrecht: Springer, 1996.

Zeillinger, Peter. "Badiou und Paulus. Das Ereignis als Norm?" *IWK-Mitteilungen* 61 (2006): 6–12.

———. "Phänomenologie des Nicht-Phänomenalen. Spur und Inversion des Seins bei Emmanuel Levinas." In *Phänomenologische Aufbrüche*, edited by Michael Blaumauer, Wolfgang Fasching, and Matthias Flatscher, 161–79. Frankfurt am Main: Peter Lang, 2005.

Zizek, Slavoj. *The Parallax View.* Cambridge, MA: MIT Press, 2006.

Zizek, Slavoj, and John Milbank. *The Monstrosity of Christ. Paradox or Dialectic?* Cambridge, MA: MIT Press, 2009.

Zovko, Jure. Review of *Gegenständlichkeit*, by Günter Figal. *Theologische Literaturzeitung* 135 (2010): 72–74.